Introduction to
MOVEMENT
EDUCATION

Second Edition

Introduction to
MOVEMENT
EDUCATION

Glenn Kirchner
Simon Fraser University

Jean Cunningham
University of British Columbia

Eileen Warrell
Simon Fraser University

wcb
WM. C. BROWN COMPANY PUBLISHERS
Dubuque, Iowa

GV
443
.K468/56,428
1978/

Consulting Editor
Aileene Lockhart
Texas Woman's University

Copyright © 1970, 1978 by Wm. C. Brown
Company Publishers

Library of Congress Catalog Card Number:
76-16211

ISBN 0-697-07265-7

Printed in the United States of America
10 9 8 .7

Contents

Preface   vii

Acknowledgments   ix

SECTION 1   Movement Education in the Physical Education Program

Chapter 1   Physical Education in Contemporary Education   3

Role of Movement Education   3
Value of Movement Education   4
Competition and Creativity   6
Purpose of this Book   7

Chapter 2   Structure and Methods of Movement Education   9

Movement Analysis   9
Sequence Building   16
Lesson Planning   17
Methods of Teaching   20
Teaching by Themes   21
Observation and Evaluation   22
Planning the Program   24

SECTION 2   Movement Education in the Primary Grades

Chapter 3   Gymnastics   31

Theme One: Safety Training   31
Theme Two: Adding to the Range and Understanding of Movement   58
Theme Three: Understanding Space and Directional Movements   76
Theme Four: Qualities   94

Chapter 4   Dance   105

Theme One: Safety Training   106
Theme Two: Adding to the Range and Understanding of Movement   114

Theme Three: Understanding Direction   124
Theme Four: Qualities   133

Chapter 5   Games   147

Theme One: Safety Training   148
Theme Two: Adding to the Range and Understanding of Movement   155
Theme Three: Understanding Direction   158

SECTION 3 Movement Education in the Intermediate Grades

Chapter 6 Games: Setting the Stage 171

Phase One: Existing Games Program 172
Phase Two: Introducing a New Teaching
  Format 176
Phase Three: Introducing the Problem-
  Solving Method 182
Phase Four: Introducing Movement
  Terms and Concepts 192
Sample Basketball Unit 195

**Chapter 7 Gymnastics: Building a Movement
Vocabulary 203**

Phase One: Existing Program 204
Phase Two: Introducing the Movement
  Education Vocabulary 210
Phase Three: Building Themes 239

**Chapter 8 Dance: Using the Movement
Approach 243**

Phase One: Sequence Building 243
Phase Two: Phrasing and Rhythm 244
Phase Three: Accompaniment 244
Phase Four: The Lesson Plan 245
  Folk Dance 245
  Creative Dance 251
  A Dance Drama 266

SECTION 4 Appendixes

Appendix A Bibliography and Films 278
**Appendix B Definition of Movement
  Education Terms 284**
**Appendix C Apparatus, Equipment, and
  Supply Companies 286**

Index 289

Preface

The purpose of the second edition of *Introduction to Movement Education* is no different from that of our first edition: to provide teachers who wish to introduce Movement Education into their programs with a basic understanding of this approach. A suggested program is outlined with many sample lessons, illustrations, and helpful hints.

A basic understanding of the meaning and structure of Movement Education is provided in Section One. Since there are differences between the primary and intermediate physical education programs, we have organized the remaining sections to cope with the main differences between these two age groups. Section Two will illustrate how primary teachers can begin with an integrated approach, combining Movement Education principles and concepts with gymnastic, dance, and game activities. It has been our experience that grades four through six with established formal teaching patterns, present major problems to teachers wishing to introduce the informal, problem-solving methods of Movement Education. We have given these transitional grades special attention in this revised edition.

Section Four has been retained but with some appropriate changes. Appendix A includes written and film resources. Appendix B has been enlarged to include a greater variety of terms now used in contemporary Movement Education programs. Appendix C contains up-to-date information relating to the purchase of equipment and apparatus.

We have attempted to lead both primary and intermediate teachers toward the guiding role in a systematic and gentle way. Initial emphasis is on direct teaching with a gradual introduction to problem-solving methods and a new movement vocabulary. Consideration is given to the existing physical education program and how teachers can adapt, modify, or integrate the concepts, principles, and vocabulary of Movement Education within their respective programs.

Acknowledgments

It is virtually impossible to express our gratitude to all the teachers who have arranged demonstration lessons, tried our lessons, and provided invaluable suggestions throughout the revision of this text. And, to the hundreds of children who are represented in our illustrations, our sincere thanks.

We would like to express our special thanks to Mrs. Sherry Fulton, Mrs. Paulette Strim, and Mr. Norm Ellis of Ranch Park Elementary School; Mrs. Arlene Taylor, Westover Elementary School; Mrs. Birthe Kulich, Community Music School; Mrs. Darlene Webster, Hastings Elementary School; Mr. John Richmond, Trafalgar Elementary School; Miss Ruth Rout, Gleneagles Elementary School; Mrs. Fran Heath, Frome Elementary School; Mrs. Ruth Parker, Lincoln Elementary School; Mrs. Lynn Bullis, A. R. Lord Elementary School; the children and teachers of Maplewood Elementary School; and to Marlene McCracken and all the teachers in the Bellingham Triad of the University of North Dakota Followthrough Program. We wish to thank our patient typists Ms. Christy Cunningham and Mrs. Josephine Cook. Finally, our special thinks to Mr. Lee Mann for some of the photographs used in this edition.

Section 1

Movement Education in the Physical Education Program

Chapter One: Physical Education in Contemporary Education

Chapter Two: Structure and Methods in Movement Education

Chapter One

Movement Education in Contemporary Education

The Role of Movement Education

Value of Movement Education

Competition and Creativity

Purpose of this Book

Education today is characterized more than ever before by an inquiry approach to learning. Through a process which may include guided experience, experimentation, observation, and selection, children make many important discoveries for themselves. The teacher uses concrete materials and visual aides where suitable and available, to link abstract thought to the "real" world. In the interests of understanding rather than isolated memorization, the teacher today classifies and groups ideas in such a way that children learn to link information to meaningful concepts. At the same time they learn the skills of classification and analysis. In the selection of subject matter the teacher pays greater attention than ever before to the intellectual development of the children and to the enormous range of skill and maturity that is to be found among the individuals in any class.

In physical education the "new" approach which we call Movement Education is based on the same educational principles that are mentioned above and which have already been accepted in the classroom setting. Numerous labels have been given to this new approach.

Some teachers specifically refer to it as an "inquiry approach," while others use such terms as "individualized learning" or "child-centered" teaching. Many teachers in the past and at the present time employ the teaching strategies which are associated with such terminology, without attaching any specific label to their own methods. Implicit in all these terms, including Movement Education, are the fundamental premises that children learn at their own rate, and that discovery as well as practice and repetition brings about the understanding and self-confidence necessary for successful learning.

ROLE OF MOVEMENT EDUCATION

The three main content areas in elementary school physical education are games, gymnastics, and dance. If we apply the "new" teaching methods and concepts of Movement Education described in the next chapter to each of these three content areas, we find several basic similarities, as well as a few very important differences. In order to provide a balanced program in physical education, all three areas should be taught and their relationship to each other fully understood. Games, gymnastics, and dance, each in their own way, guide and challenge the physical energy and drive of "play," and provide vital opportunities for social interaction. To be more specific, the goals of Movement Education are to:

1. Assist children to become physically fit and skillful in a variety of situations.
2. Assist children to understand the principles of movement and give them an awareness of what their bodies can do.
3. Encourage self-discipline and self-reliance.
4. Provide opportunities for self-expression and creativity.
5. Develop confidence in meeting physical challenges.
6. Encourage cooperation and sensitivity to others in the course of partner and group work.

Figure 1.1 The goals of Movement Education are evident in even a simple task.

VALUE OF MOVEMENT EDUCATION

The values of this approach to physical education are numerous and can best be considered first from the student's viewpoint and then from the teacher's viewpoint.

Values to the Student

1. The muscular and organic systems of the body will be exercised in a natural and functional way. Through the application of this approach, a child's physical attributes (such as strength, endurance, coordination, and flexibility) are developed in a natural and functional manner.
2. The level of motor skill of each child will be increased according to ability, readiness, and interest. This approach permits the outstanding performer to progress as rapidly as he or she is capable of, since he or she is not held back by slower members of the class. Equally important, the less able students are not measured against an arbitrary standard or norm, so they too can achieve success and personal satisfaction while participating in realistic tasks and challenges.
3. The social awareness of each child is fostered by the natural and informal setting of the group. A child must learn to work as an individual, to adapt to a partner, and cooperate with groups of varying sizes. As a result the child develops self-reliance, cooperation, and tolerance for others.
4. In gymnastics the possibility of accidents and injury, particularly on apparatus, is greatly reduced. One of the most important features of this approach is the "built-in" safety that is fostered and emphasized. A "movement task" or challenge is first given by the teacher, to which each child is allowed to respond in his or her own way. To illustrate, a teacher presents a challenge such as "Can you find a balance position using your head and two other parts of your body?" A child who has sufficient arm and shoulder

Figure 1.2 Children develop skills while learning to work with each other.

ences in children, a much greater sense of accomplishment and enjoyment can be experienced by the class as a whole.

Values to the Teacher

1. Through the Movement Education approach the teacher has an opportunity to learn more about each child's personality. The child can be observed in situations where there are greater opportunities for self-expression and inventiveness. Many teachers utilizing this approach have commented that they see the "low achievers" and "problem cases" of the classroom in quite a different light in the gymnasium. Furthermore, the personal success experienced by these children in the gymnasium tends to bolster their confidence, and in turn, they begin to do much better in the classroom. Although these are opinions, related research indicates that success achieved in one area may genuinely motivate achievement in another area.

2. Classroom methods and mannerisms are carried over into the gymnasium. One of the most distinguishing features of Movement Education is the teacher's use of a natural, conversational, speaking voice (instead of formal commands) and the elimination of the whistle as a means of gaining attention and control. In addition, teachers are not required to wear physical education apparel since few demonstrations need to be given by the teacher. Where the problem-solving method is used, careful planning is necessary, and *observation* rather than demonstration becomes the key to successful teaching.

3. The teacher has time for individualized instruction. Since there are no formal lines or commands which require all of the children to perform the same movements at the same time, the teacher continuously circulates among the children. There is no front or back of a class. From any position in the gymnasium the teacher may present a movement problem. Once the problem is understood, all children are actively engaged in its

girdle strength may respond by doing a headstand. Equally correct, however, would be a position in which perhaps a less able child uses the head, one foot, and a hand to form a three-point balance position. This method of teaching provides "built-in" safety, since children who are given the freedom to evolve their own solutions, will not attempt a movement which is beyond their capabilities.

It must be emphasized that the above statement is not just an opinion held by the writers of this book. Several studies in England, where Movement Education has been taught for over thirty years, have shown that the incidence of accidents is dramatically lower than in other programs employing more traditional teaching practices.

In traditional gymnastic programs, all children are required to perform the same stunt. Asking a child who is grossly overweight or physically weak to perform a headstand not only invites accidents but also creates poor attitudes. As the approach used in Movement Education allows for the physical and intellectual differ-

solution in accordance with their own physical abilities and imaginations. While the children are working on their movement ideas, the teacher moves about giving suggestions or individual attention wherever the teacher or child feels assistance is necessary.

Most teachers will find the transition to this informal setting difficult, particularly during the early stages when children are learning to work on their own. Gradually, however, a teacher will be able to eliminate structured formations and replace the whistle with a natural, conversational tone of voice. The end result of this transition is an informal atmosphere in which the teacher becomes a guide to the learning experience, applying many methods and techniques according to the needs and interests of the children.

4. As the children become accustomed to independent work and to cooperating with a partner or a group, these same attributes and attitudes reinforce similar behavior in the classroom.

Figure 1.3   An informal teaching atmosphere.

COMPETITION AND CREATIVITY

While games can be creative (children invent their own challenges and make up their own rules in a variety of situations), the ultimate purpose of games is to challenge oneself or an opponent. In this way games are competitive, and if the skills involved have been mastered by the class, this form of competition can be very enjoyable. The teacher has the responsibility of making the competition as equal as possible, in order to increase the development of skill and to provide opportunities for children to experience success and defeat. Continual defeat causes despair and a strong dislike of the subject. Continual success can lead to a false sense of superiority and conceit. Because of these dangers the teacher must always be on guard to place a strong opponent with a strong player. In addition, the physical education program must be strongly balanced by its noncompetitive and more creative components, gymnastics and dance.

Gymnastics cannot thrive in an atmosphere of competition. Control and the ability to work within one's own limitations are of paramount importance for both safety and aesthetic reasons. Where movement tasks or problems are set, each child works out his or her own response, making winning and losing totally irrelevant and out of place. It must be stressed however that acceptance of a child's response does not imply that the teacher accepts a poor effort in the gymnasium any more than in the classroom. Each child must be continually encouraged to work at maximum capacity, and the highest expectations of effort, concentration, and behavior should be established.

Of all the content areas in the physical education program, dance is potentially the most creative. As in gymnastics however, creativity should not deter the teacher from demanding effort and concentration. There is no place for competition in the dance lesson, although this can creep in if just a few dancers are selected to "perform" for parent-teachers' evenings. Dance in education is primarily concerned with experiencing and understanding the expressive aspects of movement. It also provides many opportunities for integration with other areas of the curriculum, most frequently with language arts, music, and art.

Movement Education can be described as a contemporary approach to the teaching of physical education, where the fun of discovery has replaced much of the drill, and where invention and creativity has reduced the competition. The result is more enjoyment and satisfaction for all children and a higher level of physical skills in games, dances, and gymnastic activities. This in turn produces a confident attitude towards physical activity out of school and an enthusiasm for physical education in school.

PURPOSE OF THIS BOOK

The essential purpose of this book is to provide the teacher who is beginning to utilize this new approach with lesson plans and practical advice. We appreciate and sympathize with those making this transition from the "formal" to the "informal" approach, and for this reason initial emphasis is on direct teaching, while allowing for informal and scattered formations. Gradually the limitation and indirect methods are introduced until an informal atmosphere is created with the teacher acting as the "guider" of the learning experience of each child.

Chapter Two

The Structure and Methods of Movement Education

Movement analysis

Sequence building

Lesson planning

Methods of teaching

Teaching by themes

Observation and evaluation

Planning the program

Movement Education is more than a new method of teaching children physical activities. It is an approach which involves a new analysis of movement, combined with an adherence to several important principles and methods of instruction. This chapter will describe the main ingredients of Movement Education and will show how lesson themes are developed for primary and intermediate level children.

MOVEMENT ANALYSIS

There is a fundamental distinction that must be made between the organizational structure of most physical education classes and Movement Education. In traditional physical education classes, the *activity itself* (volleyball, track and field, or folk dance) provides the *structural basis* for developing a curriculum. Skills within each area are arranged from the simple to the complex and presented to children in accordance with their physical maturity and general readiness.

Based upon the analytical work of Rudolph Laban, Movement Education utilizes the media of games, gymnastics, and dance to foster the child's physical and emotional development through the movement concepts described as *body awareness, space, qualities, and relationships*. These categories of movement thus become the *framework* of a Movement Education curriculum. (See film *Introducing the Elements of Movement Education* in Appendix A.)

> WHAT the body can
> do: BODY AWARENESS.

> WHERE the body can
> move: SPACE AWARENESS.

> HOW the body can move:
> QUALITIES of movement.

> RELATIONSHIP to other performers
> and to apparatus.

1. *WHAT the body can do: body awareness.*
    In this category we consider the basic
    ways in which our joints allow movement.
    a. *Bending and stretching, twisting and
        turning.* These actions can be done
        with isolated parts of the body or
        with the whole body. The actions of
        stretching, curling, and twisting in-
        volve the body in very specific shapes.
        These shapes may be maintained
        whether the body is still or moving.

Turning is differentiated from twisting. Twisting involves rotation of one
part of the body against another part.
Turning simply involves a rotation of
the whole body to face a new direction.

b. *Transferring body weight.* Action
    usually involves a transference of
    weight from one part of the body to
    another. Sliding on the feet or seat
    is an exception to this. Transference of
    weight can take place from one foot
    to the other as in walking. It can take
    place with a variety of step-like actions
    using various permutations of feet, or
    hands and feet. It can also take place
    when one body surface receives the
    body weight from an adjacent part
    of the body as in rolling actions.
c. *Balancing.* The body can balance and
    maintain a variety of positions in still-
    ness. The positions involve varying de-
    grees of skill according to the number
    of parts of the body that are used
    and the size of those parts. For ex-
    ample, a child can balance on his
    back, side, or seat with greater ease
    than on an elbow-knee combination.

Figure 2.1   Stretching.

Figure 2.2   Twisting.

Figure 2.3 Transferring body weight from the shoulders . . .

Figure 2.5 . . . to the feet.

Figure 2.4 . . . to the back . . .

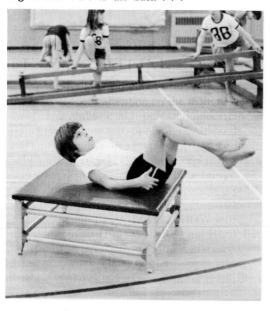

Again there will be a greater or lesser degree of skill required, according to the body's center of gravity. When the center of gravity and the position of the body are low, as in balancing on all fours, there is less skill involved, than in maintaining a handstand position where the body's center of gravity is higher.

The examples shown in Figures 2.6, 2.7, and 2.8 illustrate a variety of ways a child may balance on the floor or on small or large equipment.

d. *Flight.* The body can defy gravity in a number of ways. It can jump or leap off the floor from one or both feet, and it can also land on one or both feet. The body can be thrust into the air from the feet with the weight received by the hands (as in the "cat spring" or jumping onto a rope or vaulting box).

The body, even when it is in the

Figure 2.6 Balancing on the floor.

Figure 2.7 Balancing on small equipment.

Figure 2.8 Balancing on large equipment.

air, has shape, which can be varied in a number of ways. It can assume three basic shapes; stretched, curled, or twisted. It can be stretched long and thin, or spread in a number of directions. The positions and actions of the limbs in flight will also alter the shape of the body. Furthermore, the body can perform complete or various degrees of revolution in mid-air.

Finally, attention must be given to landing. The body's weight can be brought back to the floor by one or both feet, or the hands. The depth of landing or the degree of body resilience can also vary. All landings require "give" or flexion of the leg joints, especially the knees. When jumping from a height, children should be

Figure 2.9 The body in flight.

encouraged to make a deep landing, which brings them into a full knee bend position. This allows them to continue to absorb the momentum of the fall and the shock of impact by rolling.

If the landing can be easily controlled or does not involve much height, a smaller give in the knee, ankle, and hip joints will provide the necessary resilience to avoid shock in the legs and spine.

Figure 2.11   Using personal space.

Figure 2.10   Jumping from a height.

Figure 2.12   Using general space.

2. *WHERE the body moves; space awareness.* Awareness of space can be divided into:
   a. *Personal or limited space.* This refers to the space around the body that can be reached from a fixed position.
   b. *General space.* In contrast to personal space, general space refers to the floor area that is available for use by the children.
   c. *Directions.* The body can move within personal and general space in a variety of directions (forwards, backwards, sideways, up and down).

Figure 2.13   Moving in a variety of directions.

d. *Levels*. The various levels of movement refer to movement which takes place low to the ground, such as rolling; movement that takes place at a middle level such as moving on the hands and feet; and high level action such as cartwheeling or leaping. The floor or apparatus can be used as a base for variations in level. Balls or other small equipment can be used to create movement at different levels relative to the child.

Figure 2.14 At a low level.

Figure 2.15 At a medium level.

Figure 2.16 At a high level.

e. *Pathway*. Movement as it travels follows a pathway. If the soles of the children's feet were painted, we would become more conscious of this pathway as they travel in the general space of the gym. These pathways can be curved, straight, or a combination of the two. Pathways are also created in the air as a result of gestures or the body moving at different levels.

3. *HOW the body moves; qualities of movement*. This category gives expression to movement. Its parts may be likened to the varying shades of soft and loud or quick and slow, which characterize expression in music.

a. *Time or speed of movement*. At one end of the scale, movement may be

Figure 2.17   Creating pathways.

Figure 2.18   Relationship between the child and apparatus.

very quick and sudden. In contrast, it may also be very slow and sustained.

b. *Effort or the force of movement.* Effort is concerned with the amount of force involved in an action; the extremes being very strong or very light.

c. *"Flow" and "bound flow."* A single movement or series of movements may be performed in a manner which emphasizes discontinuity. This is referred to as "bound flow." In contrast, where movements blend harmoniously, with one running smoothly into the next, we describe the action as having "flow."

4. *RELATIONSHIP.* The relationships which are found in games, gymnastics, and dance are continually changing.

a. *With apparatus.* There is a relationship in gymnastics and games between the child and the apparatus. Relationships also develop in all three content areas as children work with partners and in groups.

b. *Matching movements.* In gymnastics and dance, a variety of relationships

occur as children build sequences in pairs and in groups. They may *match* movements, working opposite each other in mirror image, or they may match movements but work beside or even at different levels from each other.

c. *Contrasting movements.* The children may contrast actions; one making a

Figure 2.19   Matching shapes.

Figure 2.20 Wide and narrow shapes.

narrow shape for example, while a partner does a complimentary wide shape.

d. *Simultaneous and successive movements.* Further contrasts in relationships may be made by moving simultaneously or successively. Action—reaction or "question and answer" responses are different ways of moving successively. Shadowing or following the leader is a way of moving simultaneously.

Every teacher of physical education should understand this analysis which can be considered the structure or "grammar" of movement. In movement, as in spoken language, grammar cannot be assimilated quickly or easily, nor can it be taught without an infinite number of concrete examples. The teacher will acquire an understanding of this new movement analysis in a systematic way as the class progresses through the lessons provided in sections Two and Three of this book. It will be helpful to refer back to these pages as the teacher plans an overall program and more detailed lessons.

The five body actions listed below have direct relevance to the teaching of gymnastics, games, and dance, although the emphasis and intention of the actions will be different:

1. *Jumping and landing.*
2. *Traveling or locomotion.* Transfer of

body weight from feet to feet, feet to hands, or by rolling.
3. *Twisting and turning* with a consequent change in body shape.
4. *Stretching and curling* with a consequent change in body shape.
5. *Balancing* or holding the body in stillness.

In gymnastics we are concerned with the manipulation of the body in a variety of settings; on the floor and with small and large apparatus. For this reason the following categories are added:

1. *Hanging.*
2. *Climbing.*
3. *Pushing and pulling.*
4. *Swinging.*

Dance involves the first five categories mentioned as well as two others:

1. *Gesture* involves movement of the limbs where there is no transference of body weight.
2. *Rising and Sinking.*

In the games lesson all five categories are used, although there is little variation in the transference of body weight other than with the feet. As games are primarily concerned with the manipulation of a ball with part of the body, a stick, or a bat, we find ourselves emphasizing:

1. *Rolling.*
2. *Catching.*
3. *Throwing.*
4. *Bouncing.*
5. *Kicking.*
6. *Hitting.*
7. *Dodging.*

SEQUENCE BUILDING

Exercises for specific parts of the body have for many years been an accepted way of building physical strength and gaining mobility. Usually one exercise at a time is repeated for a set number of repetitions. Within the Movement Education approach children are given an opportunity to explore their own ideas in response to a given movement problem. They may find a variety of ways of doing this. Later they will select some of these actions and link them together to form a sequence or a "movement sentence." As in written language, the movement sentence can vary enormously in length and skill. Having decided upon the actions that form the sequence, children then work to make each individual action blend smoothly with the one that follows. Repeated practice is essential to improve the quality of performance and provide a sense of achievement. Thus we have four separate stages:

Exploration   Selection   Repetition   Polish

As children build their own sequences they are getting as much physical exercise as they acquired through traditional methods, but now there is much greater kinesthetic satisfaction in the flow of their movement. In addition, children work harder at a sequence which they have completely, or in part, designed themselves.

LESSON PLANNING

In the Movement Education approach, the lesson plan is considered to be a flexible guideline. Basically it consists of three parts which are described in the following paragraphs in reference to a gymnastic lesson.

Free Practice

One of the most striking characteristics of a Movement Education lesson is the immediate participation of children as soon as they enter the gymnasium. Since every teaching situation varies with respect to where and how long it takes children to change their clothes and enter the gymnasium, a simple procedure is established to cover this situation. As soon as each child is in the gymnasium, he or she is allowed to practice any previously learned movement pattern or to experiment with small equipment such as balls, beanbags, or hoops. During this time the teacher has an opportunity to supervise the changing, talk to the children, or provide assistance and encouragement wherever it is necessary.

The following suggestions may be helpful to teachers in the planning and general supervision of this phase of the lesson:

1. The length of free practice will vary from class to class depending upon the ages of the children and the dressing room conditions. As a general rule, the length of this part of the lesson should be approximately three to four minutes.
2. Restrict practice to individual movement skills, with or without a partner. Do not allow practice in groups or on large apparatus.
3. Have all equipment, such as balls, beanbags, hoops, and small mats arranged in the gymnasium prior to the arrival of the children.
4. Do not allow "horseplay" during this period. It should be a time for constructive practice.

	Part 1	Part 2	Part 3
Free time to play, practice, and limber while waiting for slow changers	Introductory Activity	Movement Training	Apparatus (in the gymnastics lesson) Group games (in the games lesson) Dance (or some group composition in the dance lesson)

5.   Create a few clear-cut rules regarding changing and entering the gymnasium and insist that the children abide by them. When procedures are well established, the teacher can spend time observing and providing individual assistance.

6.   Children's feet and ankles need strengthening and loosening. So much of the work in physical education depends on good foot work that a little time should be devoted before the Introductory Activity begins, to rotating the ankle joints, stretching the toes down to the ground and up to the ceiling, and opening and clenching the toes. Strong, healthy feet are important all through life, not only in physical education classes.

The Introductory Activity

The first part of the lesson, which should last about three to five minutes, is comparable to the "warm-up" of a traditionally planned lesson. It should be simple to understand, so that the children can get started quickly and energetically. It has the same physiological purpose as the warm up; it increases the circulation and

provides a much-needed burst of activity after prolonged sitting. Also the Introductory Activity should incorporate a few basic concepts:

1.   The theme of the lesson should be represented. (This will become apparent when the reader starts to use the lesson plans in Sections 2 and 3 of this book.)

2.   Small apparatus such as hoops, beanbags, or balls are frequently used in the gymnastics and games lessons, while music can be used in the dance lesson.

3.   The Introductory Activity, although simple and energetic, should not be devoid of skill or thoughtfulness. (See film *Introducing the Elements of Movement Education* in Appendix A.)

Movement Training
(or skill development)

Part 2, Movement Training, should last about ten minutes. It is used to introduce one or more movement skills involving individual or partner activities. In games, specific skills are practiced, while in gymnastics and dance the process of

Figure 2.21   Vigorous introductory activities.

Figure 2.22   Flight over small equipment.

sequence building takes place. The main as well as the secondary themes of the lesson are explored in as much depth as the maturity and skill of the class allow.

Exploration must not only be encouraged by the teacher, it must be guided as well. This direction will be the result of observation. (See page 22.) In questioning the children, the teacher should keep movement analysis in mind. For example:

"Can you do the same thing from a different starting position?
Using a different part of the body?
Do it more quickly?
Go in a different direction?"

When a movement idea or problem is given, sufficient time must be allowed for the children to think and practice. If children are not enjoying the process of working out their own ideas, it probably indicates that not enough guidance has been given or that the problem is not clear to the children.

Teachers should never be afraid of taking command of the situation and teaching in a direct way if the class is not ready to work independently. (See film *Using Small Equipment in Movement Education* in Appendix A.)

Figure 2.23   Flight from large apparatus.

young children, this part of the lesson will usually involve work within a group. (See film *Using Large Apparatus in Movement Education* in Appendix A.)

Group or Apparatus Work

Part 3, Apparatus work, takes up the remaining fifteen to twenty minutes of the lesson. It utilizes the skills and ideas that have been practiced, but places them in a more challenging and complex setting. For example, in a gymnastic lesson, the children should be given the opportunity to apply the ideas they developed on the floor to the new medium of large apparatus. This should provide an exciting and stimulating variation of the lesson theme. In the games lesson, groups of children develop their own game or play a game that is taught to them. In dance there will be a unification of the work that has gone before. Except for very

Allocation of Time

Since the length of physical education periods varies from fifteen minutes to one hour, allocating time to Parts 1, 2, and 3 must be done in a general way. Although each part of the lesson is considered of equal importance, the rate of learning and the children's experience with this approach to physical education must be considered. When a theme is first introduced to a class, allow proportionately more time for Parts 1 and 2 and less time for part 3. As the theme develops, more time can be given to Part 3. Numerous modifications of the following diagram will, of course, be worked out by each teacher.

←	Length of Movement Education lesson →		
Part I Introductory Activities	**Part II** Movement Training		**Part III** Apparatus or Group Work
	Devote more time to Parts I and II during initial stages and gradually decrease as movement ideas develop.		Devote less time to this section during early stages and gradually allow more time as skill and movement ideas develop.

METHODS OF TEACHING

If children are involved in the process of invention and exploration and are putting together their own movement sequences, the teacher must provide a stimulus rather than a direct command. This is done by proposing a task or a challenge, such as "How many ways can you balance using three parts of your body for support?" or "Can you catch a bean bag using different parts of your body?" The teacher decides upon the range of skills the children are to practice but allows them to think out some possible answers for themselves. Later the teacher may select one child's idea and have the entire class practice this particular skill. The children may also be invited to put two or three of their ideas together to form a sequence. In these situations, the teacher is using a *limitation* method of teaching. That is to say certain important limits have been set on their choice of responses, *but room has been left for some selection and discovery.*

Limitation Method

The limitation method is used most frequently since it allows skills to be learned in an informal setting with the teacher placing limitations and emphasis according to the needs of the children. The following advantages seem to support the general adoption of this method of instruction:

1. It allows for some direction to be given by the teacher, yet the inventiveness of the children is not stifled.
2. It provides for differences in physical ability and encourages personal interest in each child.
3. In spite of individual variations, the general response of the class will fall within certain limits. This makes the task of observation easier and thus general teaching points can be identified.

Figure 2.24 "Travel from one end of the bench to the other, keeping one foot in contact with it."

Direct Method

In the direct method of instruction, the teacher structures the class formation, chooses the type of activity, and prescribes what and how each child shall perform.

Figure 2.25   Attempting headstands on rubber mats.

Let us imagine a lesson where forward rolls are being performed. Many children appear to be banging their heads, instead of tucking them under. The teacher should stop the whole class, give relevant teaching points, and invite everyone to try again.

The preceding case is an example of the direct method since all children are required to perform the same activity.

This method of instruction has many shortcomings with respect to developing initiative and self-direction, however:

1. It allows the teacher to introduce specific skills or rules to all the children at the same time.
2. It is relatively simple to observe only one type of skill.
3. Children sometimes enjoy being told exactly what to do (in contrast to problem-solving).

Indirect Method

The indirect method of instruction allows the children the opportunity to choose the activity or movement to be practiced. They also have the freedom to use any piece of apparatus that is available in the gymnasium.

The distinguishing feature of this method is the freedom or opportunity given to each child to practice on the floor or on any apparatus that is available. The indirect method:

1. Recognizes individual differences in abilities and interests.
2. Allows the teacher to determine what movements the children like to perform.
3. Encourages initiative and self-direction.

The three methods of instruction should not be considered as separate entities even within the framework of a single lesson. In Movement Education, a teacher will often use a combination of all three, depending upon the maturity and skill of the class.

Figure 2.26.   Various activities involving apparatus.

TEACHING BY THEMES

A movement theme may be defined as a concept or an idea which becomes the main focus of a lesson or a series of lessons. Having selected the concept to be stressed, the teacher may add interest and variety by introducing one or even two subthemes. These themes will be devised from the concepts within the movement analysis. To illustrate, the main theme for a series of lessons might be flight, with an emphasis on jumping and landing. A subtheme could be shape (the body can assume a variety of shapes when it is in flight). As part of this theme, the five basic jumps should be explored. The jumps are from one foot to the other, one foot to the same foot, one foot to two feet, two feet to two feet, and two feet to one foot. Flight can also take place from the feet to the hands. This adds a further dimension to the theme, while it strengthens the arm and shoulder girdle muscles. The subtheme of shapes can develop ways of stretching, curling and twisting on the floor as well as in flight.

Having worked on the floor, the idea of flight is then transferred to apparatus. Here a great array of ideas are possible, using objects to jump off, over, and onto. Ropes can be effective, as well as the top of the vaulting box, for flight from the feet onto the hands.

Once the children begin to work independently and can use their ideas to form sequences, the teacher will be able to take a main theme and develop it over five or six lessons. In general, the greater the child's ability to work independently, with a partner, or in a group, the more time the child will need to work out his or her own ideas.

Teaching by theme gives the exploratory approach to learning a framework and a purpose. It also helps to make relationships clear. Differences are sharpened and similarities are strengthened as the activities in one theme are utilized, adapted, or abandoned to fit the changing problems of the next theme.

The lesson plans in Section 2 and 3 have been developed in such a way that there is a natural flow between the four main elements of Movement Education. An unhurried development of games, gymnastics, and dance should characterize primary physical education. A wide "movement vocabulary," work with various equipment (including large apparatus), and themes involving percussion and music are all important for a broad education in movement. They allow children to develop mastery in movement skills, as well as control and confidence in their physical abilities.

With the intermediate grades, the teacher's approach to theme development must take into consideration the nature of the students' pre-vious experience. In most elementary schools, children have been taught units of games, dance, and gymnastic activities. These units normally range from three to six weeks in duration and stress the appropriate skills of each respective activity. In addition, the teaching approach is usually formal with emphasis on the direct teaching method. Some children may be acquainted with the problem-solving method, but few have had any exposure to movement analysis and its terminology.

Older children can be extremely conservative and resentful of change. For this reason, Section 3 gradually leads the teacher and the class from a direct teaching method towards the new Movement Education approach. It begins with a structured games unit and gradually introduces a new format and progression of teaching. The problem-solving method is then introduced, along with a few Movement Education terms. It does not change the basic terminology used in game activities. Once the children have become familiar with the problem-solving method, the new approach is then transferred to gymnastics, where movement terms are gradually introduced. As soon as the children have learned the new vocabulary and how to develop movement ideas, they may be given a theme with a partner or in a group, which may extend over six to eight lessons.

Finally, the teacher and children are introduced to dance. Once children have attained self-discipline in the gym and are used to thinking for themselves, the introduction of dance, with its unique links to the classroom, should be a natural and enjoyable extension of their physical education program. (See film *Theme Development in Movement Education* in Appendix A.)

OBSERVATION AND EVALUATION

Before the teacher or the class can be evaluated, the teacher must become familiar with observational skills and techniques.

Observation

The purpose of observation in physical education is the same as in any other aspect of the curriculum. Teachers assess the overall response to the task at hand and the degree of skill, understanding, and enthusiasm with which it is carried out.

Physical education, being a practical subject, is relatively easy to observe when all the children are doing the same thing at the same time. It is easier in fact than in the classroom where it is often difficult to assess the degree of participation and concentration in the child's mind.

The Movement Education approach incorporates problem-solving techniques that call for exploration and individual response. How then, can one teacher be expected to see the efforts of some twenty to thirty children? First, even the most inexperienced teacher can assess the children's immediate response to the problem or challenge. The teacher can tell if they are interested, excited, puzzled, or apathetic. The teacher can also know *at once* whether the assigned task was suitable for that class's experience.

Once the children are working at a variety of different things, the teacher must employ some specific techniques to observe and evaluate the children's activities. Having made the initial assessment as to the suitability of the task, the teacher must now watch one or two children

Figure 2.27   The teacher may observe a variety of activities.

closely to assess their behavior. Of prime importance is to notice how much effort the children are expending on the task. The class should keep practicing for the length of time it takes to observe two or three other children. The teacher will now have enough information to stop the class and make some relevant suggestions.

Next the teacher may wish to observe half the class at a time. This will allow the rest of the class to rest and incidentally sharpen the children's own powers of observation and understanding. The class will be asked to look for one or two specific things and encouraged to give fair and constructive criticism. Observing half the class at a time will allow the teacher to see many more details in the children's work.

As the children practice (repetition is vital for the physical exercise of the body), the teacher will soon be able to assess the quality of work that is being performed and estimate the degree of concentration among the children. It is at this point that movement analysis will become invaluable. Using this analysis, the teacher has a simple checklist with which to evaluate the potential of the movement. What would happen if the *direction* of the movements were altered? Could better or more exciting use be made of changing levels? What use has been made of *speed* and *strength of actions*? If partner or group work is in progress, the teacher can watch for the different uses of *relationships*. In this way, the teacher observes and evaluates the quality of movement and can make appropriate suggestions and decisions.

In the games lesson, the teacher observes the specific skill that is utilized in the game activity. Are the children successful in aiming; if not, are they releasing the ball from their hands too early or too late? Are they making sensible use of space when throwing and catching with a partner or in a group. If they find throwing and catching difficult, they should reduce the space between them (or increase the space if they are skilled).

Encouraging and stimulating effort is a vital aspect of observation as children must be encouraged to work to their capacities. They must seek out the most skillful responses they are capable of making. Fortunately, children encourage each other in this respect. They watch and see others in the class and most children know at once whether they can also perform the same activity. They certainly know if they would like to try. Through encouragement from the teacher and the stimulus of other children's ideas, the range and the quality of performance should grow hand and hand.

Evaluation

Evaluation is concerned with the assessment of each child's effort, skill, and understanding. Imagination and social awareness are also important aspects of the "new" physical education and should be considered in connection with any evaluation. Most of these qualities, skills, and attitudes take time to develop, and initially the teacher must depend upon an assessment of each child's effort, as this is most easily recognized.

In the process of evaluating the class, the teacher cannot help but assess the suitability of the material and methods of teaching. For this reason, observation, evaluation, and further planning are all part of a continuous process.

PLANNING THE PROGRAM

Once the teacher understands the new methods of teaching and the potential contribution of games, gymnastics, and dance to the physical education program, it is hoped that he or she will gradually move to an equal balance of these three areas within the curriculum.

Teachers who find that they enjoy this approach to physical education may wish to experiment with curriculum planning. Planning a Movement Education curriculum involves teaching games, gymnastics, and dance concurrently. The fact that these areas of study are *not* taught by the unit method (where each unit is taught separately) allows for a steady development of all the skills as the year progresses. Many teachers believe that by the end of the year the overall standard of work is higher than it would have been otherwise. Furthermore, as children tend to prefer different parts of the physical education program, the "concurrent design" means that each child has a favorite lesson at least once a week.

In conclusion, we hope that the philosophy of this book will prove thought-provoking, and that the lesson plans and ideas it contains will be of genuine help to teachers in the elementary school.

Section 2

Movement Education in the Primary Grades

Chapter Three: Gymnastics

Chapter Four: Dance

Chapter Five: Games

The format of Section 2 has been changed slightly in this edition in order to provide the teachers with an outline of the material to be covered by listing the movement tasks and by presenting a very simple analysis at the beginning of each lesson.

LESSON OUTLINE

The analysis of each outline is presented to help the teacher focus attention on the main movement ideas and to gain insight and understanding of the movement principles. Although movement analysis is complex, it is very useful in helping the teacher with little experience or background set up a physical education program. In the primary lesson plans, stress is put upon the WHAT and WHERE in gymnastics and games, and the WHAT and HOW in the dance lessons. WHAT, WHERE, and HOW the body moves are equally important in dance, gymnastics, and games, but for inexperienced teachers it makes more sense to work gradually at understanding how to analyze movement by taking one stage at a time.

ORGANIZATION AND TEACHING POINTS

Each chapter in Section 2 is divided into themes. The themes, in turn, are composed of various lessons, designed to aid the teacher in preparing activities and goals according to the Movement Education approach.

The three chapters in this section are devoted to gymnastics, dance, and games. In the primary grades there should be an equal amount of time given to each. Because teachers usually have less practical experience in gymnastics and dance, they sometimes have difficulty in preparing these lessons. To assist the teacher with these lessons, a greater number of detailed lesson plans have been included for gymnastics and dance. Teachers will be able to augment the games lessons from their own experience, adapting the material as necessary.

TIME ALLOTMENT AND FACILITIES

Some teachers attempt to complete each lesson plan in one twenty-minute session and then move on to the next lesson. Certainly most material can be taught in one forty-minute period to some classes. However, each class varies, and if large equipment is available, the same material may be used for four or five lessons with slight variations.

The age and prior experience of the children will determine the amount of time spent on each lesson. The tasks are listed in order of difficulty in each part of the lesson; the first task in each part being the easiest and the last the most demanding. Only the teacher can decide what is suitable for each class and how long the children will remain absorbed and interested. The teacher may, therefore, spend only thirty seconds on some tasks and five minutes on others.

Discussion with beginning teachers of Movement Education reveals that most of them feel more successful and enthusiastic teaching twenty minute lessons, particularly those who have to work in a classroom or hallway. Their reasons for this seem to be: (a) they feel the children work better during a shorter period, (b) daily lessons can be arranged using the classroom for some activities and the gym or out-of-doors for others, (c) teachers feel they can manage twenty minutes of the unknown, but forty minutes can be demoralizing for both teacher and children, and (d) the lessons often fall apart when it comes to the apparatus section.

To overcome problems in the apparatus section, many teachers find it satisfactory to have the Introductory Activity and the Movement Training in a twenty-minute period on one day, followed on that day or the next by a twenty-minute apparatus period.

ADAPTATIONS

Some schools do not have an activity room or gymnasium. Teachers should realize that many of the lesson plans may be adapted to the classroom by omitting some of the tasks and substituting others.

Many teachers who could work in a gymnasium prefer to begin their physical education programs in the classroom. This is because they find it easier to establish behavioral attitudes in the classroom and move to the gymnasium later, when they feel more confident about working in the larger space.

Teachers may like to experiment with having the class work in only half of the gymnasium. This restricted, but ample area may allow teachers to feel more confident and able to teach successfully.

In selecting equipment tasks for gymnastics groups, a useful rule of thumb is to attempt to provide the following for each class:

1. Section A: work at a task that directly relates to applying the Movement Training to a new situation, for example, with a partner or with small or large equipment.
2. Section B: work on tasks where arm strength is developed; supporting own body weight on arms and legs, travelling or balancing, or hanging onto and climbing up large equipment.
3. Section C: practice tasks where leaping, landing, and rolling develop leg strength and safety.
4. Section D: develop tasks where balance is the skill.

In the first few lessons diagrams show suggestions of this type. Mix and match tasks to suit the child, your class, the equipment, and the facilities available.

Chapter Three

Gymnastics

Theme One: Safety Training

Theme Two: Adding to the Range and Understanding of Movement

Theme Three: Understanding Space and Directional Movements

Theme Four: Qualities

The gymnastic lessons in this chapter are built around four main themes. The "Safety Training" theme is used as an introduction to the philosophy, methodology, and organization of Movement Education. "Adding to the Range and Understanding of Movement" emphasizes the WHAT, "Understanding Direction" emphasizes the WHERE, and "Qualities" emphasizes the HOW of Laban's analysis of movement.

Greater detail is given for the planning and organization of the gymnastic lessons, but these details apply equally to the dance and game lesson plans.

THEME ONE: SAFETY TRAINING

Before a teacher embarks upon the first theme entitled "Safety Training," it is imperative that the meaning of this term is fully understood. In its broadest interpretation, it includes not only the attitudes of the teacher and children toward their work in the gymnasium but an understanding of how to protect oneself on or off the apparatus. Safety Training, therefore, is an integral part of any lesson in Movement Education.

Figure 3.1 Jumping from a height.

The Attitude of the Teacher

What should the attitude of the teacher be toward the use of the time spent in the gymnasium? Should the gymnasium be regarded as an extension of the classroom where thoughtful learning takes place through careful guidance? Is it a place where the teacher motivates the students by allowing them to discover things by themselves, by building their confidence, and by stimulating their interests and imaginations? Is it a place where opportunities are provided for responsible and considerate behavior? Perhaps a teacher may feel that the classroom situation creates a strain on the children and that their time in the gymnasium must provide a release in the form of noisy and unrestrained activities. If the latter is the teacher's goal for gymnasium activities, then a Movement Education program should not be considered, since its goals are totally incompatible with this point of view.

Any teacher who does not capitalize on the time spent in the gymnasium to extend and often initiate the learning process is losing a most valuable opportunity. Those who teach physical education have one of the easiest tasks in making learning both interesting and enjoyable. Yet it has often been stated that not all children enjoy physical activity. It is the writers' contention, as well as that of many leading experts, that it is not the activity which children learn to dislike, it is the way it is taught that creates negative attitudes. When one observes kindergarten children, particularly at the beginning of the year, one is left with no doubt that the desire for movement is a wonderful and natural phenomenon. However, this phase needs proper guidance and direction as children grow. In most instances, when children are given unsuitable activities or forced into competitive activities before they are ready, or made to stand still in a long line before they can have a turn, then the foundations are laid for negative atti-

Figure 3.2   Carrying benches correctly.

tudes toward physical activity, which may last a lifetime.

Learning and learning theories do not suddenly stop outside the gymnasium doors; children can learn wherever they are. Few teachers would think of using a whistle to control children in the classroom or tolerate a noise level where only a whistle could restore order. Why then is it often thought essential in the gymnasium? (Apart from sports such as volleyball and basketball, where the whistle is used for officiating.) The range of the human voice can much more effectively express approval or disapproval. One simply cannot build confidence or stimulate imagination with a whistle.

In addition to the attitude of the teacher, what can be done to extend the classroom into the gymnasium? The following paragraphs do not contain radically new ideas for the teacher who has already individualized learning in the classroom. Many of the suggestions are very simple, but the experienced teacher will recognize that often the simplest suggestions are the most effective.

Let us look at the types of situations that force a child to go beyond his or her abilities, or those where the teacher, rather than the child, assumes the responsibility for safety.

1. A situation arises where the whole class becomes so excited that something which originally was considered fun becomes uncontrolled and the children end up having an accident or in tears. This often occurs in the primary grades with running games which involve chasing. To stop this type of activity may sound as though we are trying to take all the fun out of the gymnasium. This is not the case; however, one must make sure that the type of activity is suitable to the maturity and experience of the children. For example, in one popular Introductory Activity, children had "tails," tucked in the back of their shorts, then ran all over the gymnasium floor trying

Figure 3.3   "Run anywhere in the gym."

to catch as many of the other children's bands as possible without losing their own. One could see from their faces how much they enjoyed it. The activity, however, was not introduced until the children had been working in the gymnasium for about three months. If this game had been played before the children understood and had experienced safety training, there might have been trouble and accidents.

Figure 3.4   Tails.

2.   A teacher may become overly concerned with the children's safety; hence, instead of creating situations where the children gradually learn to accept responsibility for their own safety, the teacher overprotects the children in order to make the gymnasium a "safe" place. For example, if children are arranged in lines for calisthenics, the spacing is often arrived at by putting the hands on the shoulders of the child in front. The children learn to reason that because they have done this, they are not likely to touch or bump into other children. Hence, in this type of formation the child feels relieved of any responsibility. Another example of overprotection is children who have been trained to run around the gymnasium in one direction only. Again, the *teacher* has taken the responsibility for their safety. The teacher will say "Run clockwise around the gymnasium," whereas, by telling them to "run anywhere in the gymnasium

taking care not to collide" makes the children responsible for their own space awareness.

Kindergarten and first-grade children coming into the gymnasium for the first time do not naturally run in the same direction around the gymnasium. They run at different speeds because some are more physically mature and capable than others. It is interesting to watch how very few run fast at the start. That is not because they cannot go faster; it is because they are conscious that they may collide with someone else. Children who start by being allowed to run freely where the teacher emphasizes no collisions soon learn to run quickly and safely anywhere in the gymnasium.

Older children who have been conditioned to running around the gymnasium in one direction may take longer to adapt. This was particularly noticeable in one third grade class. It was apparent that they had little idea of how much space they needed to move in and how fast they could travel and still maintain control. Although they had lots of imagination and several good movement ideas, they had many problems moving apparatus, and working without encroaching on another child's space. It was necessary to stress this side of safety training for a much longer period with this group.

3.   Another potential danger exists when children are "spotted" or helped physically

Figure 3.5   "Travel in and out of the beanbags."

by the teacher or another classmate in performing a movement. Here part of the responsibility for safety is shifted from the performer to the spotter. Children should be taught to help one another but only *after* the child has first been taught to be responsible for his or her own personal safety. Few children are really physically capable of preventing a child from getting hurt. Needless to say it is also unfair to place a young child in such a position of responsibility.

4. Perhaps the most common cause of accidents occurs when children are forced to attempt tasks beyond their capabilities. This can happen if the children feel they are letting their teammates down, or they think that it is the only way they can gain teacher approval. Not all children are physically capable of performing the same things simply because they are the same chronological age.

The Attitude of the Children

How then can a teacher inculcate the attitudes of self-control, self-discipline, responsibility, and consideration? Perhaps the very first lesson in self-control for the child should be stopping and starting. This can be taught so that children enjoy it. Suitable activities will be found in the lesson plans for primary and intermediate grades. Keep the activities short, and include lots of starting and stopping, making sure all the children are involved. Insist on immediate response when you say "stop." The teacher may find children who try to take an extra turn. This must be discouraged as it is time wasted and unfair to other children. Usually, when working in groups, the other children exert the necessary pressure to prevent a recurrence. Sharing and taking turns leads to self-control and is usually stressed in the apparatus section of each lesson.

Self-discipline is fostered by allowing children to solve appropriate and meaningful problems. To accomplish this, the problems set by the teacher must be sufficiently broad to enable the least able as well as the skilled to find a solution.

Responsibility can be taught in many ways. A teacher must provide opportunities for each child to learn to run without colliding, to fall without getting hurt, and to carry apparatus carefully.

Consideration is linked so closely with responsibility it is often difficult to draw the line. Perhaps it is most easily shown in the sharing of equipment and movement ideas.

Figure 3.6   Cooperating and sharing with a partner.

One word concerning working in bare feet and on hard surfaces without mats should be noted. Young children adapt to this very quickly and show sensitivity and careful handling of themselves when landing and rolling without mats. Older children take longer to adapt because of their previous experiences. Children and teachers are encouraged to work in bare feet where the surface of the floor makes it possible.

Figure 3.7 Jumping from apparatus.

The authors have experienced all types of undesirable teaching situations, particularly where children rush into the gymnasium in a noisy, uncontrolled fashion and with an attitude which precludes any form of genuine learning and teaching. The battle with this type of class may be long and uphill. The teacher may have to rely upon more formal activities while attempting to inculcate desirable attitudes. On the other hand, many classes react well to the very first lesson taught with a Movement Education approach. It might be of interest to know, in the case of most of our student teachers who were introducing this approach in the various schools, the first three weeks were often spent battling noise, lack of sensitivity, and an indifferent attitude toward learning in the gymnasium. After this initial three-week period there was usually a transition to an enormously exciting atmosphere for both teacher and class. The children had become interested and challenged,

and consequently accepted their new responsibilities. At the same time the student teacher began to see genuine spontaneity and creativity from the children.

So far we have said a great deal about the attitudes which are so necessary to ensure the safety of the children, but little on action. The accompanying lessons will describe some ways to teach children to perform the safety sideways roll and how to land from heights. These are the main activities that are described in detail in the accompanying lesson plans.

The following lesson plans are suitable for any primary class which has not been in the gymnasium before, or for a class which has been conditioned to run in one direction in the gymnasium.

It should be realized that in the initial stages the average time for kindergarten and grade one to change into gymnasium clothes is almost twelve minutes. Grades two and three will take approximately eight minutes. However, this is not time wasted as they learn to tie shoes, fasten back buttons, and many other tasks which, with practice, can be speeded up to three to four minutes for the whole class. Encourage children to ask their parents to time them when they get dressed in the morning. Also reward those who are quick by allowing them to join into free play with balls or hoops, until all are ready to begin the lesson.

Apparatus work should always include some

Figure 3.8 "Change as quickly as you can."

work from the previous lesson. The teacher can introduce one or two new ideas in each lesson when all groups have worked on the previous activities. The list of tasks shows how different apparatus can be used for this lesson plan.

Each lesson provides an infinite variety of movement challenges, hence the teacher can easily teach many lessons from this base, according to how quickly the members of the class think their way through the various tasks. Working with a partner will stimulate ideas and a feeling of flow can be stimulated by asking the children to link one solution to another.

Movement sequences develop naturally from these activities and as with all these lesson outlines, the teacher must decide whether the children have made sufficient progress in one lesson to enable them to be ready for the next, or whether the lesson should be repeated.

The children should spend at least five minutes on *each* piece of apparatus before new work is introduced. It may be that the Movement Training part of the lesson may exceed ten minutes or longer in order for the children to have sufficient background to work on the apparatus. If this is the case then the second lesson should begin with the Introductory Activity, followed by a brief revision of the Movement Training, and then twenty minutes spent on the apparatus, thus allowing them to cover four sections. By this stage all classes (of twen-

ty-four children or more) should be working in the four sections broken into subgroups. It is, therefore, possible in a gymnasium to organize eight different apparatus activities. To cover any one of the lesson plans the teacher could spend three or more lessons developing the basic material.

It is very important that the teacher does not present a series of new ideas which give the children a chance to explore and discover **without** giving time for repetition and refinement. Each teacher must *teach* and by this we mean clarify and expand the children's basic movement ideas. Unless some of the sequences that embody the basic ideas are developed through questions by the teacher which lead the children to a wider range of understanding, much of the potential will be lost. Further, they will not derive the satisfaction that comes with creating and working hard to produce a movement or sequence that has shape and form and can be performed at a high standard. Perhaps the best four guidelines a teacher can use to

Figure 3.10   Partner work on large apparatus.

Figure 3.9   Balance sequences on benches.

determine whether the class is ready to move on to a new lesson plan are:

1. "Have they had time to explore?"
2. "Have they had time to discover and invent?"
3. "Have they had time to repeat?"
4. "Have they reached a good standard of performance?"

Ask the children to run anywhere in the gymnasium without bumping. (See Figure 3.11.) They should stop quickly and stand still when the teacher says "stop." Continue for three to four minutes. The purpose of this activity is to establish class control as the children must *listen* for your voice. Explain that sometimes you will say "stop" loudly while at other times you may speak very softly. Keep the interval between "stop" and "go" quite short (5-15 seconds) according to how sensibly they run. If the class does not respond quickly ask them to sit down instead of standing still when you say "stop" and make it a "musical bumps" game. Use "stop, sit, and listen" as the task (See Figure 3.12.)

Figure 3.11 Run anywhere without colliding.

Figure 3.12 "Stop, sit, and listen."

LESSON 1

Analysis: WHERE?   Use of general space.

WHAT?   Whole body actions to avoid collisions and log rolls.

Lesson Outline

Introductory Activity Tasks

1. "Run, using all the space, and without colliding with anyone."
2. "Stop, sit, and listen."

Movement Training Tasks

1. "Find a space, lie on the floor, make yourself long and thin."
2. "Roll like a log, go smoothly and slowly to avoid collisions."

Apparatus Tasks

Select from these or other tasks.

1. "Find a partner as you walk about the gym. Use all the space and keep on walking with your partner."
2. "Stop, sit, and listen."
3. "When I say 'go,' take one piece of equipment to a space and play with it."
4. "Put your equipment away and sit in your section place."

Section D Beanbags for hand- eye coordination	Section A Hoops for leg work, skipping, or jumping
Section C Skipping ropes for leg and footwork	Section B Balls for hand-eye, foot-eye coordination

Introductory Activity

Teaching Points

1. Praise the first child you see who stops each time. This is the beginning of your observation.
2. Notice the child who is last to stop, only commenting if the child improves, as "John was the first to stop that time and Susan was much quicker than she was the last time."
3. Praise a child who does not collide and explain why she is good. Watch to see if any child repeatedly collides and if so make him walk until he has two turns without colliding.
4. Observe whether *all* the space of the gymnasium or classroom is being used. Are they running around the edge of the area

leaving a great crater of space in the center? If so, ask the children to make zigzag patterns with their feet as they run.

5. Emphasize good footwork. Running on balls of feet is essential in order to train the sensitivity in footwork which is a foundation of good movement, whether in games, gymnastics, or dance.

"What!" you are saying, "All this in three minutes?" "Yes," we are saying, "but perhaps not all at once." In the first lesson it may be enough to accomplish just "stopping and starting" but suppose they are good at this, then check collisions, use of space, and footwork. Of course much will depend on each respective class. Nevertheless, as you will see in this Introductory Activity many things can be varied to keep the children's interest and, at the same time, will give the teacher an opportunity to emphasize these points. Bear in mind the purpose of the Introductory Activity is to provide a general warm-up period for the children, to establish class tone, and to stimulate interest.

6. If the children are better than you expected, let them know this. Also indicate that since they were so clever in stopping and starting you are going to look for two things, stopping and starting and *no* collisions. Then make it three by adding space and zigzag floor patterns. Add this only when *real* progress is apparent.

General Comment   To link this back to the explanation of safety training, the Introductory Activity first required the self-control to stop and start when told. Next we have borrowed twice from the space theme (Theme 3) by emphasizing running without colliding and running in zigzag patterns. Finally, we have borrowed from qualities (Theme 4) by requiring lightness of feet. All of these activities, however, specifically relate in a direct way to safety training.

Movement Training
(approximately five minutes)
Ask the children to find a space of their own, and make sure it is big enough for them to lie

down without touching someone else. You must *look* to see that they are well spaced and, if necessary, ask children to move into larger spaces.

If you are working in a very small space, have the children find a partner; ask one to lie down and the other to remain standing. Wherever the task is performed, ask the children who are on the floor to make themselves very long and very thin. Some will stretch their arms above their heads, while others will not. Choose a child who is performing it with arms well extended and ask the others to sit up and observe the child's demonstration. Point out that the "demonstrator's" fingers are stretched as well as his toes.

Observe that most of the class will automatically lie on their backs to do this movement. Hence, ask them to try the same movement while lying on their stomachs. This will lead the class to the next stage which is "Roll on to your side and stay there (Figure 3.13). Next, roll on to your back, over to the other side, and back on to your tummy."

Children enjoy doing this and you can get them to change from tummies to backs as well as introduce left and right side at the same time. Now, allow them to roll across the floor for a very short time. Stop any child before he collides with another. In this instance, it is helpful to stand by two who are about to collide and ask the others to sit up and look. Ask them what would have happened if you hadn't said

Figure 3.13   "Roll onto your side."

"stop." Can they think what these two should do? Some will say "roll the other way and in grades two or three you may have one child who will say "find a larger space." If no child volunteers the answer you could say, "Instead of bumping, wouldn't it be fun to jump up and find another large space where you could start rolling again? Try that this time." Often you will find they will do this just for fun whether they are about to collide or not. Finally, make sure that they do not roll in one direction too long as they will become dizzy.

Classroom Adaptation Once half the class begins rolling, those standing may run in and out carefully avoiding the "rollers." The children should change positions with their partners after short turns. This may be developed into running and jumping over the *feet* of all the "rollers" for grades two and three. This is for safety and to prevent them from stepping on heads or tummies.

Figure 3.14 "Run in and out among the log rollers."

General Comments Let us link this sideways roll to safety training and to future themes.
1. The children had to select a space large enough to lie down without touching anyone else. This promotes responsibility since they must make the initial decision.
2. We have borrowed a theme of "body awareness" (Theme 2) by stressing tummies,

backs and sides, and stretching fingers and toes.
3. We have introduced rolling in the safety training theme.
4. We have repeated no collisions as in the Introductory Activity which requires self-control and self-discipline.

In later lessons we will be able to draw upon the "borrowed themes" by referring the children back, by saying to them "Do you remember how you had to stretch for the log roll?"

Apparatus Work
(approximately five minutes)
Tell each child to take a friend's hand and sit in a space anywhere in the gymnasium. Be quick to spot those without a partner and join them in twos. Now, make four groups in the center allocating three or four pairs to each group according to class size. When in four groups explain that these will be their "section places" (or teams or homes) for apparatus work and they must remember where their places are and who is in their sections. Give them time to look and see who is in the same group. Then see if they can play the game of "section places." Here they can run, skip, or walk anywhere without colliding and when you say "section places" (or whatever term you wish to use) they run to their right places. (Figure 3.15)

Figure 3.15 Section places.

Figure 3.16   Free play in section places.

In kindergarten and grade one this will require lots of practice. If the class can remember section places quickly and accurately three times in a row, then let each section have a minute or two free play with small apparatus. Section places will be arranged as follows:

Section one: A ball for each child
Section two: A hoop for each child
Section three: A beanbag for each child
Section four: A skipping rope for each child

When you say "apparatus away, and back to your section places," each child must return his apparatus, then sit in his section place. Keep the storage box away from the wall and section places to allow for free circulation.

Classroom Adaptation   Use only two types of equipment and divide the space in two, so that two groups use hoops in one and the other two groups use beanbags in the rest of the space. You may have to restrict the activities to those which take place in their own space, for example, skipping with a hoop or jumping in and out of it, while the children with beanbags could practice throwing and catching on their own or with a partner.

General Comments   The apparatus work is related to safety training in the following way:

1.   Sitting with a partner in a space requires cooperation and relates to the space theme.
2.   Children begin to develop group responsibility for sharing apparatus, learning to take turns, and getting out apparatus. If a different child (or two) from each section puts the apparatus box into position and two other children put it away at the end of the period, this provides more opportunities for developing responsibility as well as self-confidence.
3.   Remembering their groups encourages individual responsibility.
4.   Each group working freely in one quarter of the gymnasium and not going into another group's space provides opportunities for practicing self-control and self-discipline.
5.   Free play here entails working in a space by oneself without getting in another child's way, thus using freedom with consideration.

How much each teacher can do in the first lesson will, of course, depend upon the class. Some will be capable of doing *all* in the first lesson particularly at the grade three level; however, kindergarten children will need much practice, so it will be unlikely that they will work on any apparatus in this lesson. It will be difficult for these younger children to remember section places quickly enough. Also, they will be happy to play "section places" much longer than would third grade children.

This is where we can only make suggestions. Each teacher must decide whether the class is ready to move on to a new challenge. If the children need more practice on a particular item, then you should choose another way of presenting the same material, still teaching and stressing the points you are trying to develop. You will soon learn which activities produce good results from your own class. Do not be afraid to try out your own variations as you go along.

This first lesson is based mostly on the direct and limitation teaching methods. The only indirect method came at the very beginning of the period where those who made a quick change were rewarded by having time to choose and play freely; and at the end, if there was time to go into actual apparatus work, to play freely with the apparatus.

"How" you are saying "can I remember all this and teach at the same time?" The movement tasks in the outline will provide a simple, quick guide to use when you are teaching.

If you feel the children are not sufficiently at ease moving to section places and working freely with one set of apparatus, repeat apparatus work for Lesson 1. Before moving on to new work, rotate each section, after they have had a short turn with their apparatus, so that they may experience playing with a different set. After each turn, the children should return equipment to the box, then return to section places. When everyone is sitting in their section places, tell Mary's section that they are going to play with beanbags in John's section place. With kindergarten you may say "Let's watch and see if Mary's section can go to John's sec-

tion place. Good, then come back again, and sit down. Now let's see if John's section can go to Bill's section place," etc., until all have practiced moving one place around. Emphasize no pushing, then let them have a short turn with their new apparatus. If possible allow the class to go to all four section places. They may not have too many ideas to start with for each piece of apparatus. At this stage you should be stressing safety, class organization, and freedom to choose for themselves. If they can work by themselves even for a short period, this is good—two minutes at each section is probably enough. Getting apparatus out of the box quickly and without fuss and putting it away is also important. Comments such as "Do you know in grade one, John's section had much longer to play with their apparatus because they didn't push each other trying to get it" and "Bill's section was very quick at putting their apparatus away neatly so that it is ready for Mary's section to use," are particularly helpful at this stage.

LESSON 2

Analysis: WHERE: Own space within general space.
           WHAT?   Elbows, noses, knees, log and safety rolls.

Lesson Outline

Introductory Activity Tasks

1. "Run anywhere without colliding; when I say stop, hide your nose so that I can't see it."
2. "Who could think of another part of your body that you could hide this time?"
3. "This time I am going to make it really hard. When I say stop, hide your nose, elbows, and knees."

Movement Training Tasks

1. "Find a space on your own and practice log rolls."

If individual mats, 3' x 18" or 4' x 2', are available:

2. "Find a partner, collect a mat, take it to a space, and practice log rolls."
3. "Roll as quickly as you can from one end of the mat to the other."
4. "Bend your arms and tuck your elbows into your tummy this time as you roll."
5. "Start in a log position, curl up into a safety position as you roll."

Apparatus Tasks

Select from these or other tasks.

1. Section A: "Keeping in your section's space, try to go through the hoop while it is moving."

and/or

2. "Try skipping with your hoop, backwards or forwards."
3. Section B: "Take a ball to a space and play with it. Be sensible and careful not to spoil other's activities."

and/or

4. "Can you log roll and make the ball move as you roll?"
5. Section C: "How many ways can you find to travel along the bench and do a safety roll on landing?"
6. Section D: "How many different rolls can you do?"

and/or

7. "Faint and safety roll."

Section D Mats for application of Movement Training and observation for development	Section A Hoops for agility
Section C Bench or balance beam for arm strength	Section B Balls for coordination

Introductory Activity

The emphasis here will be running and stopping, hiding elbows, knees, and noses. Before they start to run tell them which part of them they must hide when you say "stop."

You are still stressing the same safety ideas as in the first Introductory Activity, which are:

1. Quick response to "stop."
2. No collisions.
3. Sensible use of space.
4. Good footwork. The teacher uses this Introductory Activity to lay the foundation for the sideways safety roll (which follows later in this lesson) in a very simple fashion. It may be developed by posing the following questions:
   a. "Hide your nose this time when I say 'stop.'" Walk around and comment on those whose noses are really hidden.
   b. "This time I am going to make it more difficult. Noses were easy to hide, but as you run think how you can hide your knees when I say 'stop.'" Again walk around making sure all can do it. If not, select a child who is really hiding knees.
   c. "Good, this time it is going to be more difficult. I wonder who will be able to think of a really good way of hiding their elbows when I say 'stop.'"
      They usually find this the hardest to do. After they have had a try, select

a child who tucks her elbows into her tummy, as this is the best position for the safety roll; ask them all to try it this way. Practice each task two or three times.
   d. "Show me how clever you are; can you hide all three—elbows, knees, and noses at the same time when I say 'stop.'"
      This usually produces many giggles. Walk around and check that all parts are tucked in. It may be necessary to say "Michael, I can see your nose," or "Sally, your elbows are not tucked away." You must *observe* what is going on so that you can help the children and prepare them for the next stage.

General Comments We are borrowing from the body awareness theme by identifying certain parts of the body, but again the stress is on safety.

Movement Training

Practice log and tucked-sideways safety rolls (5-6 minutes). Continue posing questions:

1. "Is the space large enough for you to lie down and practice the log rolls as we did in the last lesson? If not, go into a bigger space

Figure 3.17 "Hide your nose."

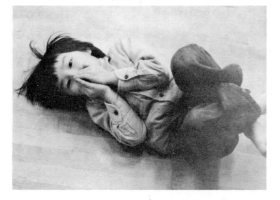

Figure 3.18 "Hide your elbows, knees, and nose."

and start practicing right away." Let them have a short turn, remind them of the main points (see previous lesson). Give another short turn watching to see that they are not colliding and are using the space.

2. "This time log roll with your elbows tucked into your tummy." If working on a mat with a partner, have one child roll from one end to the other, while the other child runs in a semicircle from the opposite end and is ready to start his roll as the first child finishes. This can become a continuous cycle and in some places is known as "keeping the kettle boiling." If you encourage them to go as quickly as they can, usually one child (or more) will begin to tuck up her knees, therefore doing the safety roll. Use these children to demonstrate how they roll into the safety position. Emphasize tucking up knees, and safety rolling becomes easy. Make sure that they keep elbows and noses, as well as knees, tucked in so they are round like a ball.

Figure 3.19   "Tuck your arms in as you roll."

Figure 3.20   Tucked safety-roll position.

Apparatus Work

In this lesson grades two and three should be ready to apply safety rolling to apparatus work. Use two benches and two large mats. Keep the balls and hoops for the other two sections and arrange as follows:

1. Rolling hoop: (keeping in their quarter of the gymnasium).
   "Try to go through it while moving." Encourage rolling as soon as they go through.

Figure 3.21   "Safety roll on the floor when you have gone through your hoop."

2. Balls: Free play or gently moving ball along against tummy by doing log rolls and not letting ball travel too far (a ball the size of a volleyball is best for this).

3. Benches: Travel along bench using any method but taking care to land with safety roll on floor. It is not necessary to have mats at the end of the bench but if you have more than two, use them. Moving benches is serious business. *Five* children to each bench for all primary grades, possibly more in kindergarten and grade one. Lay down firm rules. These are some suggestions:
   a. *Nobody* lifts the bench until *all* are ready to lift.
   b. The child at either end must look to see that the rest have hands underneath the bench ready to lift. Stress

that *all* children must help and be very strong.

c. The two children at the ends say "lift."

d. One of the "ends" usually has to walk backwards. He must look over his shoulder to see where he is going. Also the "end" who is walking forwards should also make sure that they will not walk into another group or piece of apparatus. The forward "end" should act as the pilot.

e. When putting the bench down they should remind themselves and each other to keep their toes out of the way.

f. The bench should be put down *carefully and quietly.*

g. If not well done, make them put it back and get it out again, while groups who did it well get on with their work.

4. Large Mats: Any type of roll along mat. Encourage lots of quick turns. If the mats are the large (4' × 8') then two children can roll across each mat simultaneously. With some groups of grades two and three (and this depends on individual classes), the children can have fun developing good safety rolls by asking them to "faint" and as they flop onto the mat, turn their movement into a safety side-

Figure 3.22   Stress safety rules when moving benches.

ways roll. Another way is for them to deliberately trip up on the edge of the mat and then curl up and roll. This is one of the best ways of getting nearest to a "real-life" situation, and by stressing that hands and elbows must be tucked in and not touch the mat, the teacher can get the safety training across. Ask them to watch each other to see who tucks his hands in so they do not touch the mat. (Individual mats may be used if available.)

General Comments   Remember that you must keep an eye on all four sections. Do not become so involved with one section that the others feel you have forgotten them. Some children find it more difficult than others to work by themselves; hence, the teacher should watch for those who need the extra boost until they can confidently work alone. Also, discipline problems will develop if you neglect the rest for one group, particularly in the beginning stages and if the class has been accustomed to a formal setting where they all did the same thing at the same time. At the same time cut short any type of silly behavior. Kindergarten and grade one adapt very quickly; however, children of this age level will tend to seek the center of attention by very obvious methods, hence, the teacher must tell the child to go back to his section place and work there and the teacher will watch him from a distance. This simple technique makes them realize that the teacher does not have to be standing next to them to see what they are doing.

Most teachers will feel quite at ease with the Introductory Activity and Movement Training parts of the lesson but may feel out of their depth with the Apparatus section. This is a familiar feeling to all beginning teachers. For your own security, if you have enough equipment you may decide that you would feel more at ease if every child worked freely with the same type of apparatus. For example, if you have a class set of beanbags, divide the children into sections as in Lesson 1, then have four boxes of beanbags and proceed from there. Next lesson, if you have a class set of balls, let them work the same way. When you feel ready, have two groups using the one type of apparatus while the other two use a different type and gradually build towards four groups working with four different types of equipment.

Teachers, like children, learn at different rates; some can observe a wider range of activities more quickly than others and therefore can have four different things going on and also will be able to subdivide these four sections. The latter may be necessary when there is a limited amount of one type of apparatus. If children have something to work with, they soon learn to work independently and discipline problems usually disappear.

LESSON 3

Analysis: WHERE?   General space, levels.

WHAT?   Parts of the body, run, leap, land, roll.

Lesson Outline

Free play until all are ready.

Introductory Activity Tasks

1. "Run without colliding and when I say 'stop' make your knees the highest part of you."
2. "This time when I say 'stop' make your elbows the highest part of you."
3. "Can you suggest a part of the body you could make the highest?"
4. "Choose for yourself this time."

Movement Training Tasks

1. "Take a piece of equipment to a space and practice jumping over it."
2. "Run and leap over your equipment."
3. "Run and leap over your equipment, then land and roll."

Apparatus Tasks

Select from these or other tasks.

1. Section A: "Take a rope to a space and practice tying a bow with your hands."

and/or

2. "Tie a knot in the rope using your feet only."
3. Section B: "Work with a partner and one hoop. One of you hold the hoop while the other goes through it. Take turns."
4. Section C: "Jump off the equipment, land, and safety roll."
5. Section D: "Run along the broad side of the bench, jump off, land, and roll."

and/or

6. "Step onto bench, leap off, land, and roll."

Section D Bench or beam for balance or leg work application of Movement Training Changing levels	Section A Skipping ropes for improving motor skills
Section C Any large equipment or stage with chairs and mats for application of Movement Training Changing levels	Section B Hoops for application of Movement Training or free play

Free play until all are ready. However, you may now like to suggest practicing rolls on the floor or mats. This period of time should be getting shorter, particularly with grades two and three (ten minutes).

Introductory Activity
(3-4 minutes)

Practice running then stopping with different parts *high*, such as elbows, knees, and noses. If you choose knees first, this will help to get them started. Questions that will help to extend their movement experiences are:

1. "How can you make your elbows highest if you are lying down?" (On tummies or backs, and get them to experience both.)
2. "How can you make your knees highest when you lie on your backs?"
3. "Can you do it with your nose too?"
4. "Now you choose one part of you, *not* your nose, knees, or elbows and make that highest and we will guess which part you have chosen." (Figure 3.23)
5. "Now work with your partner, one placing one part high and the other guessing, then change and give your partner a chance." Pick out interesting ones.

Figure 3.23 "Choose which part you will make highest."

This activity borrows heavily from the theme "Adding to the Range and Understanding of Movement," but is very necessary as the children are soon going to start to land and roll off apparatus from various heights. Knowledge and skill in this area increases their safety. It will still be necessary, however, to stress the safety factors of previous Introductory Activities.

Movement Training
(5-6 minutes)

Having spent three lessons working on rolling, it is time to turn our attention to footwork for landing. This can be taught more effectively if the children work *without* shoes and socks. Begin by having them leap over beanbags, bands, individual mats, hoops, or whatever you have enough of to enable each child to jump over something. Stress landing big toe first, and bending the knees. A few quick turns and then work on "peeling" feet off floor one at a time, bit by bit, with the heels coming up first and the big toe last. This will come if big toe leaves the floor last. Next have the children run and leap over beanbags trying to land with the big toe first, bending ankles and knees as they land. Make sure they understand that by doing this they will not jar themselves when they land.

Classroom Adaptation In situations where no small equipment is available, children may cut circles, triangles, squares, and rectangles out of colored construction paper (about 12" in size) and use one of these objects to jump over. If their spacing is reasonably good, you may have all the class active at once, encouraging them to run or jump in their own spaces until larger ones become available.

Apparatus Work
(6-8 minutes)

1. Skipping ropes: (one per child). Have the children tie a knot in the rope using only their hands, then only their feet, either standing up or sitting down. This is very good for

keeping feet supple and strengthening the small foot muscles which are important for landing.

2. Hoops: One hoop should be shared between two children. The hoop should be held horizontally about one foot off the ground by one child, while another jumps into it and then wriggles out underneath without touching it. Encourage those who can jump into the hoop when it is held higher than one foot off the ground to roll out underneath.

3. Mats: (Individual or large mats). If the gymnasium has a stage and steps without a railing, the latter can be utilized for gradually increasing the height of the jump for landing and rolling. Children can select the height they feel most confident to jump from. Always make them start from the lowest even if they have one turn before going higher. Make sure their landings have "give" and elbows are tucked in when rolling. Do not allow too many children to wait for their turns. Use both ends of the stage or have four working on another mat away from the steps and four working from the steps. Rotate

these children before changing section places. Make sure that mats are carried by handles and not dragged. For children who do not wish to jump or if a stage (or suitable substitute) is not available, suggest "Invent a way of rolling."

Figure 3.25 "Invent a way of rolling."

Figure 3.24 "Leap from the stage, land, and roll."

4. Benches: Encourage running along broadside, then jumping off and landing with "give" and rolling. Use as many benches as you have to give maximum number of turns. Reinforce safety rules for carrying benches. Also make sure each turn is quick and, at the same time, the mat is clear before each person starts his run and jump.

There will probably be only enough time in this lesson to work at *one* section place. Nevertheless, train them to remember how many sections they cover each lesson (you should make a note yourself), so that time is not wasted in the next lesson while everyone tries to think where they finished in the previous lesson.

From now on no further reference will be

Figure 3.26 "Leap onto the benches, land, and roll."

apparatus and movement activities as well as to work independently. A specific task given by the teacher may be used to reinforce a technique or movement idea. For example, "Take out a beanbag and practice jumping over it, remembering to 'give' when you land." During this time the teacher can help individual children work at landings, and, at the same time, encourage the slower changers to be quicker. Psychologically this method has an interesting effect on the children. If the teacher stays close by the children until all are changed they are much slower than if the teacher goes and works with the quick "changers." Encourage one child to undo another's back buttons rather than you doing it. As in all things a happy balance is required. Some children have difficulty in dressing when first coming to school and will become frustrated and sad at the beginning if left completely alone to manage by themselves. In that case the teacher should come back and give encouragement and help whenever necessary.

made to time for changing at the beginning and end of lessons. On a two-lesson-a-week basis, with encouragement from classroom teachers and parents, it will take approximately twelve lessons before they can change in three or four minutes. Whether the teacher asks the children to practice specific tasks when they are ready or allows them free choice will depend on the progress of the class. Free choice is desirable since it encourages the child to select her own

Classroom Adaptation   Chairs may be used as a substitute for large apparatus to jump from. Stepping squarely onto the seat of the chair so that it doesn't tip will prevent accidents. Half the class could work at this, while the others use thick string or rope for tying knots and bows.

Games such as hopscotch are possible if colored, construction-paper shapes are used instead of floor markings.

LESSON 4

Analysis: WHERE?   General space and change of levels and direction.
            WHAT?   Running, jumping, rolling, climbing, swinging, and landing.

Lesson Outline
Free play until all are ready.
Introductory Activity Tasks
1. "Run, leap, land and roll."

Movement Training Tasks
1. "Find a way of traveling across the room without using your feet."
2. "Think of another way."
3. "Find a way of traveling backwards without using your feet."

Apparatus Tasks
If large equipment is available select from:
1. Section A: "Start on the bottom rung and practice jumping off, landing, and rolling. Increase height one rung at a time."
2. Section B: "Find one way of getting onto the box and a different way of getting off."
3. Section C and D: "Travel up the bench, jump, land, and roll."
4. Section E: "Run, reach, and jump up on the rope, swing, then land and safety roll."
5. Section F: "Run, leap, land, and roll."
and/or
6. "Travel under and over the canes."
7. Section G: "Travel along the bench without using your feet."

	Section F Canes, chairs, or wooden blocks Application of Introductory Activity and Movement Training	Section C Climbing ropes and bench Arm strength and agility Application of Introductory Activity and Movement Training	Section A Wall bars and mats Change of level Application of Introductory Activity control
Section G Benches Application of Movement Training Arm strength	Section E Climbing ropes Agility	Section D Benches for storming Application of Introductory Activity, also Movement Training Arm and leg strength	Section B Top half of vaulting box Application of Movement Training agility

Introductory Activity

(2-3 minutes)
Running, leaping, landing, and rolling. You will find that most children will instinctively put their hands out as they get ready to roll. We are attempting through this safety roll to prevent cut hands, grazed elbows, and broken wrists when children fall and tumble in out-of-school activities. This can be done by making a game out of being able to land and roll without hands

touching the floor. Sometimes asking them to run with their arms folded will help the landing and rolling although it hampers their running and jumping.

Movement Training
(4-5 minutes)

As you have seen, safety training depends on many other themes. We have now reached the stage where it is possible to move toward increasing the range and understanding of movement.

"Choose any way you can think of to travel across the floor *without* using your feet." Pick out two or three different ideas and get each child to demonstrate, then allow the whole class to try the ideas. When selecting ideas try to find one child who is wriggling along on his tummy and using his hands. Find one who is on her back or is sitting and wriggling with her feet off the floor. The third should be a child who lies on her side. The teacher should now begin to make comments about each movement and select those to be demonstrated. For example, (1) "Look, Mary is on her tummy. Which part of her does she use to make herself travel? Yes, that's right, her hands." (2) "David is on his back and what does he use to move himself? Yes, just the upper part of his arms and elbows." (3) "Robert is on his side and observe how he travels; he bends and stretches all of

himself, rather like a caterpillar." (4) "Jane was a clever girl, do you know what she did? Show them, Jane. Yes, a log roll, and she is right, isn't she? She is not using her feet to travel at all."

We have used some of the children's ideas to extend their range of movement by asking them to travel, taking their weight on just hands and knees or hands and feet. The latter has many different varieties which can be drawn out of the children. For example, children can move with either face down or face up, and legs can be straight or bent. They may travel forwards, backwards, or sideways. Other different types of movement could be elbows and seats, backwards, forwards, or sideways. Ask the children to think up movements that have not been used and ask them to demonstrate. Remember to pose each movement task in words rather than by a demonstration of the type of movement desired. This technique will help the children to think of different ways of fulfilling the task on their own, since you have not given them a visual image.

Apparatus Work

Select from the tasks given in the lesson outline. In the primary grades, changing for the first few weeks takes up a lot of the lesson time, hence apparatus time is short. However, freedom from clothing, learning safety factors such as taking care of themselves and of the apparatus, cannot be stressed too much. Young children enjoy being helpful and being made responsible for certain tasks. The standards you set in these early stages are most important. High standards set now will save time, temper, and equipment throughout the rest of the year. Furthermore, much of this training is applied to the apparatus part of the lesson. Do not accept banging down of benches from any grade level. All the children should be capable of lifting and carrying benches carefully and quietly. Do not accept mats being dragged across the floor. Also, do not allow beanbags, hoops, or balls to remain scattered all over the floor.

Other possible variations in apparatus work for safety training are listed below. Obviously

Figure 3.27   "Run, jump, land, and roll."

you will use what is available and substitute wherever it may seem necessary.

1. Wall bars. Start jumping off lowest rung, landing and rolling either with or without mats, and increasing the challenge by going up one rung each time. Emphasize landing by rolling.

2. Tie ropes through the benches. Start by having the bench one foot off the ground at one end, and increase the height as they become more skilled. Emphasize landing and rolling (Figure 3.29).

3. Practice any method of getting onto the box. Land and roll when jumping off.

4. Storming. Two benches inclined and hooked on to a third bench turned balance side up and at right angles to other two.

5. Ropes. Swinging and landing backwards going into backward diagonal roll. This should be done only after the backward diagonal roll has been taught.

6. Three bamboo canes balanced on chairs or small wooden 9" blocks. Leaping over, landing and rolling.

Figure 3.29   "Leap off inclined bench."

Figure 3.28   "Find ways of getting on and off the box."

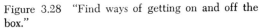

LESSON 5

Analysis: WHERE? Use of space using directions and levels.

WHAT? Running, jumping, landing, rolling, and other locomotor skills.

Lesson Outline

Introductory Activity Tasks

1. "Find a partner, one of you sit on the floor, while the other hops around the 'sitter'."
2. "Change with your partner."
3. "Jump, skip, or walk around your partner."
4. "Change with your partner."
5. "This time run once around your own partner, then around the others who are sitting on the floor. Take care not to collide."
6. "Stop, sit, and listen."

Movement Training Tasks

Use individual mats if available.

1. "Find a partner and sit."
2. "One of you make yourself long and thin, the other person stand up."
3. "Those lying on the mats practice log rolls, those standing up walk (run) in and out of the 'log rollers,' taking care not to step on them."
4. "Change with your partner."
5. "Can you jump over your partner's legs as he rolls towards you?"

6. "Tuck yourself up into the safety roll position, make sure that your head is well tucked in. Stay still and let your partner jump over you."
7. "Now try rolling sideways in a safety roll, so that your partner can jump over while you are moving."

Apparatus Tasks

Select from these or other tasks.

1. Sections A and B: "Free play with stocking bats and balls."

and/or

2. "Find as many ways as you can to go over your beanbag."
3. Sections C and D: "One of you hold the hoop for your partner to go through. Find as many ways as you can."

and/or

4. "Throw the ball to your partner. Invent tricks to do before you catch the ball. Then find other ways of throwing."

Section C and D Hoops—arm strength, agility and cooperation	Sections A and B Stocking bats and balls— Hand-eye coordination
Beanbags—hand-eye coordination and cooperation	Beanbags—arm and leg strength

Introductory Activity

If the classroom is very small, it is often impossible to have the whole class running at once. To overcome this difficulty, have the children work with a partner, so that one can travel while the other remains on his mat practicing balance positions or jumping patterns. If small mats are not available, use sheets of construction paper or hoops as "home bases," one for each pair.

Vary the locomotor skills and improve the quality of their footwork. For example, "Run on the balls of your feet," "Push with your toes as you skip." (Bare feet are essential when working in confined spaces.) Keep turns short, 15 to 20 seconds, and encourage quick change-overs.

Movement Training

Encourage children to work with a variety of partners. Do not force boys to work with girls or vice versa, but encourage a "no discrimination" policy.

The tasks in this section provide opportunities for children to work within their own capabilities, yet challenges the most able children.

As you see individual children succeed, suggest the next progression. Emphasize the following.

1. Jumping over a partner's legs as a safety precaution.
2. Jumping over a still partner is easier than a moving partner.
3. "Safety rollers" *must* have their heads tucked in.
4. The "jumper" must select the position his partner should assume from the following:
log, still
log, moving
safety roll, still
safety roll, moving
5. They should progress only when they feel confident. Jumping over a safety roll requires more space and this should be taken into consideration. It may require the space of

Figure 3.30   "Jump over your partner's legs."

Figure 3.31 "Leap over your partner."

two pairs, in which case they could combine to form a group taking one turn in four at jumping.

6.   Groups of four can develop the task into an "Evel Knievel" stunt by jumping over two or three others in the log roll position. To further develop this task (where space out-of-doors and mats for landing are available), have the children leap over moving "safety rollers."

Figure 3.32   "Evel Knievel" jumps.

Apparatus Work

As in the Introductory Activity, where space is limited, try to choose tasks where half the class can work at activities that require very little traveling space, yet are still vigorous. For example, jumping in and out of a hoop when the hoop is on the floor or is held by a partner. Less vigorous tasks, such as tying knots in ropes, and aiming beanbags into a wastepaper basket, which allow several children to work simultaneously, or bouncing a ball and doing a trick before catching it, either alone or with a partner, develop skill and can be done in confined spaces.

The stocking bats and balls can be made by second grade children in twenty-five minutes

Figure 3.33   A stocking bat.

and by fifth graders in six minutes! All that is needed is a wire coat hanger, one leg of a panty hose, a sheet of newspaper, and some masking tape. Cut the foot off the stocking, form the newspaper into a ball, and put it into the foot, securing it with masking tape. Knot one end of the leg and stretch it over the coat hanger pulled into a diamond shape, bend the wire hook so that it is harmless, pull the stocking taut and knot it, enclosing the coat hanger. Use the excess to pad the handle and secure with masking tape.

The previous lesson plans give the basis for safety training. Before moving to the next theme the teacher must decide whether the following has been accomplished.

1.   The class stops quickly when told and listens for instructions.
2.   The noise level is such that the teacher's voice can be heard at all times.
3.   The children understand moving in a space, traveling in different directions without colliding, and can do a sideways safety roll on landing.
4.   The children can work independently within a group.
5.   The children can move apparatus carefully and efficiently.
6.   The children show care and consideration for others' needs.

If the teacher feels satisfied with the standards the class has reached, then they will be ready to go on to the next stage. However, some classes will need more than five lessons to reach this stage, in which case the teacher may repeat any of the lessons and/or try to invent variations of those suggested here, putting special emphasis on the class's particular needs.

THEME TWO: ADDING TO THE RANGE AND UNDERSTANDING OF MOVEMENT

It should now become apparent that safety training depends on the child's knowledge of his own abilities and limitations. The teacher's task is to assist each child to add to his knowledge of movement patterns and to improve his physical skills in progressive stages. By gradually increasing a child's range of understanding of movement, he, in turn, is able to take more and more responsibility for his own safety.

Through experimentation with balancing and transferring the body weight onto different parts of the body, children can develop the skills of walking, skipping, hopping, running, rolling, balancing, and hanging. This experimentation also helps them to understand the movement principles involved. It should be recognized that all the traditional stunts will be "discovered" by the children themselves. The advantages of this type of experimentation and approach are that the movement tasks always permit the least able

as well as the most able child to find a satisfactory solution within his/her capabilities. This not only prevents accidents, but also makes it possible to individualize the program and retain the children's enthusiasm.

Figure 3.34   "Balance with your hoop high."

LESSON 1

Analysis: WHERE? On the spot, traveling.

WHAT? The whole body and parts of the body, transference of weight including backward diagonal roll.

Lesson Outline

Introductory Activity Tasks

1. "Run anywhere in the gym, when I say 'stop' balance on one foot. Off you go."
2. "Who could think of another part of the body to balance on this time?"

Movement Training Tasks

Using individual or large mats.

1. "Take a mat to a space and rock backwards and forwards."
2. "This time rock so far backwards that you put *both* knees by your right ear."
3. "Some of you might like to try rocking so far backwards that you go over doing a backward diagonal roll and land gently on your knees."
4. "Push with your left hand down on the floor close to your ear, and your right arm out straight; that will help you go over—if you have placed both knees by your right ear!"

Apparatus Tasks

Select from the following:

1. Section A: "Arrange eight bowling pins in a space on the floor. Each take a ball and practice dribbling the ball in and out without getting in each other's way or knocking down the pins."
2. Section B: "Invent as many ways as you can of picking up the beanbag with different parts of your body and then tossing it into the hoop."
3. Section C: "Travel backwards or sideways along the bench, jump off backwards, and do a backward diagonal roll on landing."

and/or

4. "Travel along the bench as many different ways as you can, roll on landing."
5. Section D: "Jump off the steps, roll on landing. Start at the bottom step, work upwards one step at a time."

and/or

6. "Jump backwards off the steps and land using a backward diagonal roll."
7. Section E: "Swing on the ropes, land, and roll." (Important, see teaching points.)

Mats and stage— safety training and application of Movement Training	Benches—balance and application of Movement Training	Hoops and beanbags— balance and control	Eight pins and balls— foot-eye coordination
	Box—free play, transference of weight, Introductory Activity	Swinging on ropes— arm strength and application of Movement Training	Skipping ropes— manipulative skills

Introductory Activity

Running and stopping with weight on different parts of the body. For example, stopping on two feet, left foot, right foot, one hand and one foot, back, stomach, seat, shoulders, elbows and knees, and knee of one leg and toes of other foot.

Figure 3.35 Weight on one hand and one foot.

This can be as easy or as difficult as you wish to make it. Since kindergarten and first grade children may have problems with left and right, this is a good beginning activity for them. Always give the children at least one opportunity to choose which part(s) they put their weight on.

Movement Training

Individual mats are on the floor for backward diagonal roll. Set a movement task such as: put weight on feet, seat, shoulders, seat, then feet. This should produce a backward rock. Once they have discovered this, get them to start with a little backward rock, hugging their knees, then a bigger one, and finally a bigger one still.

"Now this time when you do your biggest rock backward can you put *both* knees by your *right* ear?" Then repeat doing left ear. Many children will put one knee by each ear. Get a child to demonstrate and point out that both knees are by one ear. Allow several practice turns. (Figure 3.36)

"This time when you do your biggest rock backwards, see if you can go right over and land on both kness." Stress putting knees down gently. (Figure 3.37)

Apparatus Work

1. Distribute eight or nine bowling pins for the group and a ball for each child. Have the children dribble the ball in and out without getting in each other's way and without knocking the pins down. All should practice

Figure 3.36 Both knees by one ear.

Figure 3.37 Knees down gently.

at the same time. Initially, pins can be arranged without any definite shape or pattern and with lots of room between each pin. As skill increases move the pins closer together.

2. Hoops and Beanbags: (one of each per child). Invent as many different ways as you can of picking up the beanbag with different parts of the body and then throwing it into the hoop. Ask each child to invent three different ways and to practice until he can do them well.

3. Benches or Box: Traveling backward along bench, jumping off backward, and doing a backward diagonal roll on landing.

4. Large Mats and Stage: Using the stage, jump off steps backward starting from bottom and working upward using backward roll for landing.

5. Climbing Ropes: Swing on ropes, landing backward, and rolling. Here the emphasis is on safety. The first time the ropes are used have the whole class sit near the ropes so that you can explain the important safety precautions.

Make sure all children sit in front of or behind the ropes and not in the downward path where the ropes could swing out if not properly controlled. The teacher may forcefully swing a rope so that children can see how easily they could get hurt if they were in the way. One demonstration of this is a very effective way of driving this point home and usually the children are very impressed. This will also save you hours of saying "don't stand in the way of the ropes."

Figure 3.39 Getting out the climbing ropes.

Figure 3.38 "Jump off backwards."

Ropes fascinate children, so make sure that all have a chance to try them before they are put away. Stress the need for strength and lots of practice. Allow free practice on the ropes with proper supervision. Constantly stress coming down "hand over hand" *not* sliding (Figure 3.41), because the latter causes friction, burns, and accidents.

Do not allow any child to swing off the stage or anything else that will give them height. Even if children run on the floor and reach up as high as they can, they will not swing with the same momentum as they would from a height, and there will be less danger of falling.

Figure 3.40 "Lie on the floor, then pull yourself up til you are standing."

Figure 3.41 Climbing down, hand over hand.

Always drop off the rope when *swinging backward as the rope reaches the highest point of its swing.* The rope almost stops before beginning its forward swing–this is the best time to drop off and do a backward or sideways roll. The rope will swing forward away from the child as she drops.

A helpful suggestion for grade one and kindergarten is to stand at the bottom of the rope, jump up, keeping arms bent, and making the chin stay on the hands. Set "count tasks" until they can hold this position for the count of ten or more.

LESSON 2

Analysis: WHERE?   On the spot and traveling.

WHAT?   The whole body and parts of the body, and foot and leg work for jumping and landing.

HOW?   Strong, light.

Lesson Outline

Free play until all are ready.

Introductory Activity Tasks

1. "Run on tiptoes. Off you go."
2. "What other parts of your feet can you use to walk on?"
3. "Try these and travel in different directions."

Movement Training Tasks

1. "Find a space and sit on the floor with your legs straight out in front of you."
2. "Use your hands as guns and shoot your toes so that they point to the floor."
3. "Practice jumping, push with your toes, stretch your ankles. Make your landing soft by 'giving' in toes and ankles as well as knees."
4. "Watch your partner this time, help him to jump high and land softly."

Apparatus Tasks

Select from these or other tasks.

1. Section A: "Jump as high up the rope as you can, then swing with bent arms and feet and legs stretched."
2. Section B: "Find as many ways as you can of going over or across the box without putting your feet on the box. Land using a roll."
3. Section C: "Find as many ways as you can of going through the hoop at the same time as your partner."
4. Section D: "Practice jumping forwards, backwards, or sideways off the bench and roll on landing."

Introductory Activity

Instruct the children to run on their tiptoes. "What other parts of your feet can you use to walk on?" Make up a pattern using three movements such as forward on tiptoes, backward on heels, and sideways crossing one foot over the other. Try to pick out a child's idea that shows different ways and have the whole class practice it.

Movement Training

Have the children work with a partner and a ball. Begin by "shooting feet." Sit with legs straight, and backs of knees against floor. Take imaginary pistols from pockets and use feet as targets, toes sticking up until "shot at," then keeping legs straight, stretching toes down toward ground. (Back of knees must touch the floor at all times.) Start by "shooting" both together, then one at a time, seeing who can make big toes touch the ground while backs of knees are still against the ground. Next, partners watch each other jump and land. Remember: pointed toes, stretched ankles, and good "gives" on landing.

Figure 3.42 "Shoot your feet."

Apparatus Work

1. Ropes: Swinging, now stress bent arms, with feet and legs stretched and straight during swing.

Figure 3.43 Arms bent; feet and legs stretched.

2. Balls: Catapult balls against the wall with feet, chasing them as they bounce off and "re-fire."
3. Box: Get over the box without putting feet on top of box. Roll on landing.
4. Hoops and beanbags: Same as previous lesson.
5. Benches: Same as previous lesson.
6. Large or individual mats and stage. Same as previous lesson.

Figure 3.44 Balance on the box.

LESSON 3 (For kindergarten through second grade)

Analysis: WHERE?   On the spot and traveling.

WHAT?   Parts of the body, balance, and transference of weight.

Lesson Outline

Free play until all are ready.

Introductory Activity Tasks

1. "Walk and balance on one foot when I say 'stop'."
2. "A foot is a small part of your body. Can you think of any other small parts on which you could balance?" (Hands, elbows, knees, head.)
3. "Travel on three small parts." (Then two and four.)

Movement Training Tasks

Use individual mats and beanbags.

1. "Take a mat to a space and balance on three small parts, then on two hands and one foot."
2. "Make one foot go as high as you can."
3. "Are your toes and knee really stretched?"
4. "Change legs. Can you make your toes go higher?"

5. "Hold a beanbag under your chin while balancing on two hands and one foot."
6. "Still keep one leg stretched but now try to curl up so that the beanbag under your chin will touch the knee of your supporting leg."
7. "This time hold that position but bend your arms very slowly. Now take your weight onto your shoulders and you will tip over in a forward roll."

Apparatus Tasks

Select from these or other tasks.

1. "Invent different ways to roll. Some of you may like to try a butterfly roll. Think up a name for the roll you invent."
2. "Roll with a hoop."
3. "Balance on the bench."
4. "Free play with skipping ropes."

Figure 3.45 "Balance on one foot on 'stop.'"

Introductory Activity

Traveling and stopping. Travel with two parts of the body touching the floor (two feet). "Now can you travel with four small parts on the ground?" (Use both hands and feet.) "Now try three."

Figure 3.46 "Travel on four small parts."

Figure 3.47   "Balance on three points."

Figure 3.48   "Tuck your beanbag under your chin."

Movement Training

Ask the children to suggest other small parts
of their bodies on which they can travel. Also
ask for different ways of traveling, for example,
combinations of knees, elbows, hands, and feet;
tummy up and tummy down.

The tasks in this lesson plan lead directly to
forward rolls. In order to provide for varying
abilities, include broader tasks such as:

1.   Balance on two points, change to two
different points.
2.   Balance on one part, change to three.
3.   Start with the same balance as last time,
but change to a different three-point balance.
4.   Start on four points, change to three, then
two, then one.

For forward rolls remind the children to keep
the chin firmly on the beanbag, as this prevents
any weight going onto the head and also keeps
the backs rounded. The knee remaining on the
beanbag as a support also keeps the back
rounded, and lifting the other leg allows for
control of speed. Arms should bend slowly.

Allow those who are hesitant to do it on a
mat. Never force a child over. The forward roll
is harder than the log, sideways-tucked, or
backward-diagonal roll, and children may need
more time to feel confident enough to go right
over.

Apparatus Work

Include one section where individual mats or a
large mat can be used, so children can invent
different types of forward rolls while holding
beanbags with different parts of their bodies.
Encourage them to build sequences of roll-
balance-roll-balance, using any of the rolls they
can do.

The rest of the apparatus work will be the
same as in the previous lesson. Remember that
the safety of children in handling themselves
and equipment will still need attention. By this
time even the youngest children should be able
to do the log, sideways, and backward-diagonal
rolls. Many children will be able to do the for-

Figure 3.49   The butterfly roll.

4. Make sure that you observe each child during apparatus work. If there is only time for the children to work at one section then the teacher should go around to each section. However, if there is time for them to move to all four, the teacher may want to see that each child understands one particular point, in which case the teacher should stay at that section and let each group come there.

5. Remember to use time profitably at the beginning while the children are changing.

6. We have not mentioned using the large climbing apparatus such as the Southampton Cave,[1] since many schools do not have this equipment. However, if available, this apparatus can be used from the very beginning and provides excellent opportunities for safety training. Children in kindergarten and grade one can handle this apparatus very easily and love to do so.

ward roll. All should be able to move confidently in the gymnasium, be able to use space, and work independently with small apparatus. They should be able to go to "section places" quickly and cooperate when getting out large apparatus. Selecting and choosing apparatus, however, will require additional assistance.

Additional Teaching Points

1. At least one section should have a direct link with the Movement Training part of the lesson.

2. Keep apparatus in the same position until every section has had a chance to use it. In subsequent plans it is suggested that apparatus activities tie in with the lesson plans, and that as large a variety of apparatus as possible be used, and that children be allowed to select their apparatus. Never be afraid to improvise.

3. Always include one section in which children have freedom to invent and combine ideas. Children in grades two and three will often produce excellent ideas when working with a friend.

Figure 3.50   Getting out the Cave.

[1]Cave or C.A.V.E. refers to climbing and vaulting equipment.

Figure 3.51 Exploring movements on the Cave.

Figure 3.52 "Turn upside down on the Cave."

LESSON 3 (for grade three)

Analysis: WHERE?   On the spot and traveling.

WHAT?   Parts of the body, balance, and transference of weight.

Lesson Outline

Introductory Activity Tasks

1. "Find a partner and a space. When I say 'go,' travel keeping in contact with your partner and have eight 'points' on the floor between you. A point is a small part of you like a foot. Think of some others and work out a way to travel."
2. "Now travel with six points between you."
3. "Change to four points."
4. "Only two this time."

Movement Training Tasks

1. "Patches are large parts of your body like your seat. Find a way of traveling on your own where you only have patches on the ground. Help your partner to invent a way and both do the same thing."
2. "How many ways can you find to travel balanc-ing on one patch and using two points to propel you?"
3. "Make up a sequence of rolls and balances us-ing combinations of patches and points."

Apparatus Tasks

Select from these or other tasks.

1. "Travel along the bench using one patch and two points, first alone, and then using two patches and four points working in twos."
2. "Work on the ropes rolling or balancing with two points on the ropes."
3. "Go over the box using two points only on the box."
4. "Travel the length of the box using patches only."
5. "Travel along the balance beam with four points, two points, one patch and two points."

Introductory Activity

"Points" include hands, feet, elbows, knees, and head. All kinds of traditional stunts are "discovered" during these activities. For example, the wheelbarrow has four points on the floor. To ensure safety, insist that the child carrying the wheelbarrow holds the partner's legs above the knee and *not* at the ankles.

One child may support another doing a handstand. This may be used as an example of either four points or two, depending on whether the "handstander" places her hands on her partner's feet or on the floor. Again, safety training is essential. The supporter should hold the handstander around the hips, *not* the ankles, as only then can the supporter have any control. Also the handstander may come down when she wishes, which is not the case when a zealous supporter grips the ankles!

Walking with a partner is an example of four points on the ground that *all* children are capable of doing. You will find many easy examples as well as many difficult ones. Pickaback, another solution, involves two points on the floor. (Make sure they bend their knees when picking up their partner.)

Movement Training

The easiest example of traveling using only patches is the log roll. The children travel from side to tummy then to other side and back.

Figure 3.53　One patch—a large part of the body.

Figure 3.54　One patch and two points.

These parts of the body are considered patches. Other patches are the chest, shoulders, seat, shins, forearms, and, on some equipment, the backs of the thighs.

As they build sequences of rolls and balances, encourage the children to roll into a balance position that will help them initiate the next roll. Some may like to work at this task with a partner and develop interesting combination rolls. The older students in the intermediate grades enjoy these tasks.

Apparatus Work

"Seal" actions are performed on the benches, using one patch and two points. This is a good activity for developing arm strength.

Two points on the ropes can develop into somersaults, if two climbing ropes are used. Children may attempt both backward and forward somersaults. The children should then be taught to hold the ropes at shoulder height for efficiency and safety.

Crouch jumps and the beginnings of cartwheels appear as solutions to two points on the box (or bench).

Encourage these and other solutions by helping them understand the importance of body alignment to maintain balance. For example, in a handstand, hands should be shoulder width apart; the shoulders directly over the hands; the hips over the shoulders; the knees over the hips; the feet over the knees; and the head up to prevent tipping over onto the back.

Figure 3.55 Two points on the rope.

If headstands and handstands are attempted, encourage cartwheels first, as they do not require such refined balance. Cartwheels also allow children to learn to manage their bodies safely upside down. See later lesson plans for specific help with these activities.

Figure 3.56 Two points on the bench.

LESSON 4

Analysis: WHERE?   On the spot and traveling.
          WHAT?   The whole body and parts of the body, balancing, and traveling.

Lesson Outline
Free play until all are ready.

Introductory Activity Tasks

1. "Take a hoop to a space and place it *quietly* on the floor. Practice jumping in and out."
2. "Run freely in and out of all the hoops. When I say 'stop,' sit in the nearest hoop."
3. "When I say 'stop,' this time put just one foot into the nearest hoop."
4. "Who can think of another part of the body you could put into the hoop?"
5. "Last two into the hoop when I say 'stop' lose a life." (Nine Lives game, page 149)

Movement Training Tasks

1. "Find ways of going over your hoop without touching it."
2. "Think of ways to go around your hoop."
3. "Who can make their feet travel around their hoop while keeping one hand in the middle of the hoop?"
4. "Think of other ways you could do that task. Change the parts of the body that travel around and the parts that stay in the hoop."
5. "Invent ways of going from one side of your hoop to the other."
6. "Touch the hoop with as many parts of your body as you can."
7. "Balance the hoop in different ways."

Apparatus Tasks

Select from these or other tasks.

1. "Build a sequence using your hoop. Start by traveling around your hoop, then balance your hoop. Once you have done that, add two more ways of traveling and another two ways of balancing. Practice your sequence. Teach your sequence to a partner."

Note: This lesson is a suggested plan for all children using the same type of apparatus, but with slight modifications, a mixture of beanbags, ropes, or quoits may be substituted, if class sets of apparatus are not available.

Introductory Activity

It is impossible to give instructions over the clatter of thirty or forty hoops, so insist that they put the hoops down quietly and do not fidget with them while you are speaking. The same is true of beanbags and balls, so the children should be told that their hands should not touch the equipment when they are listening to instructions!

When asking them to suggest parts of the body to put into the hoop when they stop, check in your own mind the "patches and points." If the children run out of ideas, suggest the ones they have missed.

Use "Nine Lives" to sophisticate the Introductory Activity for grade three as necessary.

Movement Training

Observe whether the children take off with one or two feet, or whether any child travels over his hoop without jumping. Suggest ways to improve the quality of their jumps and provide time to practice other ideas.

The next movement task is to go around the hoops without touching them. Use the tasks suggested in the lesson plan or select the first child you see who fulfills the task and have him demonstrate. Then ask the others to see if they can go around their hoops in a different way. Observe:

1. How many run around, or use other locomotor skills
2. How many put one foot in the middle of the hoop and the other outside and run around
3. Anyone who used hands and feet, or
4. Both feet in and both hands out, or
5. Feet out and hands in, or
6. One of each on either side.

There are many possible variations here. If the children do not think of them, pose questions such as "Who can make their feet go around the hoop while keeping their hands in the middle of the hoop?" This will help the children solve their problem without always having a visual demonstration. It is most important for them to learn to work out instructions from words as it makes them think, thus increasing their independence, initiative, and creativity. However, children should not be allowed to flounder. If a large number of the children cannot think of a solution and do not start to work quickly, have a child demonstrate who has thought of a solution. It is extremely unlikely in the primary grades that this particular type of

Figure 3.57 "Stop with one foot in the nearest hoop."

Figure 3.58 "Travel around the hoop, keeping one hand in the hoop."

lesson will create any difficulty. Nevertheless, it is well to know how to handle the problem should it occur. Another solution is to rephrase the question.

If you then asked the class to go across from one side of the hoop to the other, the children may perform bunny jumps, handstands, or cartwheels, all of which are suitable responses to

Figure 3.59 Four points touching the hoop.

Figure 3.60 Three parts touching the hoop.

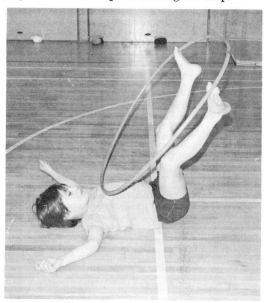

the question. Some, however, may not be able to think of a way. In this case ask them to put their hands on the floor in the middle of the hoop and move their feet from one side of the hoop to the other. This will make the task simple for them to follow, but does not allow too much scope for individual ideas.

Next, ask the children to touch the hoop with as many parts of their bodies as they can. Observe:

1. Seat, two hands, and two feet
2. Hands, elbows, knees, feet, and nose
3. Lie with tummy touching edge of hoop
4. With back touching hoop
5. Lie with side touching hoop

Select children showing these variations and then ask the remainder of the class to try each idea in turn, making it clear which parts of their body should be touching the hoop.

Apparatus Work

Note: Continue with hoop work. Set the tasks in the lesson outline or propose the following movement tasks:

1. Touch or hold your hoop with four parts.
2. Touch or hold your hoop with three parts.
3. Touch or hold your hoop with two parts.
4. Now only one part.

Figure 3.61 One way of holding the hoop.

Explain to the children they now can build a sequence using the ideas the class produced. You should give a very simple example, such as, "with the hoop on the floor, both hands and both feet touching the edge of the hoop, make a bridge shape with tummy upwards. Now turn over so that tummy is downwards and balance on two hands and one foot. Next turn sideways so that one hand and one foot are on the hoop, finally stand up and balance hoop on top of head and climb through." Make changes from one position to the next as smooth as possible.

LESSON 5
Analysis: WHERE? Own space, general space, change of levels, and directions.
WHAT? Patches and points, balance, and cartwheels.

Lesson Outline
Free play until all are ready.
Introductory Activity Tasks
1. "Take a small mat (or sheet of construction paper) to a space and travel around it in as many different ways as you can."
2. "Run in and out of the mats. When I say 'stop,' go to the nearest mat and balance on one knee and one hand (or two points)."
3. "Who can think of another way to balance where you have three parts (mixture of points and patches) on the mat? Think how you are going to do it as you run."
4. "Choose a different balance each time I say 'stop'."

Movement Training Tasks
1. "Make as many parts of your body touch the mat as you can. Then find another way."

2. "Balance with as little of your body touching the mat as you can. Now find a different way."
3. "Practice ways of going over your mat."
4. "Find different ways to go around your mat."

Apparatus Tasks
These can be done without mats. Skipping ropes or beanbags on the floor may also be used.
1. "Put your hands on the mat (or floor) and jump with your feet from side to side."
2. "Put one hand down after the other and jump with your feet across the mat."
3. "Still keeping one hand going down after the other, try to make one foot go really high into the air as you go across your mat. Count to yourself 1, 2, 3, 4, making first hand touch the mat on 1, the second hand on 2, the high foot on 3, and the other foot on 4. Think hard about your feet and make them come down gently."

Introductory Activity
This lesson may be taught in the classroom if running is omitted. You may have to rely on partner work, if space is limited. The children can take turns thinking up new balances and trying them out. Use the children's solutions for the others to try, if they are short of ideas. Since there is choice, you will often see headstands and handstands performed by the more able students. The teacher should always give the children an opportunity to think for themselves and to choose an activity which is personally challenging.

Movement Training
For the second task observe:

1. Toe of one foot, or
2. One knee, or
3. One heel, etc. (Figure 3.62)

For the third task observe:

1. Leaping with a one-foot takeoff, or
2. Jumping with a two-foot takeoff, or
3. Leaping with a turn, landing, and rolling.

Observe:

1. Locomotor skills
2. One hand, or
3. Elbow, or
4. Seat on the mat and feet traveling around.

In task 4 some children may solve the task by doing cartwheels, thus anticipating the apparatus work. If this is the case, give individual help with shape and body alignment.

Figure 3.62 "Balance on different patches and points."

Figure 3.63 "Put two hands on the mat, then jump your feet from side to side."

Apparatus Work

Note: Continue working on individual mat or the floor if mats are not available.

This is the beginning of cartwheels. Pose the following movement tasks and questions (or use those in the lesson outline):

1. Place two hands in the middle of the mat and jump, moving feet from side to side. (Figure 3.63) Allow several practices.
2. Now start from standing position and repeat (1) and end in a standing position. Next *without* turning around come back to original side. Again allow several practices.
3. From a standing position place one hand on the mat and then the other and move feet across and back to original side without turning. This helps a child to discover which hand he prefers as well as making him practice with each hand at this early stage.

At this point many children will be doing a form of cartwheel. This is where one should also stress quality by having the children begin to focus their attention on what happens to their legs when they are upside down. For those who

Figure 3.64 "Stretch your knees as you go over."

are producing a type of cartwheel, questions such as, "Can you stretch up so that your feet almost brush the ceiling?" or "Are your knees straight?" will direct the children's attention to using different parts in different ways. For the majority of the children, however, the emphasis will be on getting one leg high in the air. This is the turning "inside-out" stage. Let them choose which hand they prefer to put down first. Follow this with a slow-motion movement of putting the second hand down. Next, first foot and turning so that by putting the second foot down they end up by facing the same direction they started from.

This is where the teacher is able to give individual help to those who are finding it difficult. Ask these children to bring their mats to one part of the gymnasium while the other either practice by themselves on the shape of their cartwheels or with a partner, work on making a pattern of cartwheels. Grade three children work well together on patterns if you suggest that they fill in all sides of a square or go around together. Encourage control and balance as well as good body alignment.

Children who are already competent cartwheelers may be assigned tasks that involve cartwheeling off the end of a bench and landing on the floor or arranging hoops in such a way that each hand and foot go into separate hoops.

LESSON 6
Analysis: WHERE? Use of general space.
             WHAT?   Different parts, gripping, and balancing.

Lesson Outline
Introductory Activity Tasks
1. "Take a beanbag to a space and find how many places on your body you can balance the beanbag."
2. "Place the beanbag on the floor, when I say 'go,' run; when I say 'stop,' freeze. Go."
3. "Stop. Now here comes the tricky part. Unfreeze the top part of your body and *one* foot; the second foot must stay exactly where it is and not move. Can you reach out and touch a beanbag? It doesn't matter if two or three of you touch the same beanbag."
4. "Let's make a game of it and use the Nine Lives principle. Remember you have to keep your own score."

Movement Training Tasks
1. "How many different ways can you pick up the beanbag?"

2. "Throw the beanbag into the air one way and catch it a different way."
3. "Place the beanbag behind your heels. Now, without turning around, use both hands to pick it up and then toss it forward over your head. Make it more fun by controlling the toss so that the beanbag lands near you, then you can jump over the beanbag and start again."
4. "How good are you at tossing the beanbag off your back when kneeling on all fours? Keep your arms stiff and your knees a little way apart. Now wriggle, hump, and hollow!"

Apparatus Tasks
Select from these or other tasks.
1. "Free play with beanbags."
2. "Hold the beanbag between your feet and find ways of tossing it into the air."
3. "Toss and catch the beanbag in as many ways as you can."

Introductory Activity

For task three in the lesson plan; to prevent children from trying to stop very close to a beanbag and therefore preventing another child from being able to use it, vary the parts, such as head, nose, and ears. The latter are hard to accomplish if they have stopped too close to the beanbag. See the games section for details of Nine Lives in task four. They must keep track of their own "lives." This is helpful training in being a good loser and not cheating. Don't expect perfect results.

Figure 3.65 "Stop with your knee on the beanbag."

Figure 3.66 A new way to hold a beanbag.

Movement Training

For the first task observe:
1. Fingers,
2. Toes,
3. Teeth,
4. Trapping between elbow joint,
5. Trapping between the knee joint,
6. Both feet,
7. Both knees, or
8. Chin against chest.

For the second task observe:
1. Pick up with toes, throw to hands.
2. Pick up with teeth, throw to feet or knees.
3. Pick up with one hand, throw to other.

Task three is a useful activity for teaching the children the safe hand position needed for

Figure 3.67 "Toss the beanbag into the air."

Figure 3.68   "Shaggy dog"—hollowing.

backward somersault on the ropes and reverse hanging on the wall bars. This could be included where wall bars or ropes are used in the apparatus section of another lesson.

In task four, some of the children may be familiar with "humping and hollowing" the back, which is a useful activity for developing mobility of the spine (Figure 3.68).

Apparatus Work

Note: Continue working with the beanbags. Select tasks from the lesson outline and/or free practice or any new ideas with a partner or alone. If they run out of ideas, suggest:

1. Sitting, picking beanbag up with feet, rocking backward and trying to put it down on the floor over their heads.

2. With both hands on floor and beanbag between feet, jumping, raising both feet into the air and tossing the beanbag over their heads.

3. Have all of the class try out some of the children's inventions.

THEME THREE: UNDERSTANDING SPACE AND DIRECTIONAL MOVEMENTS

One of the most important aspects of Movement Education is the understanding and use of space. In this theme, the basic directional movements of forward, backward, and sideways are introduced. In later lessons, emphasis is shifted to understanding and using general and personal space.

Figure 3.69   Traveling in different directions on large apparatus.

LESSON 1

Analysis: WHERE?   Directions in own and general space.

              WHAT?   Running, jumping, rolling.

Lesson Outline

Introductory Activity Tasks

1. "Take beanbag to a space and play with it."
2. "Stop, sit, and listen."
3. "Make zigzag patterns as you run between the beanbags."
4. "Sit by a beanbag."

Movement Training Tasks

1. "Practice jumping forwards (direction) over your beanbag."
2. "Which other directions do you know? Show me."
3. "Make a square pattern traveling around your beanbag. Travel forwards, sideways, and backwards."
4. "How else can you travel besides running and jumping?"
5. "Make up a new sequence. You may work with a partner if you like."

Apparatus Tasks

Select from these or other tasks.

1. "Find as many ways as you can to get onto and off the box backwards or forwards."

2. "Travel in any direction along the bench, then jump off in a different direction each turn."
3. "Take four beanbags to a space on the floor. Arrange them in a pattern, jump forwards, backwards, sideways, and diagonally, always landing beside a beanbag. Teach your sequence to a partner."
4. "Take a hoop and a mat to a space. Use the mat to make the hoop stand vertically. Travel forwards and backwards over or through the hoop. Make a sequence joining these ways together. Teach your sequence to a partner."
5. "Take four pins and a hoop to a space. Balance the hoop horizontally, then find ways of going in and out of the hoop forwards, backwards, and sideways."
6. "Swing backwards and forwards holding two ropes. Land with a roll."
7. "Take a skipping rope to a space. Make up a sequence using different foot patterns turning the rope backwards and forwards. Add traveling to make it more fun."
8. "Work with a partner, make up a rolling sequence using forward, diagonal, backward, and sideways rolls."
9. "Free play."

Introductory Activity

This is a modification of an earlier lesson. Emphasis is on the use of all space; running in and out of each other in zigzag patterns. On "stop" ask the children to turn halfway round and then run in new direction. High standards in the use of space should be expected and demanded by this stage. Footwork in running and jumping should show signs of improvement. They should be able to run without a sound on the floor. Landings should demonstrate "give" in knees and ankles.

Movement Training

When the children are in a space of their own, ask them to point forward, and then by suggesting "'Who can think of another direction?" you can add backward and sideways. Grade one can even manage diagonal. Continue running and jumping patterns, emphasizing change of direction after each jump.

    You may like to select three of their ideas and build them into a class sequence or have them build sequences on their own, based on a combination of running, jumping, and change of direction. For kindergarten more assistance in sequence building will be needed than for the other grades. The inclusion of diagonal movements may be left to the following lesson if the teacher feels that four directions are too much for the class.

Apparatus Work

1. Remember to encourage rolling on landing from any apparatus.
2. One bench broad side up and one bench balance side up.
3. A safety reminder for task three, land *beside* and not on the beanbags in case they slip. Encourage the children to widen the space between the beanbags after each successful trial.
4. Choose one way of going forward either through or over hoop and a different way of traveling backward through the hoop. If no supports are available children may work in twos, one holding the hoop while the other goes through. (See Figure 3.70) Grades two and three may be able to work simultaneously, each holding hoop with one hand.

Figure 3.70 "Travel through the hoop."

5. Climbing ropes. The more adventurous children will turn upside down or do "bird nests."
6. Skip alone or with partner.
7. Large mats. Make patterns in twos or in groups using forward, sideways, backward, and diagonal rolls. Two children working from ends and two from sides of the mat.

LESSON **2**
Analysis: WHERE?   Directions.
WHAT?   Bend, stretch, twist.

Lesson Outline

Introductory Activity Tasks

1. "Take a beanbag to a space and hop forwards, backwards, and sideways around your beanbag."
2. "Run in and out of the beanbags, sometimes traveling quickly and sometimes slowly."

Movement Training Tasks

1. "Find a beanbag on the floor and make a bridge with your body over the bag."
2. "Make a different bridge. Try to think of four new bridges. Use other parts of your body for balancing apart from hands and feet."
3. "Now find ways of making the beanbag travel backwards and forwards through the arches of your bridges."

Apparatus Tasks

Select from these or other tasks.

1. "Roll on the top of the box."

2. "Travel forwards, backwards, and sideways along the bench without using your feet."
3. "Find as many ways as you can to toss the beanbag over your head forwards, backwards, or sideways."
4. "Take four beanbags and two hoops to a space. Transfer the beanbags forwards, backwards, or sideways from one hoop to the other. Which parts of your body can you use to pick up the beanbags?"
5. "Take four pins and a hoop to a space. Balance the hoop on the pins. Find ways of going under, in, and out of the hoops."
6. "Travel along the row of ropes."
7. "Take a skipping rope to a space and put it on the floor. Make up a sequence of traveling forwards, backwards, and sideways with hands and feet on the floor."
8. "Free play."

Introductory Activity

Still stressing spacing, have the children run in and out and sometimes running around the beanbags. If they can use the space well and are controlled, then introduce a variation of speed, starting slowly and ending so that they are running very quickly. Slow down at first sign of collision and remind them about safety.

Movement Training

This progression encourages the bending, stretching, and twisting of the body. Children really enjoy these contortions and these tasks produce opportunities for maintaining and increasing flexibility of the body.

These activities may be developed in a variety of ways. Third grade children are capable of developing complex roll-balance-roll sequences

where the "bridges" become balances. The beanbag can be pushed through the arches and this in turn may lead into rolls.

A simpler progression may be developed from the following: "Move your beanbag with one foot through one of the arches of your bridge." Suggest other parts with which to move the beanbag, such as hands, knees, elbows, and head.

Select one of the children who has a good, simple example, then encourage all to try.

Choose different parts and different directions. Build a sequence of three. An example of this could be:

Position 1: Standing astride over beanbag. Bending forward, pull beanbag forward with hand without moving feet.
Position 2: By putting hands on floor, then using one foot to push beanbag sideways

Figure 3.71 "No feet on the bench."

Figure 3.72 Backward roll off end of bench.

through arch formed by opposite leg and hand.

Position 3: Sit with legs crooked, reach with one hand and push beanbag sideways through arch formed by seat and feet, and catch beanbag with other hand.

Apparatus Work

According to the progress made and the number of turns the children have had, keep the same apparatus but change the task.

1. Box: Use a roll along the top of the box or bench. If a child wishes to roll off the end of the box or bench, another child should sit on the opposite end to stabilize it.
2. Benches: No feet allowed on top of bench.
3. Beanbags: Toss beanbag over head with different parts of the body.
4. Four beanbags and hoops: Transferring beanbags forward, backward, or sideways from one hoop to another, using different parts to pick them up.
5. Horizontal hoops and pins: Jump in sideways and come out underneath but traveling forward.
6. Climbing ropes: If you have a row of four ropes or more, ask the children to travel sideways changing from one rope to next. More ambitious pupils can climb up at same time as change over.
7. Skipping ropes: Sequence of forward, backward, and sideways movements, keeping hands and feet on floor.
8. Large mats: Change pattern to include jumping as well as rolling.

Figure 3.73 "Make a bridge over your beanbag."

Figure 3.74 "Change from one rope to the other."

LESSON **3**

Analysis: WHERE?   Directions and levels.

WHAT?   Rolls, locomotor skills, and balances.

Lesson Outline

Introductory Activity Tasks

1. "Take a mat to a space on the floor. Practice running, leaping, landing, and rolling on your own mat."
2. "Using a different mat each time and taking care not to collide, practice running, leaping, landing, and rolling."

Movement Training Tasks

1. "Make up a sequence using a mat. Show forwards, backwards, and sideways movements by combining rolls, locomotor movements, and balances."

Apparatus Tasks

Select from these or other tasks. (In groups of four.)

1. "Place your mats end to end in a diagonal line. Invent as many ways as you can of traveling along the mats diagonally."
2. "Backwards."
3. "Forwards."
4. "Sideways."
5. "Free play."
6. "Work with a partner in the group."

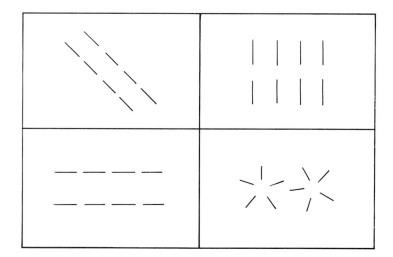

Introductory Activity

The second task requires plenty of space and experience in safety training in order to avoid collisions. If mats are not available this may be done freely on floor. Mastery in backward, diagonal, and sideways safety rolls is required. Children enjoy this task and as their skills and control increases, encourage them to run faster and leap higher.

Movement Training

This task can be simplified in many ways. For example, a sequence can be built using locomotor skills traveling in various directions; rolls only; combination of rolls and balances; combination of rolls and locomotor movements; and combination of balances and locomotor skills. All of these could show changes of direction and levels. Work for quality through the principles

Figure 3.75   "Practice leaping over your mat."

of transference of weight and flow. Partner activities will often work well for grade three.

Select two or three sequences that show variety of activity as well as direction. Have the class comment. For example, they should be able to observe whether the child took her weight on a different body part each time she changed direction or if she chose movements that linked together to give continuity to the pattern as well as fulfilling the original task.

Apparatus Work

Work in subsections, that is, with no more than four to each group and each child using an individual mat (this could also be done with skipping ropes). Whisper to each group how they are to place their mats (one in a straight line, one in a circle, and one sideways or in a diagonal line). Next, ask them to invent ways of traveling along their mats in the direction they have been placed. Leave time for each group to watch others and guess the directions. Groups must be small to do this, otherwise too much time is wasted waiting turns.

Figure 3.76   "Make up a sequence using a mat."

LESSON **4**
Analysis: WHERE?   Directions and levels.
            WHAT?   Balance.

Lesson Outline
Introductory Activity Tasks
1. "Run carrying your hoop."
2. "Find another way of holding your hoop and run."

Movement Training Tasks
1. "Balance the hoop on your head and step through it."
2. "Can you do it sideways?"
3. "Can you travel backwards through your hoop?"
4. "Where else can you balance the hoop and go through it?"

Apparatus Tasks
Select from these or other tasks.
1. "Travel along the narrow side of the bench using any direction."

2. "Find ways of going over, through, and in or out of the hoop your partner is holding while traveling along the bar."
3. "Practice forward or backward somersaults on the beams or climbing ropes."
4. "Build a sequence with a partner matching your movements getting onto and off the box. Include traveling and balancing on different parts of your body and changing directions and levels."
5. "Free play with any piece of small equipment."

Introductory Activity

Each child carries a hoop and runs in and out taking care to use all available space and not to collide. First grade boys are quite good at this and will usually produce some marvelous swerving movements in order to avoid others. Change direction after each time "stop" is called.

Figure 3.77 "Run, carrying your hoop."

Movement Training

As this activity requires little space, it is suitable for the classroom. Children in kindergarten and grade one will need lots of practice but will thoroughly enjoy working at this. Grades two and three enjoy getting a partner to balance the hoop in order to climb through. Remember to stress direction by pointing out such things as "Let's watch John and Bill. Note how John is balancing the hoop on his foot. See if Bill can go through without knocking the hoop off. Which direction did Bill use to go through the hoop?" (See figures 3.78 and 3.79.)

Apparatus Work

By this time you should be able to vary and add ideas to the apparatus suggested. Sometimes you will see children discover some activity in the free-play time at the beginning of a lesson where they may be working on the theme from the previous lesson but have combined two types of apparatus that you had not thought of and that could easily be substituted.

Figure 3.78   "Balance your hoop."

Figure 3.79   "Balance your hoop and go through it."

Either a 4″ balance beam or an upturned bench may be used in task one. If a Cave beam is available, gradually increase the height for the able children. Many kindergarten children by the end of the year are capable of walking along a beam five feet off the ground. Mats must be placed underneath and at the sides so that they can jump, land, and roll safely when they lose balance. As a safety precaution, you should make sure that the children have had plenty of practice at jumping off the top of a full height vaulting box, landing, and rolling, before permitting them to walk a balance beam that is more than two feet off the ground. Also, insist that the child jumps down from the beam at each new height before he attempts to walk along it. The children then know that they can land safely if they should lose their balance when walking along the beam. Never have two children on the high beam simultaneously unless the children have planned to meet in the middle and jump down. Most beams wobble slightly and children find this unnerving. They should only have to cope with their own wobbles!

While performing task three, have the children practice the beanbag toss to remind them how to grip the ropes for one of the rolls between the ropes. When rolling over beams or bars, insist that they change their hand grip so that their thumbs face forward. There are several grips but this one is recommended for the primary children.

LESSON **5**

Analysis: WHERE? Change of direction, level, large and small spaces.

WHAT? Body awareness.

Lesson Outline

Introductory Activity Tasks

1. "Take a band or knotted skipping rope, tuck part of it into the back of your shorts so that it makes a 'tail.' Then run anywhere without colliding."
2. "Stop, sit, and listen."
3. "This time, when I say 'go,' see how many other people's 'tails' you can capture."
4. "You have two jobs this time. Work to collect other people's tails and try to keep your own." (See notes.)

Movement Training Tasks

1. "Find a partner and put one band (rope) away."
2. "Hold the band (folded rope) in both hands and make as big a hole as you can for your partner to climb through. Change over."
3. "What other parts of your body can you join together with the band to make holes for your partner to climb through?"

Apparatus Tasks

Select from these partner tasks or set other tasks.

1. "Makes 'holes' with your body on the sides, ends, or top of the box for your partner to go through."

2. "Travel upwards, downwards, and sideways on the equipment making 'holes' for your partner to climb through. Make up a sequence so that, when you have made a 'hole' for your partner and he has climbed through it, he makes a 'hole' for you."
3. "Knot two climbing roles together. Use them to support your weight while you make a 'hole' for your partner to go through."
4. "Use the bench and the floor for making holes'."

Individual tasks.

5. "Make a continuous bridge over a slow rolling ball."
6. "Roll the ball gently, make a bridge over the ball; as soon as the ball has gone through, run, overtake the ball, and make a new bridge."
7. "Balance your hoop on three pins. Crawl or wriggle between the pins without knocking the hoop off."
8. "Use two chairs and a cane as equipment for free play."
9. "Run, leap, and land into a hoop. Find ways of making it harder for yourself."
10. "Free play."

Introductory Activity

"Tails." Each child has a band tucked into the waistband on the back of his shorts which makes a "tail." The aim of this activity is for the children to run using all the space and avoiding collisions and to capture as many tails as they can without losing their own. This game should not be played until the children have had plenty of experience in running freely in the gymnasium and can do this without any collisions. Allow sufficient time in each game for one child to capture three tails. Encourage those who have lost their tails to capture someone else's

Figure 3.80 "Tails."

tail. All children should be active since there is no "being out." Emphasize dodging sideways as well as backward and forward. Introduce this as being a quick and efficient way of keeping one's tail.

Movement Training

The tasks given in the outline may be simplified by asking each child to make a bridge shape on the floor. Find out how many arches the bridge has, that is, if both hands and feet are on the floor there will be four arches and each arch is large enough for a partner to climb through.

"Use your band this time and see if you can join together one foot and one hand."

Try to find an example of this hole made in the following manner:

1. Behind from standing,
2. In front from standing,
3. At the side from standing,
4. Sitting down,
5. Lying down, and
6. Kneeling.

Figure 3.81   "Holes" using a band.

Figure 3.82   Note the various examples of holes.

If you cannot find examples from the class ask them if they can make the same hole or "arch" in the above ways. "Can you join two or more different parts together and make some new holes? Make sure that the hole is big enough for someone to climb through. Now join up in twos, one of you make the hole while the other climbs through without touching anything."

When each has had one turn ask them to make three different holes. As soon as they have climbed through, they make the hole. When they can make continuous hole or bridge sequences using a partner and a variety of apparatus, you are leading into apparatus work. If bands are not available, use skipping ropes tied to form a circle and then double the circle so that it is about 18″ long.

This activity needs no adaptation for use in the classroom, although the energetic Introductory Activity does. Have half the class work at a time.

Apparatus Work

1. Box: Use sides as well as top working in twos within group, make "holes" for partner to climb through.
2. Wall bars or Cave: Partner travels upwards, downwards, or sideways alternately making "holes" for partner to crawl through as they travel.

Figure 3.83 "Make holes for your partner to go through."

Figure 3.84 Holes on the Cave.

3. Two climbing ropes: These may be knotted or loose, children can use these in a great variety of ways according to their ability. For example, sitting on floor holding ropes.

4. Benches: Making different "holes" with part of the body on either the broad or narrow side of the bench and part on floor. (Figure 3.85.)

5 and 6. Individually or in twos: Make a continuous bridge over a slow rolling ball, or get up and run after the first bridge to overtake ball and then make second bridge.

7. Work individually. Balance hoop on three pins and use all arches to crawl through.

8. Two canes and two chairs: Let each child arrange own way to make maximum number of arches. Kindergarden children could work on bridges made by chairs. Grades two and three would work well in twos.

All of these activities require slow, controlled movements; therefore, make sure there are other section activities such as skipping, running, and jumping, climbing or swinging on ropes to provide sufficient variety of movements.

Figure 3.85 Holes on the bench.

LESSON **6**

Analysis: WHERE?   Levels, particularly high and low, directions.

WHAT?   Body awareness and balance, locomotor skills.

Lesson Outline

Free play until all are ready.

Introductory Activity Tasks

1. "Hold onto your partner and run in the space. Avoid collisions."

2. "Still holding onto your partner, *walk* backwards."

3. "Gallop sideways holding onto your partner."

4. "You and your partner choose a way of traveling and a direction in which to travel."

5. "Find a space and a new partner, then curl up and make yourself as small as you can."

6. "When I say 'jack-in-the-box,' jump up and make your hands go as high as you can."

7. "One of you curl up small, low to the ground, the other stretch up high. This time when I say 'jack-in-the-box,' change positions."

8. "Run with your partner and, instead of saying 'stop' I am going to say 'jack-in-the-box, change positions.' Decide who will stop high and who will stop low. Ready? Off you go."

Movement Training Tasks

1. "Let's see how many statues you can make with your partner. You must remain in contact with your partner as though you were Siamese twins. If I call out 'hands,' one of you must have your hands the low part of you and the other make your hands the highest."

2. The same task as above but emphasize forwards and backwards rather than high or low.

3. "Make three different statues, the first emphasizing elbows; the second, knees; and the third, the head. Work on your own."

4. "Join up with a partner and build a sequence where you make three statues and where you emphasize the same part of the body as your partner, but you contrast either level or direction."

5. "Improve your sequence by changing from one statue to the next by 'melting' and 'freezing'."

Apparatus Tasks

Select from these and other tasks.

1. Individual or partner sequences using balance statues and locomotor movements to show high and low.

2. Individual or partner sequences to show backwards and forwards, using balance statues and locomotor skills.

3. "Make up high-low sequences on the large equipment."

4. "Free play."

Introductory Activity

So far we have not had a lesson plan dealing specifically with levels. For primary grades, the easiest way to introduce this is by contrasting high and low movements. Ask children to run holding partner's hand. On "stop," one partner makes herself as small and low to the ground as possible while the other makes herself as high as possible. Kindergarten and grade one love to play jack-in-the-box, so, for them instead of saying "stop" use "jack-in-the-box," and they will quickly shoot up high or quickly drop down.

Instead of using jack-in-the-box, use "opposites" for grades two and three. "Siamese twins" works with all grades. Adapt this for the class-

Figure 3.86   "One high—one low." Note **poor head positions.**

room by having them jump with feet together instead of running.

As soon as they understand and have the feel of being high or low, isolate different parts of the body, for example, one finger, feet. Then let each pair choose which part they will make high or low.

Figure 3.87 "One partner with feet high the other with feet low."

Movement Training

For tasks one and two, suggest all the patches and points in order to explore all the possibilities. Use task three if the partners are unable to agree on the selection of the three parts and the statues.

Changing from one statue to the next can be fun if they use slow-motion "melting" to move into the next statue. They then "freeze" and hold it before changing into the third shape. This makes the sequence more interesting to do and can lead into dance activities. It can also be used in the classroom, as well as the gym.

Apparatus Work

Apply partner work to apparatus.

1. Box: Each pair makes a sequence on top of box. Grades two and three may like to work up from floor as side of box can often be used as a support for them.
2. Benches: Invent a high-low sequence traveling along the bench.
3. Climbing ropes: Sequence of two movements so that each partner has turn at being low and high.

Figure 3.88 "Make a hole for your partner to go through."

Figure 3.89 "Go as high as you can."

4. Climbing equipment or climbing ropes: "Go as high as you can and then climb down." Allow lots of turns. Do not make this competitive—work individually.

5 and 6. Balls or Hoops: Pick up balls or hoops with different parts, taking them as high as possible and then putting them down and picking them up again with a different part. Remember to add forward, backward, and sideways to high and low for variety and added range.

7. Beanbags: Use different parts to toss beanbags into the air and then pick them up with different parts, for example, "Shaggy Dog," "Bunny Jump," with beanbag between feet.

8. Stage and large mats: Jumping as high as they can, land and roll.

9. Benches tied to ropes: Running and leaping high, landing, and rolling. (Figure 3.90)

10. Canes and chairs: Leaping over to get high, rolling under to keep low.

Figure 3.90   "Fly through the air."

LESSON **7**

Analysis: WHERE?   Levels.

WHAT?   Jumping and rolling, feet and legs.

Lesson Outline

Introductory Activity Tasks

1. "Quickly go to your section places. Each group take out a bench, put it in your space in the gym."

2. "Run along, jump over or step onto, and jump off the benches."

Movement Training Tasks

1. "Take a beanbag to a space on the floor near the bench. Practice jumping off the bench and land as close to the beanbag as you can. Roll on landing."

2. "Keep making it more difficult for yourself."

Apparatus Tasks

Select from tasks given for other lessons.

Introductory Activity

If you have four or more benches, have the children space them on the floor anywhere in the gymnasium but away from the walls. This activity should only be attempted after the initial period of safety training has taken place. Do not teach this in your first month of Movement Education. Ask the children to run and leap over, or step up and leap into the air, then land and roll without colliding and using all available space. Primary balance beams could be substituted.

Movement Training

Working individually, using a beanbag and finding a space on one of the benches, practice jumping off bench over beanbag placed on floor, and landing with a safety roll. Encourage the placing of the beanbag farther away from the bench each time they leap over and also vary the high jumps by asking them to leap high forward, backward, or sideways always landing with a safety roll. Also stress that they try to find different ways and directions of returning to the bench. Make sure that benches will not slide as children leap on and off.

Figure 3.91   "Leap over the bench."

LESSON **8**

Analysis: WHERE? Levels.

WHAT? Body shape.

Lesson Outline

Introductory Activity Tasks

1. "Find a partner and a space. Sit facing each other, holding hands, and rock so that one is sitting up and the other lying down."
2. "Can you think of another way you can go down while helping your partner to go up?"
3. "Find a way of both going up together and down together. Change direction and see if you can find two other ways."

Movement Training Tasks

1. "Curl up small on the floor. With fingers leading, stretch up slowly until you are as tall as you can be."
2. "When you can't go any higher, come down quickly and curl up small again."
3. "This time creep your fingers out along the floor and stretch out until you are long and thin. Curl yourself up small again."

4. "Stand up, stretch out sideways and make yourself wide. Try to snap yourself long and thin again, as though you were snipping with scissors."
5. "Jump, sometimes high, long, and thin, and sometimes high and wide."
6. "How many ways can you make a letter Y shape with your body?" (also X, T, I.)

Apparatus Tasks

1. "Make the shape X, Y, T, or I as you jump off the equipment. Land with a roll."
2. "Find ways of traveling on the equipment in wide or narrow shapes."
3. "Find ways of balancing on the equipment in wide or narrow shapes."
4. "Free play."

Introductory Activity

By using a slight variation of jack-in-the-box and using the words "up and down" instead of "high and low," the basis is laid for the rest of this lesson.

Movement Training

Tasks one, two, and three are suitable for kindergarten, first, and second grades. Work individually curled up in a small space. Make fingers lead the movement, gradually reach up until fingers are stretched and the child is standing on tiptoes. When he cannot reach up any higher, he comes down and curls up in a ball as quickly as possible. Practice several turns.

"Now can you stay down and take a lot of room on the floor? Are your tummies, legs,

Figure 3.92 "High and low."

head, and arms all touching the floor? This time make yourself thinner until you are long and thin and straight. Make your wide shape on the floor again. Now make your narrow shape where you are long and thin. Let me see you doing this standing up."

Experiment with different wide and narrow shapes placing weight on different parts of the body. "Can you invent a jump that goes backwards and forwards?"

Practice different parts leading up and down and experiment with various ways of being wide and narrow, and backward and forward. The teacher can select shapes to form a sequence and then have the whole class try to join them together. Finally add "quick and slow" to provide a contrast in time as well as space.

Apparatus Work

"Jump down off the apparatus and make either a wide shape or a narrow shape in the air."

Select from:
1. Box
2. Benches
3. Stage
4. Ropes and benches

Two wide shapes and two narrow shapes working sideways or upside down as well as right side up and using different body parts to support weight.

5. Two climbing ropes
6. Wall bars or climbing equipment

Figure 3.93   "Alternate going up and down."

Figure 3.94   "Make yourself long and thin."

Figure 3.95   Wide and narrow shapes.

THEME FOUR: QUALITIES

It is impossible to teach in the gymnasium or on the playground without using combinations of time, space, force, and flow. Up to this point we have taken space as a main theme (referring to where the body is moving) and have explored it in many ways. Space is also used as a quality to describe direct and flexible movements. We have used large and small spaces and emphasized how different body parts can use this space, and we have used the space in front, behind, and at the side. By including jumping activities from the ground or off apparatus, different levels of space have been introduced. For all of these activities we are unconsciously using time, force, and flow. At this stage we feel that to enable the children's movement knowledge and imagination to continue to grow we should now develop their conscious understanding and appreciation of time, space, force, and flow. This is like a chef adding seasoning which, in turn, becomes an integral and inseparable part of a gourmet dish. So too, the children learn to select and emphasize various qualities which are already a part of their movement sequences in order to produce a satisfying and complete work. It is also important for the children not to isolate the qualities. Perhaps the latter can best be illustrated by a small girl who, having played her piano piece with exactly the right notes and in strict time, turned to her teacher and asked "Now shall I play it with expression?"

How then do we set about bringing out these various qualities? One of the most effective ways we have found with primary children is through the dance approach. The majority of teachers find it easier to work toward a freer approach in the gymnasium through gymnastics. Ideally however, dance, gymnastics, and games should go hand in hand since each enhances the other.

Figure 3.96   "Flight."

LESSON 1

Analysis: WHERE?   General, own space, levels.

WHAT?   Traveling, hands and feet, balancing, rolling.

HOW?   Quick, slow.

Lesson Outline

Introductory Activity Tasks

1. "Run on the spot with very quick, little steps. Now travel making wiggly patterns on the floor with your feet."
2. "Show me a giant's step. Run with giant strides."

Movement Training Tasks

1. "Find a space and sit on the floor. Tap your hands on the floor. Start slowly, gradually going faster and faster, then slow down again."
2. "Do the same thing with your feet while sitting on the floor."
3. "Lie on your backs and shake your feet as fast as you can in the air."

4. "Make up a sequence of traveling to a new space slowly and softly. When you arrive, choose a way that you can make your feet move very quickly. Repeat this sequence lots of times."
5. "Find different ways of traveling slowly and make different parts of your body move quickly."

Apparatus Tasks

Select equipment for this task or use other tasks.

1. "Show differences in speed while using the equipment."

Introductory Activity

Small, quick-step running is more fun when changing direction and long, slow, giant strides when traveling in a straight line.

Figure 3.97   "Move your hands as fast as you can."

Movement Training

Work at the first three tasks until there is improvement in the quality of their work. In task five encourage different ways of traveling while different parts of the body move quickly. Use patches and points to remind you.

Apparatus Work

You can draw on any previous lesson and will find, as stated earlier, that certain activities lend themselves easily to stressing quality and thus making the movement more complete. For example, any balance work is more effective if slow and controlled—so benches for balance work could be one section. Balancing of balls, beanbags, or hoops and traveling also would require slow smooth movements and could be another section.

For quick movements skipping is ideal, and any form of jumping off apparatus lends itself to quick explosive movements requiring leg strength. Also making up quick foot patterns in and out of, or around beanbags and hoops, and

Figure 3.98 "Balance with the ball high."

skipping ropes can be fun. Rolling on mats as fast as possible or any apparatus activity produces lots of interesting sequences.

Grade three children are capable of making excellent sequences of rolling which show contrast of speeds.

Figure 3.99 "Slowly lift your hoop high."

LESSON 2

Analysis: WHERE? Levels.

WHAT? Jumping, parts of the body (feet and legs particularly), and arms.

HOW? Strong-light, sudden-sustained, direct-flexible.

Lesson Outline

Introductory Activity Tasks

1. "Find a space and practice jumping and landing."
2. "Push hard with your toes when taking off. Land with big toes first and bend ankles, knees, and hips."

Movement Training Tasks

1. "Shoot your feet."
2. "Find a partner, check your partner's feet and legs as he jumps and lands."

3. "One of you collect a skipping rope and lay it in a straight line on the ground. Lie on your tummies one at each end of the rope. Hold onto the rope with both hands. When I say 'go,' pull yourself hand-over-hand to the middle."

Apparatus Tasks

Select from these and other tasks.

1. "Running and jumping off your piece of equipment."
2. "Support or propel yourself using your arms."
3. "Free play."

Introductory Activity

The teacher should now be particularly concerned with developing an understanding of how to apply force in order to gain height. Movement challenges should emphasize a strong push with the legs, straightening at hip, knee, and ankle joints, and getting the final maximum lift with the push off from the toes. By this stage, children should not have any problems in running freely without collisions, hence, other points may be stressed such as lifting head and arms to help the lift. Younger children tend to try to jump high by looking at their toes. To counteract this, encourage short periods of "star gazing" as they leap.

Movement Training

A quick review of "shooting feet" is advised as this mobility in the ankle joint and toes is important to apply the force and strength necessary for jumping.

One child should jump while a partner sits and looks to see if the child's knees are straight and feet stretched with toes pointed. Children should now be able to watch each other—even grade one. Assist them to understand the need for explosive force, for example, by suggesting they shoot into the air like a rocket. Also re-emphasize that they try to land lightly even though they straightened their hips, knees, and toes in order to jump upwards, they must bend everything as they come down to prevent landing with a bump.

Figure 3.100   "Race to the middle of the rope."

Task three is a way of building arm strength that the children enjoy, however, it doesn't work on carpeted floors. Change partners every three turns. This works well as a competitive activity for grade three (Figure 3.100).

Apparatus Work

1. Benches: Run along to gather speed, jump up, land, and roll.
2. Benches: Pulling themselves along top of bench to develop arm strength ("seals").

Figure 3.101   "Run along, leap off, land, and roll."

Figure 3.102   "Seals."

3. Box: Leaping onto box, getting off by taking weight on arms (this can be done in a variety of ways).

4. Rope climbing: Using arms only for climbing up.

5. Climbing equipment: Any activity where weight is taken by the arms.

6. Hoop held by partner: Leaping into hoop and bunny-jump out so that weight is taken on arms.

7. Using gymnasium walls: Lying face downward on floor with feet against wall, pushing upon arms, and walk feet up wall. This can also be done with beanbags on edge of stage so that once their feet are as high as the stage they can knock beanbags onto the floor with their feet.

8. One child lying on back and using his feet to balance his partner. Starts by child A lying on back, legs bent with feet in air. Child B takes hold of child A's hands and leans with his tummy against A's feet. A straightens his legs slowly, thus taking B's weight and tries to balance B in the air.

Figure 3.103 Weight is taken by the arms.

Figure 3.104 "Use your feet to knock the beanbags to the floor."

Figure 3.105 "Balance on your partner's feet."

LESSON 3
Analysis: WHERE? General space.
WHAT? Whole body, traveling, and statues.
HOW? Sudden-sustained, free and bound.

Lesson Outline

Introductory Activity Tasks

1. "Run as fast as you can, making zigzag patterns on the floor. Freeze into a 'statue' when I say 'stop'."
2. "Make exactly the same statue each time."
3. "Make a different statue each time."

Movement Training Tasks

1. "Find a partner, cross hands, and twirl your partner. Break hands on 'stop' and freeze into a statue."
2. "Think how to change your statues to make them look very difficult."
3. "Build a partner sequence 'freezing' and 'melting' your statues. Make the sequence interest-ing by changing the level and the part of your body that supports your weight."

Apparatus Tasks

Select from these or other tasks.

1. "Travel anywhere in the gym using all the ap-paratus and freeze into a statue on each piece of equipment."
2. "Working as a group on one piece of large equipment, build a sequence of traveling over, onto, and around. Include statues."
3. "Traveling, freezing, and melting as a group remaining in contact with the piece of small equipment all the time."
4. "Free play."

Introductory Activity

Run quickly in zigzag patterns, freezing into a pose on "stop." Each time freeze into differ-ent pose.

Look to see that they are running on their toes with feet straight forward (neither flat-footed nor pigeon-toed) and that their arms are bent at the elbows and tucked into the body.

Remind them that their feet are not the only possible base for their statues.

Movement Training

The teacher should direct the amount of "twirl-ing" time to prevent the children from going on too long and becoming giddy. This is where

Figure 3.106 "Freeze into a statue."

Figure 3.107 "Twirl your partner."

"flow" can be emphasized, with the smooth continuous twirling followed by a jerky "stop." A greater variety of statues can be stimulated if the teacher varies height and stresses different body parts. For example, "Freeze this time with one elbow on the ground" or "'One have knees high and the other knees down low." Remember, the main emphasis is on the smooth continuous twirl and the sudden stop.

Apparatus Work

Use any available large or small apparatus. Each child should be working individually (or with a partner) traveling around, over, or on any piece of apparatus, keeping the flow of movement continuous until the "stop" signals each child to freeze into a statue. Encourage many angular or spiky shapes for the statues, then let them slowly "melt" into smooth traveling again. Make sure that all movements on and off are as fluent as possible to contrast with the "freezing" of the statues.

Task one is more suitable for kindergarten through grade two, but can be adapted to grade three by keeping turns short and stressing both quality and different ways of traveling between the equipment. Encourage statues that require difficult balances.

Task 3. Work in small groups with grades two and three, using any type of apparatus to work out a group sequence. All *must* be on apparatus or somehow in contact with it at all times. Still keep to three statues and again stress movement memory and observation.

Broom handles, large bamboo canes, skipping ropes, hoops, as well as benches, boxes, platforms, and climbing apparatus are all excellent for this type of activity.

Introduction to Lesson 4

As already discussed, direction can and does combine with flow and speed. As the children's knowledge and understanding of movement increases so does their movement imagination and creativity. It is worthwhile going back over some of the earlier lesson plans, and using ideas covered there to show how the work they have done since the earlier lesson enables them to find different ways of exploring the same ideas. For instance, by combining different parts high with wide and narrow to form sequences instead of the rather stilted and isolated movements that evolved some lessons earlier, it should now be possible for them not only to invent new solutions but to vary the speed and flow of their sequence. As their earlier attempts usually consist of jerky movements, flow would now be stressed along with a change from one shape to another.

Figure 3.108   Group statues freezing onto small equipment.

LESSON **4**

Analysis: WHERE? Levels.
         WHAT?   Whole body, shape, bend, stretch, twist.
         HOW?   Sudden-sustained, bound-free.

Lesson Outline

Introductory Activity Tasks

1. "Run and when I say 'stop' make your body the same shape as a letter T (then X, Y, I)."
2. "Choose whether you make the letter shape while standing or lying."

Movement Training Tasks

1. "Who can make a traveling X?"
2. "Who can make a traveling Y?"
3. "Join up with a partner. See if you can make all the letters in your name. You will probably need your partner to help you make some of the letters. Work with your partner and build a sequence so that you move by twisting or rolling from one letter to the next."

Apparatus Tasks

Select from these and other tasks.

1. "Find how many stretched, bent, or twisted shapes you can make on the equipment."
2. "Build a sequence with a partner showing stretched, curled, and twisted shapes as you roll, balance, and jump."
3. "Find how many words your group of four can make. Then invent ways of writing sentences."
4. "Free play."

Introductory Activity

One of the easiest ways to introduce shape is by using letters of the alphabet. Grade three children usually do this very well working with a partner, thus making it possible to form a greater variety of letters.

Figure 3.109   Making letters.

Movement Training

Xs, Vs, and Ys make useful wide shapes. Invite the children to make them standing as well as lying down. Many children in the primary grades are able to do handstands, headstands, cartwheels, and change from wide to narrow shapes in the process. Once they have decided on what narrow and wide shapes they wish to use in their sequence, the emphasis then becomes *how* they move from one to the other. Decisions must be made as to the order. Often for grade one and kindergarten, a good guideline is to ask them to choose one shape where they are lying down, one sitting, and the third one standing. Older children make much more interesting patterns if allowed to decide on their own. Again phrases that will help produce variety are "Twist from your first wide shape to your second" or "Roll into your third shape."

Permit the children to try out their own ideas first and observe any children who develop interesting ways of getting from one to the next shape. Variation of the time factor may be introduced by asking the children to change the shape suddenly or slowly.

Apparatus Work

Remember *how* they go from one shape to the other is important, but the actual quality of their shape is also very important. For example, are toes pointed if legs are supposed to be stretched? They must "feel" the movement with their whole bodies and know what each part of them is doing.

Task three works well in the classroom. It can be made more challenging by asking the whole group to make each word. For example, "I am late," the letter *I* must use all four children and they must devise ways in which the four letters of *late* are made simultaneously.

Teaching Points

1. In each lesson there should be opportunities for the children to explore, select, refine, and repeat. The balance is left to the teacher to decide by observing the needs of the class.

2. Observation is the key feature of the capable teacher of Movement Education. It is through observation that the teacher will be able to decide upon the needs of the class.

3. From this observation the teacher will have discovered many new movement patterns and ways of using apparatus and thus will have this experience to help teach the next class. Even though you are busy with a hundred-and-one things to do, jot down ideas that the children invent. Although you may feel certain that you will not forget by next year, many of those ideas will have faded from your mind. Some classes are more imaginative than others and you will be more confident with the knowledge that the activities invented by previous classes are suitable for children of that grade level.

4. We have tried to use a variety of apparatus in the lesson plans. We also realize that many teachers will have little equipment to work with at this stage. However, it is possible to work on many movement ideas with little or no apparatus and we have included the ten-cent balloon lesson to demonstrate this in the dance section.

One primary teacher who had no formal training at all in this method and no equipment, has taught valuable movement les-

Figure 3.110 Note pointed toes of a kindergarten child.

Figure 3.111 "Make a stretched shape on the apparatus."

sons to children by using a grade one science lesson where they watched water boil and then followed the freezing process by continual peeps into the refrigerator. This was immediately followed up by movement experiences in the activity room, and what fun the children had! Another lesson on the life cycle of a butterfly proved interesting to children of grade one with the boys imitating caterpillars while the girls enjoyed the butterfly part of the lesson. They both delighted in the "grub" and the "larva" stages.

If you are adventurous enough to try teaching with this method, be adventurous enough to try out your own ideas and only fall back on this book as a "prop." Improvise, capitalize, and observe, and both you and the children will enjoy the lesson.

Chapter Four

Dance

Theme One: Safety Training

Theme Two: Adding to the Range and Understanding of Movement

Theme Three: Understanding Direction

Theme Four: Qualities

Dance is an area that many teachers are discovering for the first time and are finding very exciting. Many teachers seem to find that as they integrate language arts and music with movement so easily, dance, rather than gymnastics or games, is the logical starting point for their physical education programs.

To encourage teachers to venture into dance, the same movement idea is explored using three different stimuli: music, percussion, and words. If the recommended recorded music or percussion instruments are not readily available, a dance lesson may still be taught using only words as stimuli. Therefore there is no excuse for not attempting dance at least one lesson out of every three.

The teachers will also find it fun to do all three versions if there is sufficient equipment. It is amazing to see how the children's movements develop and the ways in which a different stimulus can inspire a greater range of movement. (There has been a deliberate attempt to incorporate some of the Orff music concepts where there is a direct relationship with Laban's analysis of movement.)

The lesson outlines in both the Introductory Activity and Movement Training rely heavily upon the direct and limitation teaching methods. This has been done to enable inexperienced teachers to see *one* way in which to develop the material. However, it should be clearly understood that there are many other ways in which the same material could be developed. All teachers are encouraged to try out their own ideas. For those who lack confidence, it is encouraging to note that many teachers who have never taught dance before have successfully taught dance material directly from these outlines. As they became more familiar with the dance concepts, they began to change some of the tasks and replace them with their own. The children will also come up with ideas and should be given opportunities in the last part of the lesson to interpret the tasks for themselves.

According to the concepts of Movement Education, dance is based upon the understanding of the movement analysis. This is important in the selection and interpretation of the movement tasks. When imagery is used as a stimulus, you will note that children are not asked to *be* witches or monsters, they are asked to describe the qualities of movement associated with the image and to combine variations of time, weight, space, and flow to extract the essence of the character through movement. The movements should not be limited to mere imitative actions. For example, elephants seem to suffer from hideous misrepresentations by teachers. Children are taught to use one arm to represent the trunk and their other for the tail. That is regarded sufficient for the child to "become" an elephant. *How* an elephant moves is not considered; therefore the children do not learn about the factors of weight or heaviness and how they relate to strength and lightness.

Working from language to rhythm to music should help those teachers who lack confidence in their ability to teach dance. A tambourine is an invaluable instrument, and every teacher should have at least one in the classroom.

Tapes and records should be in every primary-grade classroom. Their use should not be restricted to music and physical education classes. If you can master a tape recorder, you may find that having music on tape is an advantage for these reasons:

a. Records may get scratched and broken.
b. The vibrations on the floor caused by the children moving can make the needle of the record player skip.

c. If the records are school property, they are often mislaid or not available when you wish to use them.

Avoid putting a lot of music on one tape, as it can be time-consuming to find the piece you want.

Combine music and movement whenever possible, particularly if the children are using the Orff music method. Encourage them to improvise accompaniments for their dance sequences.

The length of a Movement Education lesson may vary according to the needs of each class. This is especially applicable to lessons taught within the classroom. Use five minutes, or even ten or twenty minutes to try out some of the ideas suggested. The dance lessons in this chapter have been taught in classrooms and gyms, a library and even a hallway; so don't be afraid to try them yourself.

THEME ONE: SAFETY TRAINING

The lessons in this theme are designed to give the children experience in "going and stopping," avoiding collisions with others, and using the space sensibly.

LESSON **1**

Stimulus: Tambourine
Analysis: WHERE?   General space.
            WHAT?   The whole body and parts of the body, locomotor skills, going and stopping.
            HOW?   Going and stopping, quick and slow.

Lesson Outline

Introductory Activity Tasks

1. "Find a space and face me. When I tap the tambourine, see how quickly you can sit down. Ready, tap." (Figure 4.2)
2. "Stand up and try the same thing again."

3. "This time there will be two different sounds. One rattly sound like this . . . and a tapping sound like this. Run without bumping when you hear the rattly sound. What do you think you will do when you hear the tap? That's right, sit quickly. Are you ready? Off you go."

Movement Training Tasks

1. "Make sure that you are in a space. Now make your feet move as quickly as you can, as I rattle the tambourine, but stay in your own space."
2. "Who could think of another part of your body that you could move very quickly while I shake the tambourine?"
3. "This time *you* choose which part you are going to move quickly. I am going to rattle the tambourine twice with a stop in between, like this, listen . . . rattle . . . stop . . . rattle . . . stop. Decide which part you are going to move quickly. Ready?"

Development or Dance Tasks

1. "First you practiced stopping quickly, then you practiced running and stopping. Can you show me another way of going? Show me."
2. "Change the way you travel each time I rattle, stand still each time I tap."
3. "Make up a sequence using three different ways of traveling and freeze into a statue on each tap."
4. "Teach your sequence to your partner."

Figure 4.1   Learning to use space sensibly.

Figure 4.2   "Sit quickly."

Introductory Activity

Task one introduces the first sound to which they will respond. This helps establish class control and can be made into a game. After several turns of encouraging them to sit quickly, make them listen for the sound. Ask them to turn their backs and sit when they hear the sound. Vary the volume of the tap and shorten the time between turns; this makes it more fun.

Task three sends them traveling around the gym. Observe whether they (1) distinguish between the two sounds, (2) run without colliding, (3) run in a circle or use all the space, (4) run on the balls of their feet, and (5) stop quickly.

Movement Training

The first task is designed so that children learn to work in a space of their own and not crowd around the teacher. The teacher should move around to avoid directing the class always from the same spot.

The initial response is often stamping. Encourage them to pick their feet up off the floor as though the floor were very hot. This usually helps the children to become more resilient. Emphasize light, quick feet.

Draw from them other parts of their bodies they could move quickly. As soon as a child suggests one, have the whole class try it and then ask for another. Be prepared for "eyelashes" as a kindergarten solution, as it always seems to occur. Hands, elbows, heads, knees, and the whole body are the more conventional solutions.

Training the movement memory is begun in task three. Each child chooses one body part, moves it quickly, rests, and repeats. This can be

Figure 4.3   "Choose a way to move quickly."

developed by changing the part and doing hands, rest, feet, rest, and repeat. Finally a third part of the body may be added, and this becomes the beginning of sequence building for the children. Further variations of body position, for example, sitting, kneeling, or lying, may be encouraged.

Development or Dance

The children should experiment with all the locomotor movements. By asking them to show you another way of traveling, you can observe what they know and can do. Use the tambourine to accompany them and encourage quality in footwork and foot patterns. For example, the foot pattern for skipping is step-hop.

Encourage them to choose their own ways of traveling and to combine two or three ways to make sequences. Held statues as a way of stopping appeals to children in the primary grades and can give character to their sequence. Also it makes a clear distinction between their "going" and "stopping." Some grade two children enjoy working with a partner and can develop joint sequences.

LESSON 2

Stimulus: Words, rhymes, stories.
Analysis: WHERE?   General space.
            WHAT?   The whole body and parts of the body, locomotor skills, going and stopping.
            HOW?   Going and stopping, quick and slow.

Lesson Outline

Introductory Activity Tasks

1. "Find a space and face me. Show me how quickly you can sit. Ready and sit."
2. "How many of you know the nursery rhyme 'Mary Had a Little Lamb?' Say it with me."
3. "Go for a walk on your own and say 'Mary Had a Little Lamb' as you go."
4. "Do the same thing, but this time try to get back to your starting space, standing absolutely still by the time you say, 'sure to go.' "

5. "Instead of sitting when you stop, show me a different way in which to stop."

Movement Training Tasks

1. "Try to put in two stops this time before you get home. One after 'lamb' and another after 'snow.' "
2. "Do you know 'Humpty Dumpty?' Say it with me if you do. 'Humpty Dumpty. . . .' This has a different beat from 'Mary Had a Little Lamb.' Get up and skip anywhere as you say 'Humpty Dumpty.' "

3. "There are two places in 'Humpty Dumpty' when you could stop. Can you find them?"
4. "Do you know another nursery rhyme to which you could walk or skip? Say it for yourself and try to make your feet fit the words."
5. "Are there any places to have rests on the way? Make sure you are very still when you stop."

Development or Dance Tasks
1. "Find a partner and sit one behind the other."
2. "Play Follow-the-Leader. The front person is going to be the leader and the partner is going to follow the leader and do whatever she does."
3. "Now the leader makes a sequence of travel-stop-travel-stop-travel-stop. Use a different way of traveling each time and find different stopping positions. Follower, you copy exactly what your partner does."
4. "Change over, so that you each have a turn at being the leader."
5. "Mix some of the nursery rhymes together, so that you can work side by side with your partner and know what to do."

Introductory Activity

"And . . . sit" is a useful teaching technique as the *and* gives the children some warning. You can therefore expect an immediate response to "sit." This activity is fun and gives children practice in listening and following instructions. This technique becomes a great time-saver, too.

Words have a rhythm and as children are already attuned to words, they can be used to develop a sense of rhythm in movement. Most nursery rhymes have either a walking or skipping rhythmic beat. The advantage is that each child can say them at the speed that is natural for him or her. Children need to develop their natural movement rhythm before responding to formal rhythms such as those used in folk dance. Learning to keep a simple beat can be developed through walking or skipping to rhymes where each syllable is used as a step: "Mar-ry had a lit-tle lamb," "Sim-ple Si-mon met a pie-man." Skipping rhymes are those where the emphasis is on the longer syllable or word, for example, "Hump-ty Dump-ty," "Half a pound of tuppen-ny rice."

Task three allows the children to move at their own rhythm, making the words fit their feet. The children should move throughout the entire space of the gym, not merely in a large circle. Check as they walk that their feet are straight, turned neither in nor out.

Task four is designed to aid movement memory and sequence making. By traveling away from and returning to their own spaces, the children begin to acquire a feeling for and understanding of beginning and ending. A good starting position is an essential part of a movement sequence in all three movement areas, games, gymnastics, and dance. Basically this is a stance that indicates both mental and physical readiness. Sitting. when they return "home," provides a definite ending position. As they develop their movements into sequences, clearly defined finishing positions become more important. Experiment with different ways to complete the sequences.

The duration of a sequence should be considered. In the early stages, the sequences should be short, so that the children can remember the movements exactly and be able to repeat what

Figure 4.4   "Travel-stop."

they have done. The length of one verse of a rhyme is useful at this stage and helps the children to judge time and distance.

Movement Training

The purpose of the first task is to develop the idea of going and stopping by listening to the cadence in speech. For example,

Mary had a little lamb.
Its fleece was white as snow.
Everywhere that Mary went
The lamb was sure to go.

This fits the short-short-long pattern and there are natural pauses after *lamb* and *snow.* For children who do not arrive back in time, you may suggest that they travel away from their own space until *snow,* then begin to work back "home."

"Humpty Dumpty" provides a skipping rhythm. Many children have problems with the step-hop, skipping foot pattern at first. This is remedied by giving individual help and plenty of practice over a period of time.

It is not true that boys find it harder to learn to skip than girls. Any problems that boys encounter in learning to skip are usually due to a lack of opportunity. Given the opportunity, all children will be able to skip by the end of their first year in school.

Task three provides opportunities for the children to listen to sounds, find logical pauses in the rhymes, and use the rhythms as accompaniment for their movements.

"Humpty Dumpty" and "Sally Go Round the Sun" both fit the short-short-long sequence pattern and are skipping rhythms.

Encourage the children to find different ways of responding to the pauses. Sitting is a final way of stopping and makes a good ending, but after *wall* and *fall,* sitting is a difficult position to begin new movements from. Ask them to invent "stops" that are easy for "starts," for example, standing with one foot in front of the other while absolutely still.

Contrast the complete stillness of the pauses and stops with the various movements for traveling. Stress quality.

Development or Dance

Make the task of finding a partner into a game of working with the nearest person rather than encouraging "best friends" only. Repeat this task several times quickly, perhaps not waiting until all have found partners. Much valuable lesson time is lost when children do not find partners quickly.

Even the youngest children enjoy Follow the Leader. It is another means of developing going and stopping, and it gives opportunities for children to invent other ways of traveling not previously developed in this lesson. Make sure that each child has a turn at being the leader. Different ways of pausing may be included as a development of this task.

Give individual help to improve the quality of the locomotor skills. For example, suggest running on the balls of their feet or pushing with their toes in the hopping part of the skip.

Task five appeals to second and third graders' sense of humor, particularly if they mix the nursery rhymes together to form nonsense rhymes. They can then be translated into skipping and walking sequences with or without pauses.

The partner relationship has changed and is now one where both partners contribute to the same sequence. Standing side by side, instead of one behind the other, makes working together easier and is an additional challenge for the older children.

Free play with the nursery rhymes also permits children to perform them literally if they wish. A drawback is that they may try to fit dramatic actions to the exact words, causing their movements to become stilted and artificial. You could suggest they use the story line of the rhyme as the basis for a dance drama or perhaps they could write further adventures for "Humpty Dumpty."

LESSON 3

Stimulus: Record or tape of "Pop Goes the Weasel."
Analysis: WHERE?   General space.
             WHAT?   The whole body and parts of the body, locomotor, listening, and safety skills.
             HOW?   Going and stopping, quick and slow, direct and flexible.

Lesson Outline

Introductory Activity Tasks

1. "Sit on the floor and listen to the music. Do you know this song? Sing the words if you can."
2. "Stand up in a space. Show me how quickly you can sit on the floor. Ready . . . and sit."
3. "I am going to turn on the music so you can skip. When I turn it off, sit quickly on the floor."
4. "Now I am going to turn it off on *pop* each time. Listen as you skip, so that you will be ready to sit."

Movement Training Tasks

1. "Find a space of your own and sit. Listen to the music and clap on *pop* each time." (Figure 4.5)

2. "Skip with the music, use all the space and clap on *pop* each time."
3. "What else could you do on *pop* instead of clap?"
4. "Show me how well you can skip and choose for yourself what you do on *pop*."

Development or Dance Tasks

1. "Skip to the music but choose three things to do; a different one on each *pop*."
2. "Try galloping to the music and jumping on *pop*."
3. "Skip on your own until you hear *pop*. Then join up with a partner. Remember to keep skipping *all* the time." (Figure 4.6)

Introductory Activity

The beginning is the same as the last two lessons. Encourage the children to sing, and even if you have a poor singing voice, sing with them.

The stopping and starting of the music is often used as a party game called Musical Bumps. Here it is used to teach children to listen and respond to instructions. It could develop into a Nine Lives situation. The children will concentrate intently on the music if you tell them in advance at which point you are going to stop the music.

Movement Training

By changing the task to clapping on "pop," you are able to teach "pause" as opposed to sitting which is a final ending.

All kinds of variations, from touching the

Figure 4.5 "Clap on *pop*."

floor to jumping in the air, will occur when children experiment for themselves. Use the children's ideas; have them demonstrate and then the whole class do each one.

Development or Dance

The three different ideas the children select to do on "pop" can be built into a sequence. You may like to suggest that they skip on the spot or travel backwards and forwards as part of their sequences.

Galloping (keeping the same foot in front as you travel) is a step-hop pattern, so it requires the same kind of music as other step-hop patterns the children have practiced. Note the children's use of space as they find partners. They often have a tendency to revert back to skipping in a large circle instead of using all the available space.

Figure 4.6   "Skip with your partner."

LESSON **4** (for grade three)
Stimulus: Percussion.
Analysis: WHERE? General space.
           WHAT?   Locomotor skills, going and stopping.
           HOW?   Quick and slow, rhythm, going and stopping.

Lesson Outline

Introductory Activity Tasks

1. "Find a partner and a space. Stand side by side with one arm across your partner's shoulders."
2. "When I tap the tambourine, walk one step for each tap. Run when you hear the rattling sound."
3. "Listen to this and tell me what I have added: (tap ♩ ♩ ♩ rattle ♫ ♫ ♫ silence ♩. tap . . . rattle . . . silence.)"

Movement Training Tasks

1. "Find a new partner for Tap and Rattle Tag. Stand side by side, but not touching each other."

2. "Decide who is going to be chaser A. Listen carefully, chaser A may only move when he hears the tambourine rattle. He tries to tag his partner before the rattle stops. Partner B is going to walk when he hears the tap and run when he hears the rattle. Take care to avoid collisions."
3. "Change over so that A becomes B, and B becomes A."

Development or Dance Tasks

1. "Work out a new way of playing the game by changing the walking and running to other ways of traveling. Make sure they fit the tap-and-rattle pattern."
2. "Clap this with your partner and then work

out a movement sequence using running, walking, jumping, and stillness."

♩ ♩ ♩ ♩ | ♫ ♫ ♫ ♫ ♫ | ♩ 𝄾 ‖

3. "Invent a clapping pattern that you could use as a secret code. Work out how you could travel using that coded message."
4. "Write down your code so that you will not forget it."

5. "Join up with another pair. Clap out your message and see if they decode it by traveling the same way as you did or a different way."
6. "See if you can think up a rhyme that would make a good clapping pattern and invent a movement sequence to match it. For example, 2, 4, 6, 8, meet me at the garden gate, If I'm late, don't wait, 2, 4, 6, 8."

Introductory Activity

Begin with four taps and then rattle for four beats. After several turns, vary the number of taps to encourage the children to listen and respond. Check that they use only one step for each tap.

In task three the ♩· can be used for stopping. It could also be used later in the lesson for a jump.

Figure 4.7   "Hop."

Movement Training

The purpose of this game is:

a. To discriminate and respond to two different sounds.
b. To use both walking and running.
c. To foster rhythm.

As soon as the rattle stops, everyone should stand still whether they have tagged their partner or not. If you find that no one had time to tag their partner, vary the length of the rattle or reduce the number of tags. Begin with four taps and an equal length of rattles. If you wish, points may be scored if A tags B, or B tags A.

Development or Dance

Hopping (one foot to same foot) and jumping (two feet to two feet) will correspond to the tap. At this stage, galloping, skipping, or sliding may be used for the rattle, although ideally a different rhythm is preferred. This will be developed later.

Children who have had some musical education will find it easy to think of their own clapping patterns. Those who have not will need help. Keep the pattern short and simple. For example, the Orff music method uses language as the base, so that ♩ = walk, ♫ = running, ♩ = jump, and 𝄾 = rest or stillness. If you cannot think of suitable patterns, go to the children's reading books and select short pieces. For example,

Hambone, jawbone, mulligatawny stew,
Pork chop, lamb chop, cold home brew.

would be useful, as it combines slow and quick in a simple form.

The rhythm for skipping is long-short, ♩ ♪, with the accent on the longer first beat. If the children invent skipping to accompany the rattle of the tambourine, teach them how to tap so as to produce the correct skipping rhythm. You may find it easier in the early stages to keep the rattle as the skipping sound but have the children say "skip-pty" as they skip. This will establish the correct rhythm for the skipping movement.

THEME TWO: ADDING TO THE RANGE AND UNDERSTANDING OF MOVEMENT

In this theme emphasis is given to using different parts of the body and to rhythm patterns.

Figure 4.9   Clapping in time with the music.

Figure 4.8   Rattle and tap.

LESSON 1

Stimulus: "March of the Mods" or another quick $\frac{4}{4}$ march.

Analysis: WHERE?   On the spot and/or traveling, levels.

WHAT?   The whole body and parts of the body, meeting and parting.

HOW?   Quick-slow rhythm.

Lesson Outline

Introductory Activity Tasks

1. "Clap in time with the music."
2. "Walk and clap with the music."
3. "Sit quickly when the music stops."
4. "Kneel and use both hands to clap on the floor in time with the music."
5. "Where else on your body could you clap?"

Movement Training Tasks

1. "What is the highest part of you?"
2. "The lowest?"
3. "Stand up, clap your head and your feet and two other different parts in between. Clap four times on each part."

or

4. "Kneel on the floor, clap the floor four times, then your thighs, shoulders, and head. Reverse the order coming down to the floor again."
5. "Join up with a partner and make up a sequence, where you clap your head and feet and two other parts. Choose a starting position of standing, kneeling, sitting, or lying."

Development or Dance Tasks

1. "So far you have made both hands clap the same part at the same time. Make up a new sequence where you alternate. For example, left hand to left knee, then right hand to right knee; or use both hands simultaneously but clap different parts, for example, left hand to head and right hand to tummy."
2. "Find a new partner and make up a sequence that includes traveling away from and towards your partner. Clap with each other when you meet."
3. "Free activity with the music."

Introductory Activity

Many children are so used to music as background noise they "tune out." These tasks are to help them "tune in." Walking should be free and easy, adjusting the length of step to keep beat.

Draw from the children the parts of the body they can clap. Use all their suggestions to pro-vide a movement vocabulary for them to draw upon during the rest of the lesson.

Clapping four times on each part is suggested. However, the amount of clapping may vary between two and eight times. Let the children decide what is right for themselves.

Figure 4.11   "Clap the highest part of you."

Figure 4.10   "Clap the floor."

Movement Training

Tasks three and four are alternatives. If you don't think the class is ready to make up a sequence by themselves, use the direct method to teach task four or choose a child's solution if you began task three and decide to abandon it as the majority of children encountered difficulties.

All kinds of interesting sequences occur when a change of position is introduced. Some like to change positions during their sequences.

Figure 4.12 "Choose a starting position with your partner."

Development or Dance

Make sure that they clap accurately. For example, the elbow is the joint, not some point vaguely on the upper arm or the forearm; knees often become thighs. Insist on accuracy here. Experiment with building class sequences from some of the unusual solutions.

Have the children group in fours and teach their sequences to each other, so they can then join the two sequences together. This is good training for their movement memory.

This lesson works very well in the classroom. Vigorous activity can be encouraged in the Movement Training by joining parts together for single counts. However, do give the children a chance to use the music freely in the gym or the classroom.

Figure 4.13 "Clap different parts of your body."

LESSON **2**

Stimulus: Hop-pop-stop.
Analysis: WHERE? Traveling.
        WHAT?   Whole body traveling, parts of the body for statues and jumping.
        HOW?   Quick, light.

Lesson Outline

Introductory Activity Tasks

1. "Listen to these words: hop, stop, pop. Which is the word that tells you to travel?"
2. "Show me how you can hop."
3. "What other ways can you travel? Show me."

Movement Training Tasks

1. "How can you pop?"
2. "How does 'explode' differ from 'pop'? Show me."
3. "Run and when I say 'stop,' stay absolutely still, not even moving an eyelash. Off you go . . . stop."

4. "Make yourself into a statue when you stop this time. Make yourself into a funny shape."

Development or Dance Tasks

1. "Put the sequence together and practice hop, pop, stop."
2. "Change the rhythm. Try hop-hop, stop, pop."
3. "Change the words around and make a new sequence."
4. "What words rhyme with 'jump?' Try building a sequence with three action words."
5. "Make up action word sequences of your own."
6. "Listen to this music; invent ways of moving to it."

Introductory Activity

Clarification of terminology may be necessary here. There are five basic jumping foot patterns. Taking off from one foot and landing on the same foot is one of them, and in the primary section of the book this refers to hopping. Taking off from two feet and landing on two feet is described as jumping with feet together. Leaping is used for taking off from one foot and landing on the opposite foot.

Stress "push off with toes" and "give" in ankles and knees for take-offs and landings while hopping. As hopping is a vigorous and demanding activity, alternate it with other ways of traveling, for example, walking, running, skipping, and galloping. Observe how skillful the children are, as you may need to develop lessons around the other locomotor skills to improve their quality.

Figure 4.14 "Pop."

Movement Training

Children usually jump to show a "pop." Whatever actions they perform, stress lightness and quickness. Contrast "pop" with "explode," which is a much stronger, larger action. Children instinctively end up "splat" on the floor changing their level from as high as they can be to floor level. "Pop" can be smaller, lighter, and quicker.

You may choose to develop "smooth" or "spiky" statues on stop. Emphasis on elbows, knees, and fingers often helps produce spiky statues. Standing normally or curled up in a ball on the floor are two examples of smooth statues. Encourage absolute stillness. This however, does not require stiffness. Stillness does not always require excessive tension.

Figure 4.15 "Explode."

Development or Dance

Some of the children will elect to hop more than once when they put hop-pop-stop together as a sequence. This freedom to choose allows for greater creativity.

If they all elect to hop only once, suggest they make a rhythmic sequence of ♩♩ ♩♩ which could be interpreted either as hop-hop, pop, stop or pop-pop, hop, stop.

"Hump" and "bump" combine with jump and a sequence may be developed as follows:

a. Jumps could include (1) variety of body shapes with stretch, curl, or twist, or (2) parts of the body meeting, hands touching feet in front, at side, or behind.

b. "Hump" is a body shape with tummy, seat, or back up.

c. "Bump" can have different parts of the body taking the weight. Make sure that this is a controlled, gentle bump and not an uncontrolled, hard crash!

Figure 4.16 "Stop."

LESSON **3**   (not suitable for kindergarten or grade one)

Stimulus: Small wooden blocks and skipping ropes, tape or record of "Tinikling" (Michael Herman's *Folk Dances*).

Analysis: WHERE?   On the spot and traveling.

WHAT?   Jumping.

HOW?   Quick and slow.

Lesson Outline

Introductory Activity Tasks

1. "As quickly as you can take a block to a space and kneel facing me."
2. "Tap the block on the floor making the sound grow louder as I raise my hand and softer as I lower it."
3. "Imagine you are at a swim meet or football game where the crowd sometimes claps in unison with a steady beat. Tap your block on the floor, listen to the people around you and see how quickly you can pick up a class rhythm."
4. "Now stress the first beat of each three taps."

Movement Training Tasks

1. "Move into a space with a partner and kneel so that you are facing each other."
2. "Hit the ground twice with your block and hit your partner's block in the air on each third beat."
3. "One of you take both blocks, the other stand up facing your partner. The kneeling partner taps the rhythm pattern of two beats on the floor and the third in the air, while the standing partner invents a jumping pattern to match the blocks."
4. "Change over."
5. "Now try to make your feet do the opposite thing to the blocks. When the blocks are apart, your feet should be together, and when the blocks are together, your feet should be apart."

Development or Dance Tasks

1. "One of you keep the beat with the blocks and the other invent a jumping pattern that travels towards and away from your partner."
2. "Collect two skipping ropes and place them parallel on the floor 12"-15" apart. One of you work out a jumping pattern traveling forwards, backwards, and sideways along the ropes, while the other keeps the beat."
3. "Invent different foot patterns."
4. "Listen to the music and keep the beat with your blocks or your jumps."
5. "Join up with another pair, use two skipping ropes and four blocks. One person kneels at either end and ties ropes around their wrists and holds blocks. Practice ropes and blocks first. Kneel far enough apart to keep tension on ropes, otherwise the ropes will become tangled. The other pair will then develop jumping patterns in and out of the moving ropes. Change places after a short turn."
6. "Practice with the blocks and poles."
7. "Free play with blocks and/or ropes."

Introductory Activity

Chalkboard erasers or grass-hockey balls may be substituted for wooden blocks. This activity could cause chaos in a class that has poor listening and observing skills. Stress the point that they must watch your hand and not their blocks during this activity.

The slow, steady beat of the blocks in task three is usually the correct speed for the "Tinikling" music. Accenting the first of each three beats, results in $\frac{3}{4}$ time. Make sure they change positions frequently, and check that they keep an even beat, while stressing light, resilient footwork.

Movement Training

The basic jumping pattern is feet apart and then together. Encourage hops and crossed feet as a final development after they have mastered the apart-and-together pattern. Making their feet do the opposite of the blocks is a challenge, but it is necessary if they are to use ropes or the poles. How far each part is developed will depend on the class. Many third graders are content to use only blocks to invent highly complex foot patterns as they travel toward and away from their partners. They enjoy making blocks "talk"; one forward, one backward, turned inwards, outwards, or crossed over while their partners match their actions.

The children with ropes tied around their wrists should be reminded to maintain ample tension on the ropes. Inadequate tension makes it impossible for their partners to jump across the ropes.

Figure 4.17 "Invent a jumping pattern while your partner taps the rhythm."

Development or Dance

Give each group a chance to experiment freely with blocks and/or ropes. Watch as they invent a wide variety of interesting jumps and patterns.

Figure 4.18 "Tie ropes around wrists and hold blocks."

Figure 4.19 "Invent jumping patterns in groups of four."

LESSON 4

Stimulus: *The Judge* by Harve Zemach, "Its paws have claws."
Analysis: WHERE?   On the spot, traveling, and directions.
            WHAT?   Bend, stretch; the whole body and parts of the body.
            HOW?   Quick, strong, sustained stillness.

Lesson Outline

Introductory Activity Tasks

1. "What words do you associate with claws?"
2. "Suppose you were having a tug-of-war and you were gripping onto the rope as hard as you could. Show me what you would look like."
3. "What words can you think of that describe how a creature captures its prey?"
4. "Run, leap, land, and grip."
5. "Swoop and clutch."

Movement Training Tasks

1. "Find a space and curl up. Suddenly, reach out, snatch, and pull in."

2. "Slowly and stealthily reach out, grip onto the floor, hold there and then slowly drag your hands back."
3. "Find a new starting position where you could suddenly stretch out arms and legs and slowly pull them back."
4. "Contrast round, soft, gentle shapes with angular, stiff, and strong shapes. Freeze and melt from one to the other."

Development or Dance Tasks

1. "Make up a sequence using the idea 'Its paws have claws' on your own, with a partner, or in a small group."

Introductory Activity

The most commonly used words children associate with claws are sharp, dangerous, fierce, strong, curled, and gripping.

The tug-of-war idea helps the children feel the gripping action. This calls for strong, curled movements, feet firmly on the floor and bent, strong legs, back, arms, and hands. Teeth are usually clenched. Sharpness can be implied by the sudden incisiveness of the action.

Pouncing, clutching, and swooping describe the capturing of prey. Run, leap, land, and grip may produce a fair simulation of pouncing. Emphasize the quickness and the suddenness of the jump and the strong stillness of the grip.

"Swoop and clutch" may be done with beanbags. Running, bending down, and picking up the beanbag in a quick, smooth, continuous action is quite difficult but children enjoy practicing it.

Figure 4.20 "Leap, land, and grip."

Figure 4.21 "Reach out and snatch."

Movement Training

These tasks stress bending and stretching movements with variations of speed in order to show different types of clawing actions.

Development or Dance

Here the children may develop other ideas of their own. Give individual help as necessary.

LESSON **5**

Stimulus: *The Judge* by Harve Zemach, "Its tail is hairy."

Analysis: WHERE? On the spot or traveling.

WHAT? The whole body and parts of the body, shapes.

HOW? Time, space, weight, flow.

Lesson Outline

Introductory Activity Tasks

1. "Do you know what happens to a cat's tail when it is frightened? It fluffs out and makes itself wide and stiff, then when it feels better the hairs smooth out and lie flat again."

2. "When I tap the tambourine, make your arms stick out to the sides so they are stiff and straight."

3. "As I scratch the tambourine, let them float down to your sides."

4. "This time jump and land making a statue with both arms and one leg stiff and straight. Let them float down and be ready to jump again into another statue."

5. "Turn as you jump, so that you land in a new space each time."

6. "Find a different starting position. Try sitting or lying down. Remember to stick arms and legs out suddenly and let them slowly float back to where they started."

Movement Training Tasks

1. "What words can you think of that describe the way in which an animal moves its tail?"

Development or Dance Tasks

1. "Join up with a partner or small group and invent a sequence where you show stiff wide shapes with swinging and flicking movements. You may work on the spot or travel."

or

2. "Make up a sequence on your own, with a partner or in a small group, showing 'Its tail is hairy.' "

Introductory Activity

Emphasize change of body shape and contrast quick, sudden, wide, and stiff movements with slow, sustained, flexible, and soft movements.

Jumping and turning can be done with quick,

Figure 4.24   "Flick."

Figure 4.22   Wide, stiff movements.

Figure 4.23   Soft, gentle movements.

explosive jumps. Contrast these movements with stiff, still statues, then melt to prepare for the next jump. Many interesting wide shapes occur from sitting or lying on backs, tummies, or sides. This can be developed in the last part of the lesson as group work if desired.

Movement Training

Children use flick and swing most often to describe the tail action of animals. Encourage whole body actions. Turning jumps that are quick, light, and flexible make good flicking movements. Relaxed, bouncy, heavy, upward, and downward swing using the whole body make an interesting contrast.

Development or Dance

Besides the "hairy" type of tails already discussed, another interesting development of this lesson would be the crocodile type of tail. The flicking movements of the hairy tail can be contrasted with the slashing, cutting movements of the crocodile tail.

The older children enjoy "group tails" that travel, but be sure they have decided on the movement characteristics of their tail, so that it doesn't become merely a conger line.

THEME THREE: UNDERSTANDING DIRECTION

Up-down, rising-falling, backwards-sideways-forwards are the key movement words in this section.

Figure 4.25   Noses lead up and down movements.

LESSON 1

Stimulus: Tambourine.
Analysis: WHERE?   Levels.
            WHAT?   Parts of the body, rising and falling.
            HOW?   Quick and slow, direct and flexible.

Lesson Outline

Introductory Activity Tasks

1. "Run when I rattle the tambourine, freeze when I tap."
2. "Run when I rattle the tambourine and jump as high as you can when I tap."
3. "Run, jump, and collapse."

Movement Training Tasks

1. "Find a space on your own and curl up small."
2. "When I rattle the tambourine, make yourself take up more space until you are tall as you can be. Collapse and become small again when I tap the tambourine."
3. "What could you make the highest part of you this time?"
4. "This time, instead of rattling the tambourine, I am going to scratch it. Listen to the sound. . . . Try getting higher slowly this time."

5. "Draw me a line using one finger going from the floor up to the ceiling." (Figures 4.28 and 4.29)
6. "Listen to the sound I make with the tambourine and decide whether to draw the line quickly or slowly."
7. "Draw a wriggly pattern in the air with one finger. Make it go up and down and round about."
8. "What other parts of your body can you use to draw lines or wriggly patterns?"

Development or Dance Tasks

1. "Go quickly to your section places."
2. "I am going to give one tambourine to each group and each one of you will have a turn to use the tambourine. When it is your turn, make one sound for the others to rise up and another sound will tell them to collapse."

3. "You are going to make a sequence this time. Choose a starting position, decide which part you are going to make go high, and whether it is going to go straight up high or whether it is going to wriggle up high."

Introductory Activity

Encourage the children to discriminate between the two sounds, rattle and tap. As they become experienced, vary the locomotor skill used while rattling the tambourine and suggest they freeze, explode, or collapse on the tap.

Figure 4.26 "Jump as high as you can."

Figure 4.27 "Try going higher slowly this time."

Movement Training

Have the children vary: the parts of the body leading; the starting position (lying, sitting, kneeling); the speed (slow-up, quick-down, quick-up, slow-down); the space (straight-up, straight-down, flexible-up and straight-down); and the weight (strong, punch or press up, light, float or glide down). Introduce a third sound by scratching the tambourine.

Development or Dance

If tambourines are not available, improvise percussion instruments that could be rattled and tapped. Bottle caps make good rattles and plastic tubs can be used for drums.

Figure 4.28 "Draw a line from the floor to the ceiling."

Sequences may be developed according to the age and experience of the children. You may find it easier to build class sequences first. One activity that a younger age group really enjoys has the children lie on their backs, "running" in the air until their feet are as high as possible. Then the children bring the feet down slowly (knees bent or straight), "painting" a straight line with their toes.

Figure 4.29 "Paint a line with your fingers."

Figure 4.30 "What part could you make highest this time?"

LESSON 2

Stimulus: *Listen and Dance*, record three, side two, bands two and three.

Analysis: WHERE?   Levels and directions.

WHAT?   Parts of the body, rising and falling.

HOW?   Dabbing, gliding.

Lesson Outline

Introductory Activity Tasks

1. "Listen to the music. What does it do? Yes, it goes up and down."
2. "Start low with your hands on the floor. Make your hands go higher as the music goes up, and lower them back to the floor when the music goes down."
3. "Try that again and listen carefully to the music so that you don't go up and down too quickly."
4. "Instead of using your hands, think of a different part of your body you could make go up and down."
5. "Some people were trying to make their feet go high. Start lying on your back, then it is easier to make both feet go up."

Movement Training Tasks

1. "Listen to the music again and tell me whether you can hear a smooth part and a jerky part."
2. "Lie on your back again and imagine you are running upstairs on the quick, jerky sounds and

sliding down on the slow, smooth sound coming down."

3. "Invent other starting positions and use different parts of your body to lead up and down."

Development or Dance Tasks

1. "Join up with a partner and invent other ways of going up high with quick, jerky movements and coming down low with slow, smooth ones."

2. "One child from each pair collect a loop of elastic. Instead of just going high and low, invent ways of moving away from your partner and coming back to him. You may hold the elastic with your foot, hand, or waist, but it must fasten you to your partner."

3. "Remember to find jerky ways to go away from your partner and smooth ways of going back. Start low to the ground and finish low to the ground."

4. "Build a sequence with your partner, so that you travel forwards, backwards, and sideways as well as up and down."

Introductory Activity

Use band two on side two of the record for all the tasks in this lesson. The other selections are suitable for development in later lessons.

There is always one child, even in kindergarten who recognizes that the music goes up and down. The starting position may be sitting, kneeling, or lying. Let them choose their own. Usually the children arrive at their highest points and lowest points before the music. Have the children practice moving and listening to the music to make them match.

If children don't attempt shoulders, seats, sides, and tummies, suggest they try these. Some children will always try feet, usually by taking their weight onto their hands and kicking their feet into the air. This can be dangerous if they are in a small space, so change the starting position to lying on their backs.

Figure 4.32   "Make a different part of your body go high."

Figure 4.31   "Make your hands go up as the sound gets higher."

Figure 4.33   "Can you make it go higher?"

Movement Training

The quick, ascending sounds may be used for dabbing and the slow, descending sounds for gliding. Encourage quick and light, and slow and light movements with different parts of the body.

Figure 4.34   Quick, jerky movements going up.

Figure 4.35   Slow, gliding movements going down.

Development or Dance

Children enjoy partner sequences and will invent sequences where they make hands, seats, elbows, and feet meet their partner's as they go up and down.

If elastic is used, it should be the inexpensive variety, ⅛″ or ¼″ thick, and knotted into circles. Allow three feet for each loop.

The children find this task fun, but teachers should insist that the elastic does not go around the neck as this could be dangerous.

It is possible to develop the quality of movement with these elastic loops, as well as sensitivity to others. The ideas could be used without the music as the elastic itself provides a stimulus.

"The Monster"
A horrible thing is coming this way,
Creeping closer day by day.
Its eyes are scary, its tail is hairy,
Its paws have claws, it snaps its jaws,
It crawls, it groans, it chews up stones,
It spreads its wings and does bad things,
It belches flame, it has no name.
I tell you, judge, we all better pray.

"The Monster" is taken from the story by Harve Zemach entitled *The Judge.*

There is sufficient material in this story for a minimum of seven lessons. The two lessons in Theme Two and these two in Theme Three are given in detail. Brief suggestions follow for another three lessons:

Themes: Directions, meeting and parting, qualities.
Stimulus: "It chews up stones."
Vocabulary: Pounding, grinding, crunching.

Themes: Large-small, stretch-curl, wide-narrow, qualities.
Stimulus: "It spread its wings."
Vocabulary: Spread, swoop, beat, flutter.

Themes: Rising and falling, directions, qualities.
Stimulus: "It belches flame."
Vocabulary: Roars, flickers, smolders.

Figure 4.36   "It . . .

Figure 4.38   . . . its . . .

Figure 4.39   . . . wings."

Figure 4.37   . . . spreads . . .

The teacher should realize that the children may, and often do, have very strong ideas of their own about this monster and should therefore be encouraged to invent their own interpretations.

Please note that all seven lessons would fit equally well into Theme Four and it will depend upon the experience and interest shown by the children as to how far you may develop these ideas.

This series also provides many opportunities for integration with language arts, music, art, and handwork. Also a science class based on prehistoric creatures is an excellent way to combine Movement Education with other areas of study.

LESSON **3**

Stimulus: *The Judge* by Harve Zemach, "Its eyes are scary."
Analysis: WHERE?   On the spot, directions.
            WHAT?   The whole body and parts of the body, circles, side to side, up and down.
            HOW?   Quick-slow, direct-flexible, strong-light, going and stopping.

Lesson Outline

Introductory Activity Tasks

1. "How can you move your eyes?"
2. "Can you roll your eyes around in a circle?"
3. "Draw a circle with your hand. How many places can you draw a circle?"
4. "Draw two circles simultaneously, one with each hand."
5. "Move your head around in a circle."
6. "Look from side to side without moving your head."
7. "Make one hand dart from right to left."
8. "Now both hands."
9. "Jump from side to side."
10. "Close your eyes and open them suddenly."
11. "Curl yourself up small and stretch out and up. What part of you could you use for eyelashes?"

Movement Training Tasks

1. "Tell me what things would make you find eyes 'scary?' "

Development or Dance Tasks

1. "Work with a partner. Each collect a hoop."
2. "Use the hoops for the monster's spectacles and make up a sequence to fit 'Its eyes are scary.' "

Introductory Activity

Explore side to side, around, and up and down as directions in movement and the ways in which eyes can move. The children enjoy watching each other's eyes move. This is a good starting point to begin the tasks of the Introductory Activity.

Experiment with drawing circles above the head, around the feet, and out to the sides. The circles can be small or large, slow or quick. Contrast slow, sustained movements from side to side with quick sudden movements.

Work from small, curled, round shapes to large, stretched, wide shapes. Arms make good eyelashes!

Movement Training

Use the movement analysis to clarify the movement quality of the words they suggest.

a. Rolling round, use slow, continuous, flexible movements.

b. Darting from side to side, use quick, light, direct, and sudden movements.

c. Popping out, move backwards and forwards with quick, light, direct, and sudden movements.

d. Cross-eyed, use diagonal, slow, and flexible movements.

e. Flashing, use up and down or sideways, strong, direct, quick, and sudden movements.

Give individual help as necessary. Use some of their solutions as class sequences.

Figure 4.40 "Its . . .

Figure 4.41 . . . eyes . . .

Figure 4.42 . . . are scary."

LESSON 4

Stimulus: *The Judge* by Harve Zemach, "It snaps its jaws."
Analysis: WHERE?   Levels, up and down.
       WHAT?   The whole body and parts of the body, shape, meeting and parting.
       HOW?   Sudden, strong, direct.

Lesson Outline

Introductory Activity Tasks
1. "Run, leap, and land."
2. "Make a stretched shape in the air when you jump."
3. "Touch your feet with your hands while in the air."
4. "Clap your hands when you leap."

Movement Training Tasks
1. "Make a wide shape with your body. Change it to a narrow shape."
2. "Find a different starting position and do the same thing."
3. "Invent three different wide shapes and three narrow shapes. Practice changing shapes sometimes quickly and sometimes slowly."
4. "Do you remember in the story it says the monster 'snaps its jaws'? What words can you think of that describe 'snap'?"

5. "Snap your fingers. Make them very quick and strong, so that you can make a loud noise."
6. "Sit on the floor with your legs apart. Snap your legs together."
7. "What other parts of your body can you snap together? Change your starting position if you wish."
8. "Join up with a partner and invent as many wide and narrow shapes as you can. Use different starting positions."

Development or Dance Tasks
1. "Invent a way of going from a high, wide shape to a low, narrow shape on the floor, suddenly."
2. "Work with a partner or in a small group and invent a sequence of movements that fits 'It snaps its jaws.'"

Introductory Activity

If space is limited, the jumping can be done on the spot instead of traveling. These tasks are designed to introduce stretched, wide body shapes and the meeting and parting of different parts of the body. Encourage strong, vigorous jumps with stretched fingers, elbows, knees, and feet. Ask them to clap other parts of their bodies (apart from their feet) while in the air.

Figure 4.43   "It snaps . . .

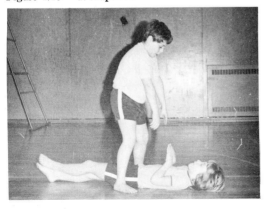

Movement Training

Permit the children to explore changing shapes and to add variations of speed and flow. Standing, sitting, and lying are various starting positions that will give the children opportunities to invent different shapes. Insist on quality of movement by making sure that the children stretch their entire bodies, including their fingers and toes. Contrast quick and slow changes, encouraging them to go faster and slower.

Snapping fingers may be used to clarify the movement elements needed. Ask them to feel

Figure 4.44   . . . its jaws."

the strong pressure of their thumbs on their fingers before they make the quick and sudden movement that produces the sound.

Have them transfer the quick, strong, direct elements to other parts of their bodies, for example, clapping hands together, snapping legs together, or clapping hands to feet.

Partner work for grades two and three works well as the children invent interesting shapes which can be used for snapping, and is good preparation for the last part of the lesson.

Development or Dance

Emphasize changes from high to low and wide to narrow, as well as changes of speed. Limit the group size to four as it becomes difficult to share ideas and coordinate movements in larger groups.

THEME FOUR: QUALITIES

Interpretations of several movement ideas and stories follows. The focus of these interpretations is on the motion factors of *time, weight, space, and flow.*

Figure 4.45   "Witches."

LESSON 1

Stimulus: A ten cent balloon.

Analysis: WHERE?   General space, directions and levels, large and small.

WHAT?   Floating, punching, bending, stretching, twisting.

HOW?   Quick-slow, direct-flexible, sudden-sustained.

Lesson Outline

Introductory Activity Tasks

1. Each time I blow into the balloon and make it take up more space, move into a larger space."
2. "What do you think you should do when I let the air slowly out of the balloon?"

Movement Training Tasks

1. "This time in a space, on your own, make yourself as small as you can. As the balloon becomes larger, make yourself take up more space."

2. "Watch how I tie the end of the balloon in a knot. Tie yourself into a knot."
3. "Burst the knot."
4. "Watch how the balloon comes down to the ground when I toss it in the air. Make your hands come down the same way."
5. "Does the balloon go higher into the air if I hit it like this?"

Development or Dance Tasks

1. "Tell the story in movement of the balloon's adventures."

This lesson plan has worked in an endless number of situations where children have had no previous experience in any form of Movement Education. In this lesson plan, time, space, force, and flow are all explored, developed, and linked together by focusing the child's attention on the antics of a ten cent balloon. No adaptations are necessary for a classroom lesson.

Introductory Activity

The children should sit in the middle of the gymnasium with the teacher in the middle of the group. "Children, I have a secret in my

Figure 4.46   "I have a secret."

Figure 4.47   "Yes, it's a balloon."

hand. If I give you a clue, do you think you can guess what it is? If I blow into it, it will get bigger. That's right, my secret is a balloon! Now, look how tiny the balloon is; it is hardly taking up any space at all, but when I blow into it, it will get bigger and take up more room. Now, you are sitting in the middle of the gymnasium and taking up very little space. Look at all the space we have left in the gymnasium. As I blow into the balloon and make it take up more space, you must move into a bigger space. There is just one rule, you can only move when I am blowing into the balloon, so you must always keep your eyes on the balloon." When the balloon is fairly large, begin to let the air out, and ask the children what they think they should do. They will instinctively start moving back to the center. This is an opportunity to emphasize spacing. As they come back they must move carefully to avoid bumping into anyone.

The second time let the air out slowly and ask them to move back slowly (introducing time). Repeat two or three times according to how well the children use the space. The last time, when they are well spaced, have them gradually get smaller on the spot until they are very tiny and curled up in a ball. Allow two or three turns at getting as big and taking up as much room as they can in their own space.

Next, blow up the balloon and have the children watch you tie a knot in the end. Ask them to ties themselves into knots. Do not keep them in this position for too long. Look at some of the different types of knots so that when they "burst" you could use one or two as demonstrations. Let them burst so they are flat on the floor. (This permits quick movements and wide shapes.) The second time ask them to tie a much more complicated knot and to start in the standing position, twisting slowly to tie a very tight, hard knot. When all are tied ask them if they can make their knots tighter still, then have them burst. Stress the quick, sudden movement needed to make a wide shape on the floor (as a contrast to the small, tight knot). Repeat as necessary, and select children who have good knots or quick bursts to demonstrate.

Figure 4.48   "Tie an imaginary knot."

Figure 4.49   "Tie yourself into a knot."

in their own spaces and that they understand that they are to punch as hard upwards in the air as they can. The direction is important as there is a risk that some boys may try a few "right hooks" on each other! Dissipate their energies by strong, hard, punching movements *upwards* or *downwards*.

Another safety precaution is to let them shout "punch" as they do it, but have them ready to punch at the same time; otherwise it is difficult to make oneself heard as they usually do this with great vigor and enthusiasm! Allow only one shout for each punch. When they gather themselves to punch, ask them to make a tight fist so that they can punch hard; emphasize the quick, explosive movement and the strength and force necessary to perform this.

If you think that they are ready, you can now suggest that they imagine how the balloon would travel if the string snapped and it was blown away by the wind. Initially, they will probably just "whoosh" around the room without making a pattern. Tell them you want to see if the wind is having fun and playing tricks on the balloon, sometimes leaving it quite still and not blowing it at all, other times blowing it up into the air, and other times blowing so hard the balloon has to go very fast.

Finally ask them what usually happens to a

Figure 4.50   "Punch the balloon in the air."

Toss the balloon into the air and let it float down. Ask them if they know the word that describes how the balloon comes down. Even at the grade one level there is always one child who says "floating." Invite them to float their fingers down as gently as the balloon floats down. Make sure they watch their own fingers. Younger children find this quite difficult.

For contrast, punch the balloon into the air and again ask them for the word that describes the action. Before you ask the children to perform this movement, make sure the children are

balloon if it gets blown into a tree, and the usual reply will be "pop."

Pop the balloon and ask the children to watch what happens to the pieces. "Do they drop straight to the ground, or do they go upwards first and then drop, or what do they do?" Then let them try popping themselves. Again you can get the children to provide the sound effects! Stress quick, explosive movements.

To be truly effective, this lesson will take thirty or forty minutes. You may like to try part of the lesson in one period, ending up with the wind blowing the balloon, and save the rest of the lesson for a second period. Repeat the wind-blowing part of the lesson during the second period. The children should now be able to perform their own actions more skillfully.

Figure 4.51 "Pop."

Questions That May Assist:

1. From which spots on the floor do they start?
2. Are they standing, sitting, or curled up in a ball?
3. Is the wind gentle or strong to start with?
4. What sort of tricks does the wind play on them?

The questions that follow give suggestions as to some points you may wish to stress and also help you to observe the many actions the children may perform during this lesson. From this you should also be able to gather some ideas regarding your class's needs. You may find, for instance, that their spacing is good (it ought to be by this stage as a result of the emphasis on this during safety training), but they may not be very good at quick and slow movements. Young children find it hard to maintain a speed which is not natural to them, so during the next few lessons you might provide opportunities for responding with very quick movements and also very slow movements.

Balloons

1. Look to see how the children space themselves within the central group.
Do they scatter evenly?
Do they improve when activity is repeated?

2. When returning to the center—
Do they rush back in uncontrolled manner pushing each other as they go?
Are they interested in controlling their movements to keep in time with the balloon?

3. When making themselves as large as they can in their own space—
Do they reach up with hands together above their heads?
Do they spread themselves, hands and feet wide apart?

4. When making themselves as small as they can—
Do they tuck in as much as they can?
Do they lie flat on the floor?

Do they crouch on tiptoes with everything tucked in?

5. When tying themselves in a knot—
Do they tie arms and legs separately?
Do they intertwine arms and legs?
Do they twist rather than bend their bodies?

6. When they "burst"—
Do they jump up as they burst?
Do they lie down?
Is it a quick movement?

7. When they "float" their hands down—
Do they watch their fingers?
Is there feeling in the quality of their movement?
Do they find it easy?

8. When they punch—
Are they strong and firm?
Can they hold the position?
Does the quality of their movement improve when they say the word as they punch?

9. When asked to punch in different directions—
Do they use the same arm, or switch to the other arm?

10. When they are moving around the room—
Do they stay on one level?
Do they leap in the air?
Do they sink to the ground?
Do they swirl around?

LESSON 2

Stimulus: "Witches' Sabbath" by Ruth Parker. This may be developed using voices only, percussion only, and/or music (*Dance Macabre* or *Night on Bald Mountain*).

Analysis: WHERE? General space, levels, directions.

WHAT? Rising and falling, individual and group work.

HOW? Thrust, slash, float, flick.

Lesson Outline

Introductory Activity Tasks

1. "Run and leap in the air, landing softly."
2. "As you leap, this time try to get your elbows and knees high into the air."
3. "Keep the twisted, angular shapes you made in the air and hold them when you land."
4. "Find a space of your own. Experiment with turning jumps. Slash with your arms and legs. Go as high as you can. You will need a strong push from the floor with your feet. Use strong arm actions to drive you around."
5. "Hold your shape on landing. Keep it firm and strong."
6. "Choose three different leaps and three different shapes for landing. Practice and repeat these to make a sequence."

Movement Training Tasks

1. "Make groups of five or six, form a circle, and put your hands on each other's shoulder joints."
2. "Stamp on the floor."
3. "Invent a rhythm for your stamping." or direct teach
4. "Clap ♩ ♩ ♫ ♩ Now stamp ♩ ♩ ♫ ♩."
5. "Invent a way of traveling and stamping as a group."

Development or Dance Tasks

1. "Now build a sequence starting with stamping on the spot. Use your three turning leaps to whirl out into a larger circle (letting go of each other), stamp and travel, then repeat the leaps."

The Witches Sabbath

Long ago in a far off land, a boy was going home across the mountain. He had started later than usual and the mist had come over the path making it hard for him to see.

"I have walked and walked but have missed the way and am lost" he said. When it began to get dark, he sat under a tall tree and tried to sleep. It was very cold on the mountain and from a long way away came the chimes of the church clock telling him that it was midnight.

"I feel scared," he said to himself. "Who is here with me? It feels eerie."

This was the night of the witches sabbath and all the evil ones had come to dance their crazy dances. They soon saw the scared boy and wanted him to dance with them, but the boy ran away. The demons chased him.

"We will make you dance with us" they told him as they whirled and stamped on the hillside, "or you will never go home again."

Faster and faster they spun, up and down they jumped, as the tired boy tried to hide his face.

Then he saw the sky was getting paler in the rays of the morning sun. The church clock chimed six o'clock, the time when all witches and demons must hide from the light of day.

"I am so glad, now I can see the path to my home," the boy said. As he passed the black rocks, he looked at them hard and wondered if it had been a bad dream after all.

This story was designed to suit level five reading. Decide when you think it would be most appropriate to read the story to the children, before either the Introductory Activity or the Movement Training.

Introductory Activity

A strong push with the toes will help improve the height of their jumps, and bending their feet, ankles, and knees will result in soft landings.

Encourage stiff, spiky fingers and angular knees, elbows, and feet while in the air and hold shape on landing. Work to produce gro-

Figure 4.52   Twisted shapes.

tesque shapes. Make sure the children are able to remember and repeat their better "horrors."

Movement Training

When they form their small circles, make sure they place their hands on the shoulder joints and not the necks, or the circle will be too small and they will not have sufficient room to "whirl" out.

Classes with some music education will have no problem inventing stamping rhythms. However, other classes may need help. The rhythm suggested is one used for clapping at some football games and is easy to pick up. You may, of course, substitute a rhythm yourself, remembering to keep it short and simple.

Children really enjoy the next task. It seems instinctive for some groups to travel around, while others travel away from and towards the center. The more able children will invent up and down.

Development or Dance

Suggest that they begin by stamping on the spot, subsequently adding their three whirling leaps. Then alternate and add different ways of stamping and traveling with their three jumps to build a long sequence.

Figure 4.53   "They leaped . . .

Figure 4.54   . . . and . . .

To establish a group pattern, suggest they chant "whirl, leap, hold," repeating this three times as they break away from their small circle into a larger one. If tambourines are available, each group should have one to accompany their whirling, leaping, and landing.

Select a passage that you think is suitable for leaping, whirling, and stamping from the music suggested. It should last approximately one and a half minutes. Ask the children, on an individual basis, to respond to the music. They should not try to use their previous sequence, but develop a new one. However, it should still include whirling, stamping, and leaping.

Figure 4.55   . . . stamped."

LESSON **3**

Stimulus: "Witches' Sabbath" by Ruth Parker.

Analysis: WHERE? Directions, on the spot, traveling.

WHAT? The whole body and parts of the body, falling, transference of weight.

HOW? Quick-slow, strong-light, direct-flexible, sudden-sustained.

Lesson Outline

Introductory Activity Tasks

1. "Practice running, leaping, and landing."
2. "What words would you use to describe mist?"

Movement Training Tasks

1. "Leap, land, and hold your shape. Make yourself stiff and strong."
2. "Gradually lose tension and relax. Let gravity pull you down and sink to the floor."
3. "Gather enough tension to lift one elbow and hand high. Keep the feeling of lightness while you let your arm float down to the ground."
4. "This time let your elbow lift and lead you into a very soft and gentle roll."
5. "Lift any part of you high that can lead you into a roll and end in a sitting position. Remember to keep the whole sequence light, soft, and gentle."

6. "Practice rolling, sinking, and rising from the floor gradually until you are standing up. Give the impression of floating by using slow, flexible, and light movements."

Development or Dance Tasks

1. "Contrast these soft, slow, floating movements with some strong, slashing leaps."
2. "Travel anywhere, running, slashing, and leaping. Then freeze into a landing position. Hold it, then gradually lose tension, and sink to the floor. Hold that position, then change to rolling and rising, using slow, light, flexible movements."
3. "Drift into groups, moving in and out of each other as well as changing your own level while using slow, light, and flexible gestures."
4. "Move away from the group back into a space of your own. Be ready to run, leap, and whirl."

The material used in this lesson is designed to give children the opportunity to explore and discover the difference between two of Laban's effort elements, punch and float.

Punching or thrusting requires strong, quick, and direct movements, while floating requires light, slow, and flexible actions. Teaching by contrast helps the children clarify and understand the concepts.

Introductory Activity

Some of the words that children suggest to describe mist are: soft, light, moist, smooth, wavy, delicate, shifting, tumbling.

Movement Training

It is important that the teacher presents this material in such a way that the children can see the value of these movements and do not view

them as silly or embarrassing. One suggestion would be to integrate the movement tasks with science lessons that involve observations and discussions of boiling water, cloud formation, and rainfall. The texture and appearance of clouds may also be appropriate material for a language art lesson.

Rolling, rising, and falling, with emphasis on light, slow, and flexible movements, appeals to children more than standing up and vaguely waving their arms about. However, later in the lesson you may wish to develop the rolling sequence by asking the children to add traveling on their feet to the sequence.

Focus on contrasting the quick, strong, direct actions with the slow, light, flexible actions. Recall the demonic leaping and stamping from the last lesson.

Scratching a drum or tambourine with the fingernails can be used as an accompaniment for the light, slow, flexible movements.

Development or Dance

Up to this point, the children have been working individually. In order to produce a group effect, it is suggested that you have the children work from the edges of the room and move to cover the whole floor space. Divide the class in two groups and have one group move about in half the space. Then have the second group move about in the remaining space, so that all the children can observe the effect of movement within a large space.

The group that is observing should be looking at the general effect of the movement and also at the quality of individual rolling or traveling movements. The movements should be light, slow, and flexible.

The groups should take turns at filling the space with thrusting, punching, leaping, stamping, floating, rolling, and traveling.

LESSON **4**

Stimulus: "Witches' Sabbath" by Ruth Parker.
Analysis: WHERE?   Pathway, directions.
         WHAT?   Whole body, traveling.
         HOW?   Quick, light, flexible and quick, strong and direct, slow, heavy and flexible.

Lesson Outline

Introductory Activity Tasks

1. "Shake your hands, . . . feet, . . . hands and arms, . . . feet and legs, . . . whole body. . . ."
2. "Swing arms backwards and forwards. Now your legs, one at a time."
3. "Walk swinging your arms, then change to standing and shaking your whole body."

Movement Training Tasks

1. "How would you know by looking at someone if he was scared?"
2. "Try making your teeth chatter, now your knees, . . . hands, knees, and teeth all together."
3. "Try again and remember to keep your 'chattering' quick, light, and flexible."
4. "How would you know by looking at someone if they were happy and confident?"
5. "Choose a starting place from which you can walk happily and confidently to a different place in the gym. Decide where your stopping place is going to be. Ready . . . go. . . . Now walk back to your starting place."
6. "Imagine that you are like the boy in the story who lost his way. Show me how you would walk then."

Development or Dance Tasks

1. "One group is going to imagine that they are the boy setting off to walk home, and after a while they realize that they are lost and scared. The others are going to spread out all over the floor. Choose a round shape or a jagged shape that you can hold, then stay absolutely still as though you were made of stone."
2. "Change groups."
3. "Build a dance drama using the whole story."

Introductory Activity

In task one encourage quick, light, flexible, shaking movements. Arms should swing freely and easily in the second task.

Movement Training

The following is a list of word and phrases that children often associate with feeling scared.

trembling	teeth chattering
shivering	running away
pale	hiding your eyes
stiff	

Children are familiar with the actions of teeth chattering and are usually eager to transfer these actions to make their knees "chatter." This transference of a movement idea from one

Figure 4.56   "Confident."

part of the body to another helps to improve the quality of the children's movements.

Phrases and words they associate with being happy and confident are:

smiling   head held up
skipping   bouncy walk

Although they do not describe boldness or hesitancy of movement in words when asked to perform movements in tasks five and six, both

these qualities emerge clearly and should be developed.

Development or Dance

Make sure that all the children have opportunities to work at all phases of the story.

When working in a large space, it is possible to have several "boys" rather than just one. Allow them to choose and take turns at the part they like best.

Figure 4.57   Stones.

LESSON 5

Stimulus: *Homer Price and the Donut Machine* by Robert J. McClousky.

   a. Improvisation by the children
      1. Words and sounds, press-hiss, jer-puck-er-ty.
      2. Clapping, stamping, snapping rhythmic phrases.
      3. Percussive sounds.
   b. Sounds on records
      1. *Listen and Move*, record four, side A, band C, "Machine Rhythms."
      2. *Listen, Move and Dance*, record four, band two, "Electronic Sound Pictures."
      3. *Modern Dance Series*, side C, selection from "Machine Rhythms."
      4. *Pageant of Dances*, side A, "Machinery."

Analysis: WHERE?   On the spot and traveling, directions and levels.
           WHAT?   The whole body and parts of the body, meeting, parting, and directions.
           HOW?   Quick-slow, strong-light, direct-flexible, sudden-sustained.

Lesson Outline
Introductory Activity Tasks
1. "Run, changing speed as you go."
2. "Make zigzag floor patterns as you travel. Alternate walking and running."
3. "Shoot up as high as you can, then sink down slowly."
4. "Find a partner, face each other, and clap hands. Make a rhythmic pattern."
5. "Travel backwards away from your partner, then meet and clap."

Movement Training Tasks
1. "Tell me the names of some of the parts you find in machines."
2. "In what directions can cogs and wheels move? Pistons? Levers?"
3. "Work either on your own, with a partner, or in a small group. Make up a sequence where you travel around, up and down, and from side to side."

Development or Dance Tasks
1. "Show variations in time, weight, space, and flow."
2. "Decide upon the accompaniment for your sequence."
3. "Read *Homer Price and the Donut Machine*, then invent machines that would do the following:
   a. Mix the ingredients together.
   b. Knead the dough.
   c. Squeeze the dough through the tube.
   d. Cut the dough into shapes.
   e. Lift up the donuts and drop them into the fat.
   f. Lift them out of the fat and drain them, and finally move them to a new place."

Introductory Activity

Give the children the experience of traveling and working on the spot. These tasks allow them to use different directions and to contrast quick-slow, strong-light, direct-flexible, and sudden and continuous movements. Stress the use of different parts of the body as well.

Movement Training

Discuss briefly the use of cogs, wheels, pistons, and levers. Ask the children for the directions in which these parts usually move. Older children usually prefer to work with a partner or in a small group. Give them the option of working on their own, with a partner, or in a small group.

Development or Dance

With kindergarten and grade one, you may choose to build a class sequence using some of their ideas, while you provide a percussion accompaniment. For grades two and three integration of movement tasks with science and language arts, as well as music and art, works well. Some children build fascinating machines with constructional toys.

To give the children some help, you may like to suggest the following words for the machines:

beat, spin, mix
knead, lift, twist, turn over
squeeze, press
sharp, punch, mark
hold, lift, release, drop
lift, grip, flick, toss, run along, glide, circular

The following tasks may be used to develop machinelike movements.

1. "Run, leap, land, and roll."
2. "Find a space of your own and beat your arms in the air."
3. "Make your arm actions so strong that they spin you around."
4. "Jump as you spin. Try to beat your legs in the air as you turn around."
5. "Instead of jumping quickly to get high, use your arms to turn you around slowly, moving downward, then upward."
6. "Make the movements bigger; use your legs to help you. Lift one knee high as you turn and press downward."

7. "Lie on the floor, press yourself down as though you were trying to go through the floor."
8. "Press your hands against the floor."
9. "What other parts of your body can you press against the floor?"
10. "Sit or stand, and bring your hands slowly together until your palms meet. Make the action slow, sustained, and strong."
11. "Have you used cookie cutters? Show me how you use them."
12. "Make a strong, straight action for cutting. You may find it fun to combine walking, jumping, and stamping to help you make a series of cutting actions."
13. "Start low to the ground with hands on the floor. Slowly and gently raise your whole body, leading with your hands, then sink down again."
14. "Use your hands to make quick, light, dabbing movements."
15. "What other parts of your body can you use to make quick, light, direct movements?"
16. "Travel, changing levels from high to low. Make it slow, soft, and gentle."
17. "Make a strong, firm statue. Grip with your hands, now your toes on the floor. Stay very still."
18. "Practice quick, light, turning jumps."
19. "Build a sequence of traveling, gripping, and flicking."
20. "Travel with different parts high, so the part that is highest appears to glide along."
21. "Lie on the floor and balance on your shoulders. Imagine that you are running along the ceiling."
22. "Stand up or sit down and find as many ways as you can of drawing circles with parts of your body."
23. "How many circles can you draw at one time?"

Chapter Five

Games

Theme One: Safety Training

Theme Two: Adding to the Range and Understanding of Movement

Theme Three: Understanding Direction

Game Skills and Competition

One third of the time allotted to physical education should be spent on games. The game skills that should be developed during the primary years are: throwing, catching, bouncing, rolling, kicking, hitting, and dribbling. Running, skipping, and jumping are also fundamental to games.

The main emphases of the individual and partner tasks suggested are to develop individual skills and encourage cooperation.

Competition is the essence of games. However, it is important that the children master the necessary game skills before they are put into a competitive situation with other children.

The lesson plans in this chapter include four categories of competition.

1. A child can compete against himself by trying to break his own record. For example, if a child can bounce a ball three times in succession, he can try to improve his record by bouncing the ball four times in a row.
2. Partners can work together to beat a joint record. For example, each child is given five chances at tossing a beanbag into a wastepaper basket. A point is earned for each successful attempt. The partners then add up their total points out of a possible ten and try to better that record the next time.
3. One child can compete against the rest of the group as in the game of Nine Lives.
4. One group of children may compete against another group of children. Relay races, dodgeball, and Empty the Basket are examples of this type of competitive game.

Twenty-four minutes out of every thirty minutes should be spent on tasks from the first three categories. No more than four minutes should be spent by the *entire* class on group competitive games.

Children should be encouraged to invent their own competitive games for small groups. Allow them to select the equipment, determine the game skills to be used, and decide upon the rules.

The teacher and the individual child are responsible for deciding when the child is ready to join others in competitive games. There is no predetermined age at which a child is able to handle competition. For this reason, the lesson plans in this section contain time for free play, which allows the teacher to provide suitable challenges for all the children. The gymnasium or playground can be divided into areas for children who wish to work alone, with a partner, or in a small group. Another section may also be set aside for small-group competitive activities such as tag games and relays.

Checklists for each of the skills are included in the Movement Training sections and should be used to assist the teacher in observing and giving *individual* help to the children. It is the responsibility of the teacher to see that each child leaves the primary grades with these skills.

It is easy to give individual help to children experiencing difficulties in performing a specific skill, once you know what to look for in the skill. Repeated practice is essential, so make sure that you have enough equipment. The invention of stocking bats and balls alleviates the problem of lack of equipment as a drawback to teaching game skills on an individual basis. Lack of space should not be considered a problem either. The teachers at Roosevelt School in Burlington, Washington have proven what can be achieved in a narrow hallway.

Oftentimes, teachers avoid using available space outdoors, because of the problems involved in organizing such a lesson. It is hoped that the following suggestions will encourage teachers to have another try.

1. If it is cold, put on your coat and boots. Keep on the move; walk around giving individual help.
2. Use a whistle if your voice does not carry. It should be used sparingly to bring the children together quickly.
3. Establish boundaries by using traffic cones, equipment, boxes, or chairs. Begin by making the area just a little larger than the classroom area. Increase the size gradually, as you and the children become accustomed to working out-of-doors.
4. Give the children clear instructions for the first task while indoors. Make the task a vigorous one if the weather is chilly. Set them going quickly, so they do not stand around.
5. If you are going to use only one type of

equipment, make each child responsible for one piece of equipment such as a ball, otherwise select children to carry out baskets of equipment at the beginning of the lesson. Check to see that all pieces are accounted for at the beginning and end of each lesson. If it is cold, this may be done indoors.
6. Use familiar tasks that the children will enjoy doing in the larger space. Avoid long instructions that cause children to become bored and disinterested, and limits the time for the activity.

The game section is shorter than the dance or gymnastic sections. This is not because games are unimportant, but because teachers usually have the knowledge and experience necessary to invent suitable game lessons. (See film *Teaching Game Activities to Primary Children* in Appendix A.)

THEME ONE: SAFETY TRAINING

Learning to use space sensibly, avoiding collisions and accidents, and employing simple safety precautions are the main emphases of this theme.

Figure 5.1 "Take a ball to a space and play with it."

LESSON 1   GOING AND STOPPING

Equipment: A hoop or other piece of small equipment for each child.
Analysis: WHERE?   Traveling.
             WHAT?   Whole body, locomotor skills for going and stopping.

Lesson Outline
Introductory Activity Tasks
1. "Take a hoop to a space and play with it."

Movement Training Tasks
1. "Place your hoop in a space on the ground. When I say 'go,' run around all the hoops without colliding, until I say 'stop,' then stand in the nearest hoop."

2. "Each of you has nine lives. Run in and out of the hoops as you did before, but the last two players to find a hoop after I say 'stop' lose one of their nine lives."

Development or Games Tasks
1. "Free play with small equipment."
2. "Grandmother's Footsteps or Red Light."
3. "Releave-Oh."

Introductory Activity

If the lesson is to take place out-of-doors, give the task to the children before they go out, so they may start the activity as soon as they find a space.

Use this opportunity to assess the children's skills and to determine what activities are popular. This provides useful information for planning future lessons and enables you to select activities suitable for the children's abilities.

Figure 5.2   "Run in and out of the hoops."

Movement Training

The many possible variations of Nine Lives makes it a useful activity for safety training. If hoops are not available, any small equipment may be used. Sitting may be substituted for standing if the ground is dry or the game is played indoors. Keep turns short, with four turns constituting a game. Play two or three games, so that the children may try to beat their own records in each game.

Games

Children need opportunities to practice in order to improve their skills. Free play enables you to give children individual help with tasks they choose themselves.

Grandmother's Footsteps is a traditional, going-and-stopping tag game that may be easily adapted to ensure maximum participation by having one "grandmother" for every four children. The grandmother may tag only children in her own group. Grandmother stands with her back to the children. The children try to creep up without being seen and tag grandmother, who then chases them and tries to tag one of them before they cross the starting line. Make sure the starting line is at least six feet away from the wall for safety.

Releave-Oh is a tag game that grades two and upwards enjoy. The class is divided in half.

Figure 5.3   "Grandmother's footsteps."

One half wears bibs or bands. They chase and try to tag the other children. Children who are tagged must stand with arms stretched out sideways until released by a member of their own team touching them.

Play for one and a half minutes and count how many children are standing at the end. Then change so that the other children become the chasers.

Figure 5.5   "Release a player by touching her hand."

Figure 5.4   Releave-Oh.

LESSON 2

Theme: Safety training, going and stopping.
Equipment: One skipping rope for each child.
Analysis: WHERE?   Traveling.
             WHAT?   Whole body, locomotor skills for going and stopping.

Lesson Outline

Introductory Activity Tasks

1. "Trail the rope on the ground while you run using all the space."

Movement Training Tasks

1. "Place your rope on the ground and find as many ways as you can to jump over the rope."
2. "Hold one end of the rope in each hand, swing the rope backwards and forwards and jump over it."
3. "Keep turning the rope backwards over your head and jump."
4. "Run turning the rope forwards."

Development or Game Tasks
1. "Free play with skipping ropes."
2. "Partner tag."
3. "Skip with a partner."
4. "Traditional skipping rhymes, use two ropes knotted together and work in groups of four."

Introductory Activity

The ropes may either be held in one hand or tucked in the backs of their shorts. Encourage them to look where they are going and to avoid stepping on other people's ropes. Make sure that they run in and out using all the space. If they hold the rope in one hand, suggest they use one finger and thumb only, so that if anyone should tread on the rope, it will be pulled easily out of their grasp. This precaution will help avoid accidents. Children find this fun to do and it can help their spacing. Add, "Stop, change direction, off you go again." You may turn it into Nine Lives by ruling that anyone who treads on a rope loses a life.

Movement Training

Young children need practice at jumping and running before combining the locomotor skills with a skipping rope. Stretch the rope out on the ground, and have the children jump over it, using two feet to two feet, two feet to one foot, one foot to same foot, and one foot to opposite foot.

Figure 5.7   "Jump over the rope."

Figure 5.8   "Make a shape with your rope and jump over it."

Figure 5.6   "Trail the rope while you run."

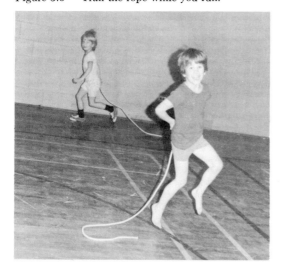

Success in rope skipping is achieved rapidly if children are taught to keep their arms straight and at shoulder level, using wrist action to turn the rope. It is easier to swing the rope backwards and forwards than to make a complete circle, so beginners should be encouraged to work on task two. Some children find it much easier to turn the rope backwards rather than forwards to complete a circle, as in this instance they seem to instinctively keep their arms outstretched. Bending arms and beginning the turning action with wrists close to shoulders restricts the circular motion and allows the rope to hit the floor and interrupt the rhythm. The rope should only just skim the floor as they skip. Have the children check the length of their rope by standing with one foot on the rope and stretching arms out at shoulder level. If the rope is too long, wind the excess around the hands. Many of the problems children encounter in learning to skip are due to ropes that are either too long or too short.

The first three tasks may be performed in a classroom. Divide the class in half and have

Figure 5.10   Arms should be straight and at shoulder level.

Figure 5.9   "Turn the rope backwards, keeping elbows straight and arms out."

Figure 5.11   Partner tag.

one half practice jumping over a stationary rope on the ground while the other half swings the rope to and fro and jumps over the moving rope. Running and turning the rope forward needs plenty of space, and is therefore unsuitable in the classroom.

Development or Game

Partner tag is a development of the Introductory Activity and can be used with grade two

upwards. The pair have one rope each, A holds his rope with finger and thumb only, while B carries his folded rope so that it doesn't touch the ground. B tags A by stepping on the trailing rope. He immediately turns away from A and trails his own rope. A gathers up his rope and begins to chase B.

When they skip with a partner, check their posture and footwork. Discourage poking heads and stiff, heavy feet.

LESSON **3**

Analysis: WHERE?   Own and general space, high and low.

WHAT?   Bouncing and catching, alone, with a partner, or in a small group.

Lesson Outline

Introductory Activity Tasks

1. "Take a ball to a space and play with it."
2. "Hold it *still* when I say 'stop'."

Movement Training Tasks

1. "Bounce the ball as many times as you can without stopping."
2. "Try bouncing it first with one hand and then with the other."
3. "Start bouncing the ball low to the ground, then make it go higher and higher."
4. "Travel while you bounce the ball."
5. "Bounce and catch the ball."
6. "Throw the ball up, let it bounce once and catch it. Invent a trick to do before you catch it."
7. "Roll the ball along the ground as fast and as hard as you can, catch it as it bounces off the wall."
8. "Throw the ball against the wall, let it bounce once on the floor and catch it. Try sometimes to catch it before it bounces."
9. "Kick the ball against the wall and catch it with your hands as it bounces back." (Figure 5.13)

Development or Game Tasks

Working with a partner or in a small group.

1. "Invent a game where you bounce the ball against the wall for your partner to catch."
2. "Throw the ball through the basketball hoop, let your partner chase after it and catch it while it is bouncing, then bring it back and have his turn at the hoop and you will chase the ball."
3. "Stand one behind the other facing the wall. The front person throws the ball against the wall and jumps over it as it bounces on the floor. The second person catches it, then has her turn at throwing and jumping."
4. "Pig-in-the-Middle. Roll the ball along the floor or throw it over the center person's head."
5. "Invent a game that involves bouncing and catching." (Figure 5.14)
6. "Bounce the ball to rhymes, for example, 'Bounce high, bounce low, bounce the ball to Shiloh'."

Introductory Activity

Observe the general interest and skill level in order to select activities from the tasks given in the rest of the lesson plan.

Movement Training

Observe and encourage:

1.   The top of the fingers are used to bounce the ball. Fingers are spread and relaxed.

Figure 5.12   "Bounce the ball around you."

Figure 5.13   "Kick the ball against the wall."

2.   The bounce is produced mainly by a downwards wrist action. The rest of the arm is used to adjust to the height of the ball.
3.   The ball is close to the body in order to control it.

Task four depends upon the space available. Walking, running, skipping, and galloping are possible if there is plenty of space. Task five requires relaxed fingers and bent knees. The child should be directly in line with the flight of the ball in order to catch it.

In task six observe whether they (1) clap hands, (2) turn around, or (3) touch the floor before catching the ball. These are simple solutions to the tasks that could be taught directly if they do not occur naturally.

Development or Game

Select from the tasks suggested or substitute traditional games which involve bouncing and catching skills. If the children invent their own games, be sure they have no more than four children in a group and that they invent rules, a system of scoring, and boundaries. The latter is determined by the amount of space available.

Figure 5.14   "Invent a game that involves bouncing and catching."

In task one suggest variations in throwing and catching positions, for example, standing, sitting, or kneeling.

Task two is an activity that kindergarten children instinctively attempt. They enjoy running after their own balls. There is usually great excitement if they hit the hoop or the net, and ecstacy if the ball actually goes through.

Some children will attempt forwards or backwards or even spinning around to the bouncing routine in task three.

THEME TWO: ADDING TO THE RANGE AND UNDERSTANDING OF MOVEMENT

Theme two is concerned with experimentation (largely self-directed) by children with pieces of small equipment (bats, balls, sticks, ropes, etc.). This experimentation helps them proceed to the development of basic game skills. It is intended to encourage the children to recognize the potential uses of the various equipment. The children should also be encouraged to develop their capabilities of catching, throwing, kicking, hitting, and rolling. Many lessons can be developed around free play of this nature making extensive use of the equipment available. The lesson given uses direct tasks and are similar to those in Theme three. This is because it is virtually impossible to show the development of a lesson based on free play. If you find free play too difficult at this stage, design your lesson according to the structure of lesson 1.

Figure 5.16 A kindergarten child experiments with small equipment.

Figure 5.15 "Eyes on the ball."

LESSON 1

Equipment: One ball and/or beanbag per child, balls for one fourth of the class, and a variety of other small equipment.

Location: Outdoors, indoors if stocking or Nerf balls are used.

Analysis: WHERE?   On the spot and traveling.

WHAT?   Throwing, running, parts of the body and the whole body.

HOW?   Time, weight, space, flow.

Lesson Outline

Introductory Activity Tasks

1. "Free play."

or

2. "Empty the Basket."

Movement Training Tasks

1. "Throw for distance."
2. "Throw from the same place each time, mark where the ball lands with a beanbag, and try to beat your best throw."

Development or Game Tasks

1. "Throw at a target. Move further away each time you hit it."

and/or

2. "Free play with any small equipment."
3. "Empty the Basket."
4. "Invent a throwing-and-catching game with a partner."
5. "Invent a partner game of throwing ball against a wall."
6. "Invent a throwing relay. Work as a team of four."

Introductory Activity

Empty the Basket is a running game. It may also be used as an enjoyable way of sorting out and putting equipment away.

Organization: Four or six containers, hoops, or small mats are spread around the edges of the playing area, but not against the walls as this could be dangerous. The children are divided into as many groups as there are containers. Each child needs one piece of any kind of equipment.

Game: Children put their pieces of equipment into their own group's container. The game starts by the children running to the other groups' containers, taking out one piece of equipment, and returning it to their own container. The game is ended when the teacher says "stop." Each group counts up the number of pieces in their own container. Then a new game begins.

Scoring: This can be done in two ways: (1) either the group tries to better its own record each time or (2) the group that has the highest number of pieces is awarded three points, the second two points, and the third one point.

Advantages: Every child is active at all times. The slowest and the fastest children can work at their own rates without the children being aware of who collects the most equipment.

This game, used at the end of a lesson, may be adapted to reorganize and sort out the equipment, either according to color or type. For example, if the beanbags are usually stored in one container and the skipping ropes in another, each section is made responsible for retrieving one type of equipment only. When a mixture of equipment is color coded and stored in one container, each section is instructed what color they are to retrieve.

This game appeals to children of all ages. Some rules may be necessary:

1. Throwing of the equipment is not allowed as children may get hurt or the equipment may be damaged.
2. Guarding of equipment containers is not permitted. This can help prevent fights.
3. Only one piece may be removed from another group's container at a time, then taken immediately back to their own group.

This increases the amount of running in the game.

Movement Training

Check the following when observing children who have difficulties in throwing overarm.

1. The ball is held by the fingertips and thumb, not clutched in the palm of the hand.
2. The opposite leg to the throwing arm is forward.
3. The thrower stands "sideways-on."
4. The nonthrowing arm is used for balance and is pointed in the general direction of the target.
5. The body weight is transferred from the back foot to the front foot.
6. The arm is extended backwards with the ball at the beginning of their throw.
7. The ball is released at a point just in front of their heads.

A ball that travels too high and too short a distance is indicative of releasing the ball too soon. If the ball is released late, it hits the ground too soon.

Give individual help and encouragement. Challenge children who can already throw competently to beat their own records and invent throwing tasks of their own. You may suggest to some that they find a partner and compete against each other, marking their throws with a beanbag. Do not insist that they pair up if they are content to practice on their own. Train children to throw into a space, away from windows and roads.

Development or Game

Children should be encouraged to experiment with other small equipment. This is essential if there is not a sufficient number of balls to permit each child to have one. The Movement Training and Development tasks may be combined and the children rotated so that they all have practice at overarm throwing for at least five minutes. The rest of the time is spent at free play with other equipment.

Figure 5.17 Compare the actions of these two children throwing for distance.

Figure 5.18

Figure 5.19 "Roll the ball backwards."

THEME THREE: UNDERSTANDING DIRECTION

Following from the previous theme, theme three utilizes the basic game skills in order to develop aim and control of small game apparatus.

LESSON 1

Analysis: WHERE?   Direction and levels.
               WHAT?   Whole body, rolling a ball.

Lesson Outline

Introductory Activity Tasks

1. "Free play."

Movement Training Tasks

1. "Roll the ball along the ground and chase after it."

Development or Game Tasks

1. "Free play with balls or other equipment."
2. "Roll the ball against the wall and field it as it comes back."
3. "Use two beanbags to make a goal and practice rolling the ball along the ground."
4. "Pig-in-the-Middle. *Roll* the ball to hit the feet of the center person."
5. "Work in a group of three. Roll the ball from one person to another." (Figure 5.20)
6. "Make up a rolling game of your own." (Figure 5.21)

Introductory Activity

Each child should have a ball about the size of a tennis ball. Stocking balls may be used.

Movement Training

The following is a checklist for rolling.

1. Opposite foot forward to rolling arm.
2. Knees are bent.
3. Eyes looking at the target.
4. Smooth arm swing working from the shoulder.
5. The ball should roll off the fingertips as it is released.

The next list is a checklist for fielding (catching ball on the ground).

1. Little fingers together, fingers spread, palms facing towards the oncoming ball.

2. Hands directly in line with the ball.
3. Flexible fingers.
4. Reach out and pull in.

Give individual help. Challenge the more able children to work on some of the tasks from the last part of the lesson.

Development or Game

Provide opportunities for practicing the skill alone, with a partner, or in a small group (no more than four to a group). In group games more than one ball may be used.

Many of the group games the children invent are traditional games and relays. Build upon them and introduce competition against self, partner, or group.

Children can invent many games rolling the ball between three players. Suggest variations of the starting position and also the direction of

the roll. For example, the children can stand in a triangular formation or a straight line. The ball may be rolled from A to B to C, or A to B, B to A, and A to C.

Balls may be rolled forward, or a two-handed roll may be used to roll the ball backwards between the legs.

Rolling a ball against a wall can be made more challenging by introducing a target or by encouraging a more forceful arm swing to increase the speed of the ball. Fielding the rebound gives practice at one of the simplest forms of catching.

If beanbags are used as a target, suggest that they use two beanbags and begin by spacing them about four feet apart. Encourage the children to move the beanbags closer together as their throwing becomes more accurate. Or they may stand further away to increase the challenge.

Dodgeball games can be used as practice for rolling. You may decide to use dodgeball for third grade children as one of the tasks in the last part of the lesson. Be sure you select a version where those who are hit are absorbed back into the game. Keep the groups small in number or use several balls simultaneously.

Figure 5.20   "Work in a group of three."

Figure 5.21   "Make up a rolling game of your own."

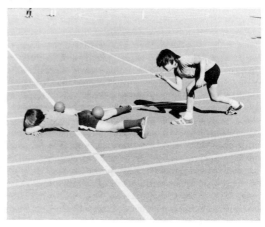

LESSON **2**

Equipment: One seven-inch ball per child (or five-inch Nerf ball for work in the classroom) and a variety of small equipment.

Analysis: WHERE?   On the spot and traveling.

WHAT?   Whole body, feet and legs, kicking.

Lesson Outline

Introductory Activity Tasks

1. "Free play."
2. "Take a ball to a space, kick it, and chase after it."

Movement Training Tasks

1. "Kick the ball against the wall or bench."
2. "Invent ways of stopping the ball with your knees and feet."
3. "Drop and kick the ball to your partner."

4. "Kick the ball to your partner."
5. "Run and kick the ball to your partner."

Development or Game Tasks

1. "Invent a game with a partner where you kick the ball against a wall."
2. "Drop and kick the ball through the hoop your partner is holding."
3. "Kick goals. Make it harder for yourself each time you succeed."

Introductory Activity

This is best done outdoors so the children can enjoy the fun and freedom to kick the ball with full force. To prevent accidents indoors, either use Nerf balls or stress that the balls must stay on the ground.

Movement Training

A checklist for kicking includes:

1. Nonkicking foot is beside the ball.
2. Arms are used for balance.
3. Head is over the ball.
4. Kicking leg swings from the hip.
5. The knee straightens as contact is made.
6. The instep (shoelaces if shoes are worn) of the kicking foot on the ball.

When wall space is not available, gym benches or chairs turned on their sides may be used so the ball will rebound.

Kick-passing to a partner requires the inside edge of the foot to connect with the ball. The kicking leg should swing diagonally across the body. To lift the ball high off the ground, the supporting leg should be behind the ball rather than beside it as the body leans backwards.

Development or Game

Suggest to the children that they use some other small equipment as well as balls. This allows more opportunities for original and creative kicking games. Some of the lead-up games for soccer may be simplified for the primary grades.

LESSON **3**

Equipment: One stocking bat and ball for each child.

Analysis: WHERE?   On the spot, traveling.

WHAT?   Hands and arms, whole body, hitting.

Lesson Outline

Introductory Activity Tasks

1. "Free play."
2. "Hit the ball and chase after it."

3. "Hit the ball along the ground and chase after it."

Movement Training Tasks

1. "How many times can you hit the ball before it touches the ground?"
2. "Hit the ball first with one side of your bat then the other."
3. "Hit the ball at a target (or through a hoop)."
4. "Run, carrying the ball on your bat."
5. "Join up with a partner. Use one ball and toss it to land on your partner's bat."
6. "Hit the ball back and forth with a partner."

Development or Game Tasks

1. "Beat your own record for hitting the ball."
2. "Invent a game with a partner."
3. "Using two chairs and a skipping rope, make a 'tennis net' for you and your partner to hit over."
4. "Play French Cricket. Four people in each group."

Every primary-grade classroom should be equipped with their own set of stocking bats and balls. Grade two children can make their own in twenty-five minutes. Younger children may need help closing the hook. All that is required are a wire coat hanger, an old nylon stocking, a double sheet of newspaper, and some masking tape.

Pull the coat hanger to form a diamond shape, then close the hook for safety. Cut off the foot of the stocking and knot one end of the stocking leg. Stretch the open end over the top of the coat hanger, pull taut over the handle, and knot it (Figure 5.22).

Crumple the newspaper into a ball and stuff it into the foot of the stocking. Seal with masking tape around the "equator" and the "poles."

Introductory Activity

As the stocking balls can do very little damage, this equipment is ideal for the classroom.

Figure 5.22   "Pull the stocking bat taut and knot it."

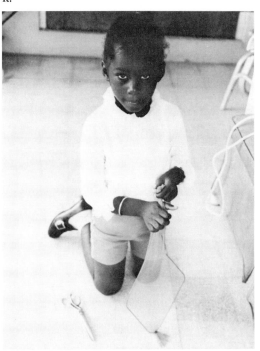

Figure 5.23   "Good hit."

Movement Training

This checklist for hitting includes suggestions for improving the distance of the hit.

1. Stand sideways in the direction of the hit.
2. Hold the bat in one hand.
3. The foot opposite of the hitting hand should be forward.
4. Eyes on the ball.
5. Swing from the shoulder.

Give individual help as necessary. Encourage children who are having difficulties to tap the ball (dribble) along the ground and chase after it. The children may progress to tapping the ball into the air with their bats. Ask the children to beat their own records by counting the number of hits before the ball touches the ground. Let the children decide whether they wish to participate in partner work.

Figure 5.24   "Eyes on the ball for a backhand hit."

Development or Game

Some children will develop complex net games and should be encouraged to do so.

French Cricket can be varied to suit the age levels of the children. It can also be played in pairs. The child protects his feet with a bat. His partner aims to hit the "batter" below the knees. When the thrower is successful they changes places. This game is also enjoyed by intermediate level children when four children make a ring around the batter.

Figure 5.25   French Cricket.

LESSON **4**

Analysis: WHERE?   General space, own space, directions.
            WHAT?   Skipping.

Lesson Outline

Introductory Activity Tasks

1. "Take a rope to a space and practice jumping over it."
2. "Show me how you can skip." (Figure 5.26)

Movement Training Tasks

1. "Stretch the rope out in a long, straight line and walk along it."
2. "Jump along the rope going from side to side." (Figures 5.27 and 5.28)

3. "Can you jump ten times before you get to the end?"
4. "How quickly can you jump?"
5. "Try jumping backwards along the rope."
6. "Make a 'bridge' over your rope."
7. "Use the same bridge or invent another bridge to travel along the rope."

Development or Game Tasks
Select from these or other tasks.
1. "Find a partner, put one rope away, and see how many ways you can find to skip with your partner." (Figure 5.29)

2. "Take a rope to a space and skip changing foot patterns and arm positions."
3. "Work with a partner, place the rope on the floor, and invent a jumping and hopping sequence."
4. "Find a partner and take out a beanbag. Tie the beanbag securely to one end of the rope. One of you swing the rope so that the beanbag just skims the floor. The other should jump over the beanbag."
5. "Play hopscotch."

Introductory Activity

Distribute skipping ropes, one to each child. Instruct them to skip on the spot or while traveling. If kindergarten or grade one children find this activity difficult, have them run and jump over a rope on the floor, as many times as they can before you say "stop."

Classroom Adaptation   If your skipping space is limited, suggest that one third of the class skip while traveling or on the spot, while the others find as many ways as they can of going over a rope within their own spaces.

Figure 5.27   "Travel along your rope."

Figure 5.26   "Skip on the spot."

Figure 5.28   "Travel along your rope."

Figure 5.29   "Skip with a partner."

Movement Training

This group of tasks provides opportunities for the children to explore possibilities for the theme, "directions." Observe what movements they invent and in which directions they travel. Do they make stretched, curled, and twisted shapes in their "bridges?" Can you improve the quality by making them conscious of exactly what their joints are doing? For example, "Are your knees meant to be straight or bent?"

Encourage children to build individual sequences or build a class sequence in the following way. Observe the "traveling bridges" and select one child who travels standing up, one who supports his weight on hands and feet, and one who has her knees on the floor. Ask the class to practice all three positions and then ask them to add one of their own. The final sequence will contain four different ways of traveling along a rope.

Classroom Adaptation   Usually there is just enough space in the classroom for kindergarten and grade one children to work individually.

However, second and third graders can overcome the space problem by working two to a rope. Cooperation and peaceful coexistence are essential.

Class Organization   Note: At the end of Movement Training, ask the class to go to their section places taking their ropes with them. Sections 1, 3, and 4 will be sharing ropes. Knot the extra ropes and leave in a pile in each section place.

Development or Game

In task one, the children can invent different ways of skipping with a rope. Partners can skip together with each child holding one end of the rope, or they can take turns skipping one at a time.

The children may work individually in task two. They can vary the ways they travel with the rope:

1. Hopping on one foot.
2. Changing feet.
3. Feet together quickly.
4. Backwards.
5. Arms crossed.

The children can create sequences by varying the patterns of hopping on one foot and jumping with feet apart and together. The starting positions can also be varied. The children may begin by each standing at opposite ends of the rope, or they can stand at the same end; side by side or one in front of the other.

For task four, have one child swing the beanbag around in a circle, changing the rope from hand to hand to prevent dizziness. The beanbag should skim approximately 1″ above the ground while the second child jumps over it. Develop this task by suggesting that each jump be different: one foot, two feet, turning in the air, backwards, bunny jump, etc. Each child should try five jumps and then change positions.

LESSON **5**

Equipment: One seven-inch ball or stocking bat and ball per child, skittles (pins), hoops and beanbags.
Analysis: WHERE?   Traveling, directions.
            WHAT?   Hands and feet, dribbling.

Lesson Outline

Introductory Activity Tasks
  1. "Free play."
  2. "Travel, moving the ball with your feet only."
  3. "Travel, moving the ball with your hands."
  4. "Travel, moving the ball along the ground with your bat."

Movement Training Tasks
  1. "Travel forwards, backwards, and sideways, moving the ball with your feet or hands in your own space."
  2. "Dribble the ball around the gym, moving in and out of the beanbags."

Development or Game Tasks
  1. "Arrange eight or nine pins in a pattern, then dribble the ball in and out of the pins. Go as close and as fast as you can without knocking them down."
  2. "Invent a game of dribbling with a partner or small group."
  3. "Play Find a Ball."
  4. "Free play."

Introductory Activity

Dribbling involves being able to keep the ball within reach and control, as well as being able to change direction quickly.

Children need plenty of practice at "nudging" the ball along. This is achieved by using the inner border of the foot and keeping the head over the ball. Encourage equal skill with both feet.

Have the children run around, alternating their hands while bouncing the ball. Another form of dribbling involves running and tapping a stocking ball on the floor with a bat. Young children find the latter the hardest as they often become so absorbed that they forget to look where they are going.

Figure 5.30   "Move the ball using only your feet."

Figure 5.31   "Now try it using only your hands."

Movement Training

Emphasize increasing speed as their ability to control the ball improves.

Have them discover and invent ways to stop the ball, so that they can change direction quickly.

Have the children run around in a circle approximately ten feet in diameter, always facing the same wall. This forces them to move the ball sideways, backwards, and forwards.

Development or Game

Any type of small equipment may be used to form a maze for them to dribble the ball through. Move the objects closer together to increase the challenge.

Find a Ball is played by the whole class. Distribute balls to two-thirds of the class. They should begin to dribble, using all the space. The other third of the children try to intercept a ball with their feet. The goal is to keep control of the ball through skillful dribbling. *No body contact of any form is allowed.* The child who loses her ball immediately tries to intercept someone else's. The children who keep one ball for the whole game are the winners.

Section 3

Movement Education in the Intermediate Grades

Chapter Six: Games: Setting the Stage

Chapter Seven: Gymnastics: Building a Movement Vocabulary

Chapter Eight: Dance: Using the Movement Approach

In Section 1, the value and application of the Movement Education approach was discussed with reference to both primary and intermediate children. Section 2 illustrated the relative ease of introducing this approach to primary children through integrating the main content areas of games, dance, and gymnastics with the concepts and principles of Movement Education. The characteristics of these younger children, coupled with their lack of experience in more formal learning environments, permits such an integrated approach.

For the typical intermediate class there is a need to consider several important factors before deciding on how to introduce Movement Education to older children. Most elementary school teachers normally teach games, dance, and gymnastic activities using a formal or direct method. Children have learned to observe demonstration and practice specific skills in a progressive and systematic manner. Where skills have an element of risk and danger, such as vaulting and climbing activities, "spotters" are used to prevent accidents or injury.

Section 3 has been organized to cope with these factors. Chapter six begins with a structured games program and gradually introduces a new teaching progression, problem-solving methods, and a few Movement Education terms. Chapter seven uses the medium of gymnastics to introduce the vocabulary of Movement Education and to lay the ground work for theme development. As the class progresses to chapter eight, the teacher will be able to teach through the problem-solving or limitation method and to understand the new Movement Education vocabulary. These new skills and terms are then used to teach dance activities.

Chapter Six

Games: Setting the Stage

Phase One: **Existing Game Programs**

Phase Two: **Introducing a New Teaching Format**

Phase Three: **Introducing the Problem-Solving Method**

Phase Four: **Introducing Movement Terms and Concepts**
Sample Basketball Unit

By the time children reach grades four and five, their learning habits in physical education have been well established. In general, they have learned to begin with a conditioning-type routine, followed by a demonstration and practice period. The lesson finishes with a modified or team game with the appropriate rules and regulations. With few exceptions, the teacher has planned the lesson and taught it through a direct-teaching method.

Since it is both difficult and unwise to completely and abruptly change a particular learning pattern, another approach will be taken. Phase One of this chapter begins with a typical structured soccer unit and illustrates the change towards a more informal and more individualized lesson format and teaching progression. Phases Two and Three are used to introduce the new teaching format and the problem-solving method. They also suggest ways in which a

30 minute lesson

Part One: Warm-up or Introductory Activities	Part Two: Skill Development	Part Three: Final Activity or Group Games
Running, calisthenics, etc. three to five minutes.	Demonstration drills, lead-up games. ten to fifteen minutes.	Modified or team game. ten to fifteen minutes.

variety of small equipment can be used in the game program. Phase Four shows how Movement Education terms and concepts can be integrated into an intermediate game program.

The new teaching format, progression, and methodology provide a foundation for the more comprehensive introduction to Movement Education discussed in the next chapter on gymnastics. If a teacher wishes to introduce this new approach later in the year, the abridged basketball unit found in the latter part of this chapter may be used. (See film *Teaching Game Activities to Intermediate Children* in Appendix A.)

Figure 6.1   Movement Education introduces varied uses for small equipment.

Figure 6.2   Using a variety of small apparatus allows students to create their own games.

PHASE ONE: EXISTING GAME PROGRAMS

A typical game lesson for intermediate children is normally divided into three parts. Part one, as shown in the outline on page 171, is commonly called the warm-up or the Introductory Activity. This three-to-five minute period is normally used as a conditioning period with emphasis on running and calisthenics or other conditioning exercises. Hence, in the first lesson of the accompanying soccer unit, emphasis is on running, general strength, and flexibility exercises. During part two, Skill Development, the normal procedure is to explain and demonstrate a particular skill such as pass and trap, then set up a practice session using a variety of drills or simple lead-up games. More time is usually devoted to this part of a game lesson. Approximately fifteen minutes are spent on Skill Development during the first few lessons, then time is gradually reduced to give more time for modified or group games during the latter phase of the unit. The latter part, known as the final activity or Group Games, allows children to play and practice skills learned in the previous part of the lesson.

For many years the general approach to teaching games has been to outline the skills, rules, and playing strategies to be covered in a particular unit. Skills were then organized from simple to complex, with lessons sequentially arranged to cover each skill through the pro-

Figure 6.3   The conditioning period allows children to prepare the skills needed in the soccer lesson.

cedure shown in the previous lesson format. Since game skills (such as those required to play soccer) were considered standard, structured lessons and direct teaching have been almost universally followed when teaching games to intermediate children.

The following soccer unit will begin with a typical structured lesson. Each succeeding lesson, however, will illustrate how intermediate teachers can gradually introduce a new teaching format and progression, create an informal atmosphere, and acquire an ability to teach games using the problem-solving method. Children, too, will learn to work independently, with partners, and in a variety of group activities. As the unit develops, the teacher becomes more of a "guide" to the learning experience as the children acquire skills in a more natural and creative atmosphere. (See film *Teaching Game Activities to Intermediate Children* in Appendix A.)

Unit A: Soccer.
Grades: Four and five.
Skill Emphasis: Passing, trapping, dribbling, tackling, throw-in.
Teaching Strategies: Direct and limitation methods.
Progression: From individual to partner to group activities with appropriate increases in the complexity of skill and general playing ability.
Length of Unit: Nine lessons.

Length of Lesson: Thirty minutes.
Equipment: One ball for each child and a variety of small equipment. *Note:* Use any type of inflated ball (utility, volleyballs, etc.).
Playing Area: Playing field.

Teaching Points The recommended 30 x 30 yard instructional area is adequate for parts one and two of each lesson. Teaching in a small instructional area helps the teacher maintain class control and encourages children to concentrate on controlling the ball and sharpening their awareness of the movements of other students.

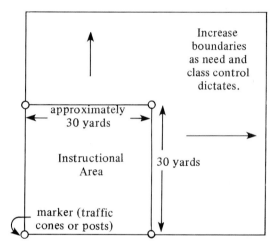

LESSON 1 PASS AND TRAP

Lesson Outline
Introductory Activity Tasks
1. "Run around inside of marked area."
2. Introduce verbal commands "start," "stop."
3. "Run around stationary balls."
4. "Calisthenics."

Skill Development Tasks
1. Demonstrate instep kick and trap.
2. "Partners, practice instep kick and trap."
3. "Practice the skill with one partner stationary and one on the move."

Group Games
1. "Play Boundary Ball."
2. Select other lead-up games.

Introductory Activity

(approximately five minutes)

This unit is based on the assumption that children in grades four and five have previously been taught through a direct-teaching approach. They are used to starting a lesson by running around the field, followed by a series of calisthenics or warm-up exercises.

The first step toward a Movement Education approach is to limit the instructional area to about one quarter of the playing area, as discussed in the teaching points. Have the children attempt the tasks in the Introductory Activity. Modify wherever necessary.

Figure 6.4   "Run around the inside of the marked area."

Figure 6.5   Assign one section group to place the balls on the field.

In task one explain to the class that you want them to run around the inside of the marked area and when you say "stop," they must stop with control and wait for you to say "go." Continue for a few moments to see if they can hear your voice. The teacher should not stay in the same spot but should walk about different parts of the instructional area. This procedure makes it imperative that all children watch and listen to you regardless of where you are located.

If you are satisfied with the class control, ask them to run in different directions—slowly, without touching anyone, and listening for the next command. Say "go," "start," or "off you go." Use "stop" or "freeze" to gain control.

In task three of the Introductory Activity scatter one ball per child around the instructional area. Assign one team or section group to get out the balls and place them on the field. Make

Figure 6.6   Introduce the command "stop."

Figure 6.7   "Run around as many balls as possible."

sure they do this quickly and without playing around with the balls.

Explain that you want them to run around as many different balls as possible and freeze when you say "stop." If they are successful at this, try "Run and jump over the balls" until you say "stop." Other variations are "Run and jump sideways over the balls," "Run and jump backwards over the balls," and "Try some running and jumping ideas of your own."

Teaching Points   These tasks may take up more than five minutes. However, as the unit develops, you will be able to cover much more in this time period.

For task four, arrange children in a circle, squads, or other formations and continue with a few minutes of calisthenics.

Skill Development
(approximately fifteen minutes)
If progressing from number three above, ask class to "Pick up a ball and find a partner. Keep one ball between partners and put the other one away." Ask them to gather around you, then demonstrate the instep pass and the foot-and-shin trap. Make the demonstration clear and brief. You may perform the demonstration or have the children demonstrate the task. Immediately after the demonstration say "Take the ball with your partner and stand about ten feet apart."

Teaching Point   It is extremely important at this stage that children learn to move about the instructional area efficiently with care and awareness of the other children in the class. If they move about recklessly or bunch up on one area, call them back and repeat the procedure. Repetition at this stage to gain efficiency, class control, and effective use of your instructional area will pay off enormously in future lessons.

Have both partners remain stationary and practice the instep kick and trap in task two. As they practice, the teacher should move through the instructional area observing and assisting where necessary. Add the following:

1. Pass with the outside of the foot and trap the ball with lower legs.
2. Pass with the inside of foot and trap with sole of foot.
3. Pass with the right foot, then the left foot.
4. One partner remains stationary while the other moves.

Figure 6.8   Foot trap.

Figure 6.9   Shin trap.

Figure 6.10 "Practice with one partner stationary; the other on the move."

The stationary partner passes while the other partner traps the oncoming ball. Have the partners switch positions and repeat. Let the children try some of their own ideas or move to last part of lesson.

Group Games
(approximately ten minutes)
This part of the lesson should be used to compliment the skills learned in the previous part of the lesson. Select lead-up or modified soccer-type activities that require passing and trapping. Also, divide large playing field into halves or quadrants to permit two or four games to be played as illustrated below.

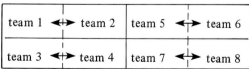

Boundary Ball may be played with eight to ten players on a team using half the field or with four to five players on a team using one quarter of the field.

Other games are soccer dodgeball and circle soccer.

Summary   Several important organizational and teaching strategies can be accomplished in this lesson. First, try to eliminate the whistle as a method of gaining control. The smaller instructional area should permit this. Establish the progression of individual to partner to group activities. Begin to make students more responsible for their own safety, when finding space to work, and when practicing a particular skill.

Each class will obviously vary in behavior and level of skill. If you feel it is necessary for your class to repeat some of the skills taught in this lesson, devise similar lessons with modifications of some of the skills and additional group games. Move on to the second lesson when you feel the class is ready.

PHASE TWO: INTRODUCING A NEW TEACHING FORMAT
The next two lessons will be used to develop a teaching format which progresses from individual to partner to group activities.

Part one, Introductory Activities, will stress individual running activities, rather than traditional calisthenics. It should not exceed five minutes in duration. During part two, Skill Development, individual and partner activities will be used to demonstrate and practice skills and to illustrate how to use a variety of small equipment. Finally, part three, Group Games will illustrate how to sequentially increase the number of players from a minimum of three to six-vs.-six games during the latter part of this chapter.

Although the direct-teaching method is used throughout the next two lessons, the teacher is creating a more informal atmosphere and the class is learning to be more responsible for their own organization and behavior.

30 minute lesson

Part One: Introductory Activities	Part Two: Skill Development	Part Three: Group Games
Use individual or partner activities and small equipment.	Use individual or partner activities and small equipment.	Gradually progress from games involving three players to six vs. six games
three to five minutes.	**Begin with fifteen minutes and gradually reduce to ten minutes.**	**Begin with ten minutes and gradually increase to fifteen minutes.**

LESSON **2**   DRIBBLING

Lesson Outline

Introductory Activity Tasks
1. "Run in different directions."
2. Give verbal commands while running "forwards," "sideways."
3. "Run around stationary balls."

Skill Development Tasks
1. "Partners, repeat pass and trap."
2. Introduce both partners moving.
3. Demonstrate dribbling.
4. "Practice dribbling slowly."
5. "Increase speed of dribble."
6. "Dribble around small equipment."

Group Games
1. "Four Corner Dribble, Dribble and Pass, and Follow the Leader."

Figure 6.11   "Run around stationary balls."

This lesson will build upon the previous lesson. It will, however, introduce the format of teaching from individual to partner to group activities. Direct teaching will be stressed throughout the lesson. Small equipment will be introduced during the second part of the lesson.

Introductory Activity

Mark off the instructional area as shown in lesson 1. No further reference will be made to the smaller instructional area; it will be assumed that you will do this in all future lessons. Ask the children to find a space (or spot) in the playing area. They should be able to move quickly to an available space without bunching up in a corner or grouping together with their friends. *Everyone should be evenly scattered in the instructional area.* Now begin the Introductory Activities.

In task one, the children should run in different directions at the command of "start . . . stop . . . go" or "away you go."

Introduce other verbal directions. After a few moments, when they have stopped to listen to your next command, say "Next time I will call out a direction rather than 'stop' . . . away you go." As they are running say "sideways, backwards (stress that they must look where they are going), forwards, right, left," and so on.

Bring out the balls as described in lesson 1. Repeat running around the balls. Let the class get used to moving around the balls without touching them, then introduce verbal directions, "forwards . . . sideways . . . backwards."

Figure 6.12   "Backwards."

Skill Development

Note: From now on we will use *only* individual and partner activities during this part of the lesson.

Arrange class in partners (put one ball away). Repeat pass and trap, first with both partners stationary and then with one partner moving.

Introduce both partners moving as they practice passing and trapping.

Teaching Points   As children practice task two they will have a tendency to move all around the playing area, lose the ball, and cause general chaos. Stress staying in their own general areas. Later, as skill develops, allow partners to move anywhere in the instructional area. However, if they are still not competent at performing the skill, increase the size of the instructional area, but stress staying in their own spaces.

Call class together and demonstrate dribbling skills. Again, be brief and to the point. After the demonstration, tell each child to get a ball, find a space, and wait for your instructions.

Instruct the class by saying "Start dribbling the ball while walking, not running . . . away you go." As they practice move about and give assistance where necessary.

Figure 6.13   "Approach the ball . . .

Figure 6.14   . . . push with the left foot . . .

Figure 6.15   . . . then push with the right foot."

While the children are dribbling at a walking pace add "Now try to move the ball a little faster, maintaining control."

Variations may be added: "Move sideways . . . backwards . . . in a circle." "Dribble and stop" (on their own or on your command).

Figure 6.16   "Dribble and stop."

Figure 6.17   "Dribble around pins."

Introduce small equipment. Ask each student to get a pin and find a new space. Any small equipment such as beanbags, hoops, or blocks, may be used in this activity.

Present the following tasks:

1. Dribble around the pins clockwise, then counterclockwise.
2. Dribble towards the pin and trap the ball before it hits the pin. Add "Trap it on the right side . . . the left side . . . on opposite side."

Figure 6.18   "Dribble and stop."

Group Games

Note: We will begin with groups of three and in each succeeding lesson gradually increase the size or complexity of the group. This procedure allows students to progressively build skill abilities, playing concepts, and strategies. It also creates various group situations which provide opportunities for the children to experience group cooperation and leadership, depending on the size of the groups and the individual child's role within his or her group.

Arrange the class in groups of three students with one ball between them.

1. Four Corner Dribble. No. 1 dribbles to No. 2's place, and No. 2 and No. 3 move one position clockwise. When No. 1 reaches No. 2's spot, he traps the ball, then passes it to No. 2. Continue pattern.

No. 1 dribbles.

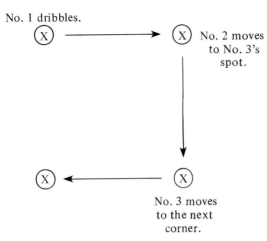

No. 2 moves
to No. 3's
spot.

No. 3 moves
to the next
corner.

2.   Dribble and Pass. Ask players to stay in their own areas, but all three must be constantly on the move. One player begins to dribble while the other two run. Player No. 1 may pass to either No. 2 or No. 3. Continue pattern.

Figure 6.19   "Dribble and pass."

3.   Follow the Leader. This game is played in groups of three and each player has a ball. Player No. 1 begins to dribble while players No. 2 and No. 3 follow his actions. Change leader every thirty seconds.

Figure 6.20   "Follow the leader."

Summary   In this lesson the direct-teaching method is still dominant. The main shift has been to begin the progression from individual to partner to group activities. Each teacher should now be able to approximate the number of tasks necessary for each lesson, to present the tasks in an understandable manner, and to observe and assist the children while moving about the instructional area.

LESSON **3**   TACKLING

Lesson Outline
Introductory Activity Tasks
1.   "Run in different directions. Jump and land."
2.   "Shadow game."

Skill Development Tasks
1.   "Review individual dribbling and trapping."
2.   "Review partner passing."

3.   Demonstrate tackling.
4.   "Practice tackling."
Group Games
1.   "2 vs. 1."
2.   "2 vs. 1, with goals."
3.   "1 vs. 2, with goals."

If you have reached the stage where a whistle is no longer necessary, and children are able to move quickly into individual, partner, or group activities, it is time to allow the children more freedom. This will be the last lesson in which the direct-teaching method will be used exclusively. The next lesson will introduce the problem-solving method.

Introductory Activity

In physical education the normal procedure is to have children change clothes, run to the playing field, and wait for everyone to be present before starting the lesson. Quick changers are not rewarded and slowpokes have little incentive to speed up their changing habits. To provide an incentive and to effective-

Figure 6.21   Quick changes are rewarded.

Figure 6.22   Shadow game.

ly use this prelesson time, utilize free play activities. Explain to the class that balls will be available in the instructional area. As soon as they arrive they may get a ball and practice any skill they have learned in the previous lesson. When everyone is present say "Balls away and into your squads" (or whatever formation you use to start the lesson).

To begin the lesson, have the children repeat running in different directions. Add "Run and jump as high as you can when you find an open space. As you land, bend your knees—then repeat run, jump, land . . . Away you go . . ."

Introduce the Shadow game. Arrange class into partners. When you say "go," one partner begins to run, dodge, change directions while his partner tries to stay three to four feet behind him. When you say "stop" or "freeze," both players must stop *immediately*. If the partner who is following can touch the lead partner without moving his feet, he takes the lead in the next game. If not, the lead player remains in front. Continue for several minutes as this exercise is a lead-in to tackling skills.

Figure 6.23   "Stop and try to tag."

Skill Development

In task four practice tackling with partners at least fifteen feet apart. Player No. 1 dribbles towards player No. 2. Player No. 2 attempts to get the ball away from player No. 1. Change positions after each attempt.

Figure 6.24   "Dribble and tackle."

Group Games

1.   Two vs. One. Arrange class into groups of three with one ball between them. Player No. 1 and No. 2 attempt to keep the ball away from player No. 3. If player No. 3 touches the ball she changes places with the last player who had possession of the ball.
2.   Two vs. one. This is the same as the previous game with the addition of goals. (See diagram.) Place two milk cartons (or other objects suitable as goals) about five feet apart. The offensive players move towards the goal to score, while the defensive player stands in front of (not in) the goal. If the offensive players manage to kick the ball within the goal area, they score and repeat the exercise. If, however, the defensive player catches the ball or deflects it away from the goal, he changes places with the offensive player who last touched the ball.
3.   One vs. two. The offensive player approaches and tries to get past the first defensive player and attempts to score. Rotate players after each attempt, regardless of score. If skill level is high enough, allow offensive player to remain in this position if he scores a goal.

Summary   By now, progression from individual to partner to group activities should be well established. Children have learned to effectively use the free play period prior to the beginning of the lesson. They have also become self-directed in performing lesson tasks: they move quickly into their small groups; they practice tasks without the need of close supervision; and they have become responsible for their own safety and the safety of others in the class.

PHASE THREE: INTRODUCING THE PROBLEM-SOLVING METHOD

At this stage in the transition from traditional physical education to Movement Education,

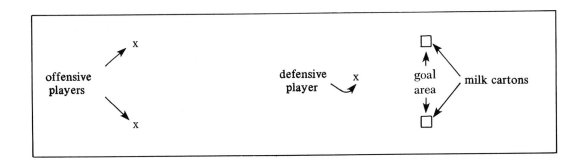

several goals should be accomplished. An informal atmosphere should be established in the gymnasium or on the playing field. The students should be able to constructively use the free play time before the lesson begins to practice already-learned movement tasks. Also, the use of the teacher's voice to gain control and give

Figure 6.25 One vs. two.

directions should have eliminated the need for a whistle. Finally, a new teaching format with progression from individual to partner to group activities should be established. It is now time to introduce the problem-solving or limitation method.

As stated in chapter two, the problem-solving or limitation method means that the choice of activity and how it is to be performed is limited in some way by the teacher. For example, when teaching soccer, the teacher presents a challenge that requires certain skills or movements, while at the same time, allowing a measure of freedom on the part of the performer to vary the skill, rules, space, or amount and use of small equipment. The degree of limitation imposed will depend upon the skill level of the class as well as their ability to use this freedom constructively and creatively.

Phase Three, although it introduces the problem-solving method, still makes use of traditional soccer terms and skills, demonstrations and drills, and the direct-teaching method. Formal teaching patterns combined with problem-solving methods, even in the context of a single lesson, can enhance the learning process.

LESSON 4 PASS AND TACKLE

Lesson Outline
Free play.
Introductory Activity Tasks
1. "Run, jump, turn in the air, land."
2. "Review Shadow game."

Skill Development Tasks
1. "Review passing."
2. Introduce inventive game with partners.
3. Change limitation and repeat task two above.
4. Inventive game with three pieces of equipment.

Group Games
1. "Two vs. two and develop game."
2. "Change equipment or rules and develop another game."
3. "Continue, changing limitations."

Figure 6.26 Inventive game with three pieces of equipment.

The problem-solving method will be introduced during the second part of the lesson with partner activities. If the children are successful with partner activities, try the suggested challenges in the section on Group Games. If not, modify the games in order to use the direct method.

Introductory Activity

In task one review run, jump, and land. Add "Run, jump, turn in the air, and land." Also review Shadow game.

Skill Development

In partners review passing—Two stationary, one stationary; and both moving.

For the inventive game in task two, have partners place two cones (or any small equipment) about four feet apart. Ask the children to make up a game with the following limitations:

    a. Involve two players.
    b. Goals are four feet apart.
    c. Play in your own space.
    d. Must involve passing.

Figure 6.27   Games must involve passing.

Teaching Points   To introduce the limitation method we have structured virtually everything but the actual skill of passing. Simply say "Make up a game then start to play it." Move about the instructional area, but do not offer advice or suggestions for their respective games. Choose one or two games (not always the best ones) and have partners demonstrate their game. Compliment them, then have partners try another game.

In task three allow the children to place the goals in any pattern they wish. Changing these limitations gives the children more freedom.

Teaching Points   Again choose one or two different games for demonstration, then try another set of limitations.

Ask the class to make up another passing game with two players within the confines of their own space. This time, however, give them three goals or pieces of equipment such as a cone, a beanbag, and a short piece of rope. Add "You must use three pieces of equipment in your game."

Group Games

There are three main points to be stressed in part three, Group Games: (1) stress tackling as a main skill; (2) group children in fours, in a two vs. two pattern; and (3) continue to use the limitation method.

Arrange the class in groups of four with the following limitations: (a) two players vs. two players; (b) stay in your own general area; (c) use one ball; and (d) include some tackling. "Away you go."

Teaching Points   Children have a tendency to request help or ask additional questions. Clarify only the four areas of limitation. Continue to visit each group, observing and encouraging. Select examples for demonstration and keep the lesson moving along.

Present another challenge with a change in the equipment, perhaps adding a piece of equipment or an additional skill. For example, you may require a tackle, a pass, or a dribble.

Continue modifying areas of limitation, making sure each challenge includes the skill of tackling.

Summary   When children are first exposed to the limitation method they may react quite slowly, ask too many questions, and at times appear to be lost. Begin with imposed limitations, then as the children demonstrate their ability to handle "freedom of choice," provide more options. Grades four and five seem to adapt to the problem-solving method rather quickly. Grade six, particularly with a strong, structured games background, may take a little longer. However, as demonstrated, this method allows both the weak and strong players to develop skills and playing strategies in an enjoyable and meaningful way.

Figure 6.28   Two vs. two.

LESSON 5   THROW-IN

Lesson Outline
Free play.
Introductory Activity Tasks
1. "Run in different directions, stop with feet parallel, then stop with one foot in front of the other."
2. "Run around balls and stop as before."

Skill Development Tasks
1. Demonstrate throw-in skill.
2. "Practice throw-in and trap."
3. "Repeat task two and change foot position."

Group Games
1. "2 vs. 3, Keep Away game."
2. "3 vs. 2 and add one new rule."
3. "3 vs. 2, with goals."
4. "Inventive game to include throw-in."

This lesson will illustrate the effective use of the direct and limitation methods. The direct method should not be overlooked, as clear demonstrations and useful drills give the children a basis for creativity. Skill and the knowledge of playing rules and strategies give a child options, which lead towards inventiveness and creative play patterns.

Introductory Activity
Review running in different directions, emphasizing change of direction and stopping with ease and control. Add "Stop with both feet parallel, then with one foot in front of the other."

For task two, scatter balls around instructional area. Ask children to run around balls and

Figure 6.29   "Run around balls and stop."

Figure 6.31   . . . move hands upward and forward . . .

when you say "stop," they should end up with their feet together in front of a ball. Repeat, this time ending up with one foot in front of the other.

Skill Development
Demonstrate the throw-in skill (a) with feet together, and (b) with one foot in front of the other.

Figure 6.30   "Begin with ball behind head . . .

Figure 6.32 . . . release and follow through."

Instruct partners to stand about fifteen feet apart. Player No. 1 stands with both feet apart and throws a high pass to player No. 2 who in turn, tries to trap the ball. Player No. 2 picks up the ball and passes to player No. 1. They repeat the sequence.

For task three repeat exercise with one foot in front of the other.

Figure 6.33   One player stands inside the hoop while the other runs around it.

Figure 6.34   The player inside the hoop throws the ball.

Arrange in partners and pose the challenge, "Make up a game with your partner; in your own playing space, with a ball, and using a throw-in pass."

Present other challenges requiring a throw-in. Vary the equipment used (add another ball or substitute a hoop) or vary the direction of the players (sideways, backwards). See Rotation game developed by a group of fifth graders.

Teaching Points   At this stage you should be able to judge how much freedom to give the class. If the skill level is very low, use additional drill-type activities. Also keep the challenges simple when using the problem-solving method. If constant behavior problems arise when the limitation method is being employed and particularly if the skill level is high, increase the complexity of the challenges. Also, if the children are competent at performing the skill, they may readily progress to larger group activities.

Figure 6.35   The player on the outside kicks the ball.

Rotation

1. You start off with one hoop and two balls.
2. Two people are involved.
3. One person stands inside the hoop and one stands on the outside, running around the hoop.
4. The man in the hoop throws the ball to the man on the outside.
5. When the man on the outside is getting the ball, he *kicks* the other ball to the man in the middle, and you keep on doing that. (Unedited version—Grade 5)

Group Games

Arrange class into groups of five. Divide each group into two players vs. three players. Begin with a simple game of Keep Away. Start with one player from the group of three throwing the ball up and between the two opposing players. Each side then tries to keep possession of the ball. As soon as there is a change of possession, repeat throw-in between players from each team.

Keep the three vs. two situation, and ask the children to add one new rule to the game.

Provide two goals and play three vs. two soccer in task three. When ball goes over side or end boundaries, require a throw-in.

Allow each group of five to make up their own game with only one limitation required, a throw-in.

Teaching Points   Children can invent very creative and useful games. Carry a notebook with you and record one or two of the most creative games for future use. Also, ask groups of five to design a new game before the next lesson. The new game may be part of a language arts lesson. Other possibilities for creative games may be related to such subjects as art or arithmetic.

Summary   Lesson 5 illustrates the effective use of direct teaching, demonstration, and the limitation method. Another possibility, such as starting with a structured game then allowing children to modify it according to their own interests, is another form of problem-solving. Also, the suggestion about relating or integrating creative games with other subjects will appeal to many teachers who favor a unified approach to education. The integrative approach may motivate students who show little interest in the language arts area. And of course, vice versa towards physical education!

LESSON 6   THROW-IN, TRAP, AND DRIBBLE

Lesson Outline
Free play.
Introductory Activity Tasks
1. Introduce Number game.
2. "Practice individual dribbling."

Skill Development Tasks
1. "Partners, review throw and trap."
2. "Partners, throw, trap, and dribble."

3. "Partners, invent game with equipment."
4. "Partners, invent game with a hoop."

Group Games
1. "3 vs. 3, with three passes."
2. "3 vs. 3, above game with modified rules."
3. "3 vs. 3, make up own games."

In this lesson dribbling is emphasized during the Introductory Activity section. A shift is made to structured drills during part two, Skill Development, in order to concentrate on all three skills. Then in Group Games, a three vs. three game is suggested with opportunities for children to invent their own games.

Introductory Activity

Introduce the Number game. Tell children to start running in different directions. As they are running, call out a number such as three. They must immediately form groups of three. Start again, with the children running independently, then call out another number. Initially, keep

Figure 6.36 "Number game."

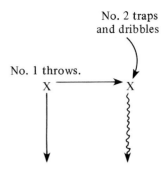

No. 2 traps
and dribbles

No. 1 throws.

your number quite small (two to five). Later, providing you have good control and rapport, try thirteen or fifteen and watch what happens.

Teaching Points What to do with children who cannot fit into a group? Calling three may leave out one or two children. Try saying "Those who do not get into a group of three will do three push-ups." Make the push-up "penalty" a form of fun rather than a punishment.

Task two gives practice at individual dribbling. Have the children dribble in different directions, concentrating on control. After a few minutes, call out "shift right," "left," "around," etc.

Skill Development

In partners, review throw and trap. Begin with two children stationary and proceed to one on the move.

In partners throw, trap, and dribble. No. 1

throws to No. 2 who traps and dribbles to next corner. As soon as No. 1 has thrown the ball, he runs to a new position shown in the diagram. Repeat with No. 2 throwing and returning to original position. Change positions and repeat.

Give partners two hoops and a traffic cone. Ask them to make up a game that includes a throw-in, a trapping skill, and a hoop (within their own personal spaces).

Repeat task three but let them make up any game so long as it requires the hoop. See the unedited description of a game invented by one group of fifth graders.

Figure 6.37 "Dribble Ring."

Dribble Ring

(It's like follow the leader.) The first person starts with a hoop and when she runs around the cone once, she drops the hoop and starts dribbling the ball. The second person does the same after the first one is finished. (Unedited version—Grade 5)

Group Games

Arrange class into groups of six. Divide into three vs. three. Use cones or milk cartons as goalposts (six feet apart). Have children play three vs. three and require three passes before any team can attempt to score a goal. If the ball goes over the side or end boundaries require a throw-in. Do not allow either team to have a goalie.

In task two allow children to add or modify the rules of the previous game. Finally, allow each group of six to make up their own game.

Summary   This lesson is similar to the previous one. The children, however, not only have greater skill but also more experience in inventing or modifying games. If their inventive games appear to be unexciting and slow, increase the complexity by adding two balls, more equip-

ment, and more specific movement patterns (pass forwards, backwards, and sideways before attempting a goal).

Figure 6.38   "Invent a game of 3 vs. 3."

LESSON 7   PASS, TRAP, AND DRIBBLE

Lesson Outline
Free play.
Introductory Activity Tasks
1. "Shadow game around obstacles."
2. "This time play the Shadow game with both partners moving backwards."
3. "Add jumping over obstacles to Shadow game."

Skill Development Tasks
1. "Individual dribbling around obstacles."
2. "Partners, develop dribbling and passing patterns."
3. "Partners, make up game with small equipment."

4. "Partners, make up new game with different equipment."

Group Games
1. "3 vs. 4 game."
2. "4 vs. 4 game."
3. "Add new rules to above game."
4. "Add three pieces of small equipment and develop new game."

The central emphases of this lesson are ball control and accuracy of passing.

Introductory Activity

Scatter milk cartons, hoops, or any other small equipment in the instructional area. In

partners, play the Shadow game. Encourage lead player to run and dodge around as many obstacles as possible.

Repeat the game in task one but with both players moving backwards.

Task three also involves the same game as task one but add jumping over an obstacle.

Demonstrate at this point. If the lead player jumps directly over the obstacle, the player following must first shift to the side before he *also* jumps over. If this is not done the next player may jump over and tag the lead player. Remember to stress control.

Skill Development

Practice individual dribbling around cartons. Start with simple dribbling around as many as possible then:

a. Dribble towards an obstacle, then circle around it and on to the next obstacle.

b. Dribble towards an obstacle, then around it sideways.

c. Dribble and create a different pattern such as forward, backward, and diagonal as you move around the obstacles.

Put small equipment away for task two. Begin with partners dribbling around instructional area and passing to each other. See if they can create a passing pattern moving forward and sideways, then forward again. Allow time for practice, then ask them to invent a new pattern.

Teaching Points   Watch for unusual patterns and allow time for demonstration. Again, concentrate on control and accuracy.

Give partners one piece of small equipment. If available, use hoops, cartons, individual ropes, and cones to show variety. Now ask partners to make up a game within their own playing area, requiring a dribble, a trap, and the piece of small equipment they have been assigned.

Provide two different pieces of small equipment and repeat the game in task three. Add passing as a skill if desired. Put small equipment away.

Group Games

Arrange class into groups of seven. Try playing the Number game ending at seven. Begin with two, then four and finally seven. Divide into three vs. four. Set up goals (but no goalie) and play a game. If the ball goes over the boundary lines, allow a defensive player to place ball on the line and kick it to a teammate.

Repeat the game with groups of four vs. four. Next, allow children to modify or add new rules.

Give each group three new pieces of small equipment and see if they can make up a new game. Provide limitations if they have difficulty with *too* much equipment. For an example, see the Skittle Ball game designed by fifth graders.

Figure 6.39   "Skittle Ball."

Skittle Ball

First—One person on one team holds hoop so it stands. Blue ring should be set three feet away from hoop. Yellow pin should be put one foot behind hoop.

Second—Object is to throw ball into blue ring so it bounces over the bottom of hoop and hits yellow pin. If you only hit the blue ring you get three points, if you hit the pin you get four points. Person on one team throws the ball to person on the other team. (Unedited version—Grade 5)

Summary   This lesson should be "the proof of the pudding!" It requires a much greater degree of accuracy and control. The obstacles also require each child to make quick judgments and to sharpen his awareness of the positions of teammates and opponents. The three vs. four, and the four vs. four games further intensify the complexity of the games. If you have followed the suggested progression of this unit, the added equipment to the latter games should present exciting challenges to each group rather than a frustrating set of obstacles.

PHASE FOUR: INTRODUCING MOVEMENT TERMS AND CONCEPTS

Throughout Phase Three there has been a conscious attempt to adhere to the teaching format and progression, and then gradually introduce the problem-solving method. The latter is accomplished by simply presenting a challenge while imposing a limitation on the skill, rules, space, or equipment. With practice, one or more limitations can be imposed in any task presented to the individuals, partners, or groups. Once children get used to this method of teaching, the fewer the limitations imposed, the greater the freedom and creativity.

The terms and concepts presented in Phase Four are not entirely new to teachers or students. What is perhaps new is the conscious emphasis of these movement terms and concepts throughout a single lesson. Thus Phase Four serves as a prelude to the next chapter.

LESSON **8**   QUICK AND SLOW

Lesson Outline
Free play.
Introductory Activity Tasks
1. Individual dribbling; introduce verbal commands of "quick" and "slow."
2. "Develop pattern of quick and slow dribbling."
3. "Repeat above adding change of direction."

Skill Development Tasks
1. "Individual dribbling around obstacles with verbal commands of 'quick' and 'slow'."
2. "Develop your own patterns."
3. "Partners, invent a passing pattern with 'quick' and 'slow' added."
4. "Partners, invent game with equipment and include 'quick' and 'slow'."

Group Games
1. "5 vs. 5 game."

Figure 6.40   Introducing the problem-solving method.

The function of this lesson is to illustrate how quick and slow may be emphasized when teaching soccer skills.

Introductory Activity

Begin with individual dribbling. After a few minutes explain to the class that when you say "quick" (or "fast"), they should dribble as fast as they can. When you say "slow," they should slow down their pace. Let them practice a few minutes then present another challenge.

Ask the class to make up a pattern (or "sequence") of quick—slow—quick dribbling.

Repeat the challenge in task two with a change in direction each time there is a change in pace. (Quick right . . . slow backwards. . . .)

Skill Development

Practice individual dribbling around small equipment. Start with individual dribbling around as many obstacles as possible. Later, add "When I say 'quick' move as fast as you can, and when I say 'slow' reduce your pace." "Away you go."

In task two allow children to develop their own patterns or sequences, moving quickly, then slowly, and with a change in direction around obstacles.

Have partners develop a routine of moving and passing with one moving quickly and the other moving slowly.

See if partners can make up a game using two hoops, cones, or pieces of rope. The games should take place in their own areas and should clearly show quick and slow movements.

Group Games

Arrange class into groups of ten. Set up goals, side and end boundaries, allow a goalie, and play five vs. five soccer. Emphasize the use of all skills.

Teaching Points   Although quick and slow movements have been emphasized during the earlier part of this lesson, specific quick and slow movements are not required in this game. Rather, start the game and look for children who consciously try to change pace, feint, or shift body movements as they play. After the game, ask the class if anyone consciously attempted to use a change of pace and what happened.

Summary   In every game situation the ability to change speed, feint, and move different parts of the body for deceptive purposes is essential for all players. In games this skill is normally called change of pace. In Movement Education terminology it is part of the Qualities of movement concerned with time (quick or slow). Both terms are synonomous as few teachers would find difficulty in using the concepts of pace or quick and slow when teaching game activities.

LESSON 9 DIRECTION AND PATHWAYS

Lesson Outline
Free play.
Introductory Activity Tasks
1. "Run in different patterns, zigzag, circle. . . ."
2. "Make up a sequence of running and dodging movements."
3. "Run, shifting from high to low."
4. "Repeat tasks two and three with a ball."

Skill Development Tasks
1. "Partners, dribble and pass, moving close together then apart."

2. "Partners, develop pathways of dribbling and passing."
3. "Partners, make up passing pattern."
4. "Partners, make up game with small equipment."
5. "Partners, repeat above and add near and far."

Group Games
1. "6 vs. 6 game."
2. "6 vs. 6, make up own game."

Perhaps one of the most common aspects of any individual or team game is a player's ability to sense where he, his teammates, and his opponents are positioned in the playing area. This is particularly true during the moment of play when a player must anticipate the next move or strategy. In traditional games this is called *positional play;* in Movement Education it is an awareness of a child's personal or limited space, as well as the general space available for individual, partner, or group movements. A performer also moves *within* the space in a variety of ways. In this unit we have stressed moving in individual ways—forwards, backwards, and sideways. A child however, may also move in a variety of pathways, such as around, through, and across. A performer moves in relation to an object or another player, such as near and far, or high and low.

This lesson will emphasize direction and pathways, two aspects of space awareness. Teachers should have little difficulty using these terms in soccer, as they are identical to game concepts and terms used in virtually every individual and team activity.

Introductory Activity
Begin with running in different directions. As the class moves in a variety of directions, such as forwards, sideways, and backwards, call out

"Move in a zigzag pattern . . . now try a circle pattern . . . and stop."

Present a challenge such as "Now can you make up a sequence of running and dodging movements?"

Try "See if you can move through the instructional area shifting from high to low." And "Can you combine change in pathway with high and low?"

Repeat tasks two and three above while dribbling a ball.

Skill Development
Dribble the ball with a partner around instructional area. Begin, keeping close together. In a few moments stop the class and ask them "Try to dribble with your partner passing close, then move apart, still passing and gradually move closer together." This illustrates near and far.

With a partner develop a sequence of pathways such as forwards, around, and diagonal. Attempt to follow this pattern while dribbling and passing with your partner.

Make up a passing pattern with your partner. Give directions if necessary.

In task four give partners two cones, milk cartons, or hoops. Ask them to make up a game involving passing and a change of direction.

Repeat the game developed in task four and add "near and far."

Figure 6.41   "Develop a sequence of pathways."

during the second half of the school year, the physical education program would follow an activity sequence of games, gymnastics, and dance. Basketball, the first seasonal sport of the new year, would be a logical choice for the first large group activity. Secondly, this activity illustrates how to adjust and modify indoor space, lead-up activities, and teaching strategies in order to better cope with individual differences in ability and motivation and to provide for maximum participation of all students.

Group Games

Arrange class into groups of twelve. Set up goals and boundaries. Also permit a goalie. Emphasize use of all skills and a conscious awareness of space and pathways of movement. Allow groups to make up their own game or to modify or add rules after several minutes of play.

Summary   The general concepts of space and directional movements are not new to soccer or other games. If these movement terms can be clarified and used, in a soccer lesson (or in the accompanying basketball unit), then the transference of these terms to gymnastics and dance should be made with relative ease.

SAMPLE BASKETBALL UNIT

The following basketball unit has been included for two reasons. First, should a teacher decide to introduce the Movement Education approach

Phase One: Existing Game Programs

The accompanying outline of a nine-lesson basketball unit will illustrate how to introduce the new lesson format, teaching progression, and problem-solving method in the same way as the soccer unit. For more detailed explanations refer to the same lesson number in the previous unit. Key references are provided within each basketball lesson.

Unit B: Basketball.
Grades: Four and five.
Skill emphasis: Dribbling, passing, shooting, checking.
Teaching Strategies: Direct and limitation methods.
Progression: From individual to partner to group activities with appropriate increases in the complexity of skill and general playing ability.
Length of unit: Nine lessons.
Length of lesson: Thirty minutes.

30 minute lesson

Part One: Introductory Activities	Part Two: Skill Development	Part Three: Group Games
Between three and five minutes throughout the unit.	Begin with fifteen minutes; as unit progresses gradually reduce to ten minutes.	Begin with ten minutes; as the unit progresses, gradually increase to fifteen minutes.

Equipment: One ball for each child and a variety of small equipment. *Note*: Use any type of inflated ball (utility, volleyballs, etc.). Playing Area: Gymnasium or suitable, outdoor playing surface.

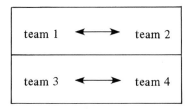

LESSON 1   PASSING

Introductory Activity
As the children run around the gymnasium, introduce verbal commands of "stop" and "start." Do not use a whistle. Have them run in different directions around scattered and stationary balls. (See page 173.) Finish with calisthenics if desired.

Figure 6.42   "Run in different directions."

Skill Development
Demonstrate a two-handed chest pass. Practice with two players stationary, shift to one on the move, then both on the move. Repeat and add bounce pass.

Group Games
Organize gymnasium floor into playing areas as illustrated. Play sideline basketball or a game involving five passes. Rotate teams to allow different groups to compete.

Phase Two: Introducing a New Teaching Format
The next two lessons will be used to introduce a new teaching format which progresses from individual to partner to group activities.

LESSON 2   DRIBBLING

Introductory Activity
Repeat the Introductory Activities of lesson 1 in the soccer unit. (See page 173.)

Skill Development
Demonstrate dribbling skill. As each child begins to practice with a ball, add "Change hands . . . change height of bounce . . . move ball in circle, but do not move feet." Use small equipment such as beanbags, bowling pins and hoops. Ask them to dribble around their own equipment, right then left. "Dribble towards and

Figure 6.43   "Dribble towards and around equipment."

around your equipment." "Dribble around the floor, circling each piece of equipment before moving to next one." Next, have partners review passing. Then shift to dribbling in a Follow-the-Leader pattern and shift again to both players parallel, with player on right side leading. If time permits, add two pieces of small equipment with Follow-the-Leader pattern around equipment.

Group Games
Arrange the children in groups of three. Begin with dribble and pass. (Same as page 179). Allow a two-handed chest or bounce pass. Shift to Follow the Leader. Finish with Pig-in-the-Middle.

LESSON 3   CHECKING
See comments on page 181.

Introductory Activity
Refer to the tasks described in lesson 3 of the soccer unit (page 306). Introduce free play activities before the lesson begins. Play the Shadow game. This time have partners face each other as they stand three to four feet apart. Player No. 1 moves in different directions while Player No. 2 attempts to stay in a checking position, maintaining the same distance.

Figure 6.44   "Shadow game."

Figure 6.45   "Try to tag your partner."

Skill Development
Start with bouncing the ball to music. Select a popular record with a 4/4 beat. Begin bouncing the ball to the rhythm, then add (1) change hands on fourth beat, (2) bounce while kneeling, and (3) move around the floor. Demonstrate checking and pivoting skills. In partners, practice checking and pivoting skills.

Figure 6.46   "Bounce while kneeling."

Figure 6.47 "Two vs. one game."

Group Games
Arrange in groups of three. Play Keep Away (2 vs. 1). Set up a modified goal such as hoops, bowling pins, or milk cartons. Player No. 1 defends the goal while players No. 2 and No. 3 attempt to score. Change game to 1 vs. 2 with player No. 1 trying to get past two opposing players and score.

Phase Three: Introducing the Problem-Solving Method
Review the tasks of Phase Three in the soccer unit. (See page 182.)

LESSON 4   SHOOTING
Introductory Activity
Review modified Shadow game. (See page 197.)

Skill Development
Review dribbling individually and in partners. Demonstrate two-handed chest shot. Practice shooting a ball against the wall then passing in high arc fashion to partner. Introduce the problem-solving method. (See page 183.) Say "In partners, with one hoop, make up a game in your own area and use a two-handed chest

shot." Allow time to invent and practice, then add "Can you modify your game to involve one player checking the other?" Continue pattern, changing skill requirements, space, or equipment.

Figure 6.48 "Make up a game."

Group Games
Arrange class into groups of four. Play two vs. two using buckets or any other small equipment to form goals. Allow all skills, but require an arc on the ball before it counts as a score. As the ball leaves the hands of the shooter, it may be intercepted by an opposing player. However, once it starts its downward arc, players must wait for it to land before attempting to gain control of the ball. Present other challenges, modify rules, equipment, and playing space.

LESSON 5   DRIBBLE AND SHOOT
Introductory Activity
Review running in different directions around balls. Add jumping over, forwards, sideways,

etc. In partners review Shadow game. (See page 197.)

Skill Development

In partners, practice dribble and pass. Add music (4/4 beat) and have partners make up dribbling routines to the music. Give partners two pieces of small equipment and ask them to make up a game requiring dribbling and shooting. Repeat previous game and add one more ball. Allow for experimentation and practice, and add other challenges as desired.

Figure 6.49   "Require dribbling and shooting."

Group Games

Arrange class into groups of five. Play two vs. three using modified goals. After a few minutes, ask each group to add one new rule to their game. Finally, allow each group to make up their own game.

LESSON 6   DRIBBLE AND PASS
Introductory Activity

Introduce Number game (page 188). Individual dribbling, stopping, and pivoting.

Skill Development

Demonstrate and have the children practice a one-handed set shot. Have partners develop a matching routine to music. The routine should include a dribble, pass, and pivot. Add other combinations of skills. Instruct partners to develop drills or creative games (with modified goals) that require passing and shooting. (See page 189.)

Group Games

Arrange class in groups of six. Begin with three vs. three Keep Away, then add modified goals and play a game requiring all skills. Allow children to add or modify rules, or you may add additional limitations to each succeeding game.

Figure 6.50   Three vs. three.

LESSON 7   DRIBBLE, PASS, AND SHOOT
Introductory Activity

Begin Shadow game with small equipment scattered around instructional area. Repeat game with lead player dribbling the ball.

Skill Development

Begin with partners dribbling and passing, then add a pattern of forwards, sideways, and backwards. Ask partners to mark a circle on the wall and play a game that requires shooting at the target. Allow players to make up a new game that requires the target. Add small equipment such as milk cartons or bowling pins and ask the children to include them in their games.

Group Games

Arrange class in groups of seven. Play three vs. four using all skills and modified goals. Allow groups to modify or add new rules. Add your own limitations as the situation dictates.

Figure 6.51 "Add your own limitations."

Phase Four: Introducing Movement Terms and Concepts

Review the concepts of Phase Four of the soccer unit. (See page 192.)

LESSON 8 QUICK AND SLOW

Introductory Activity

The Introductory Activity should include individual dribbling around the instructional area. Add fast music (4/4 beat), then change to a record with a slower beat. Without music, ask the class to develop patterns of moving quick and slow in a forward direction. Allow time

for experimentation, then add a change of direction.

Skill Development

Ask the children to dribble around small equipment in time to the 4/4 music used in the Introductory Activity. Change to music with a slower beat. Now ask the children to develop patterns of quick and slow around the small equipment. Next stress passing between partners, without music or equipment. Have partners make up a game with a ball that requires change of pace. Vary the game skills by adding small equipment.

Group Games

Arrange class in groups of eight. Set up modified goals for crosscourt basketball and play a game. Impose limitations as desired.

LESSON 9 DIRECTION
AND PATHWAYS
Review skills learned in lesson 9 of the soccer unit. (See page 194.)

Introductory Activity

Begin running in different directions. Add "Move in a zigzag pattern . . . move in a circle pattern . . . move diagonally." Repeat these instructions with a ball. Have the children make up a sequence using pathways. The complexity of their sequences may be increased by adding different directions and switching from a high bounce to a low bounce. Also add a change of pathways, high and low.

Skill Development

In partners, have the children dribble and pass around the instructional area. Explain "near and far" and see if partners can dribble and pass as they move together and apart. Create games with one piece of small equipment and demonstrate near and far as part of game. Develop other limitations but still require near and far.

Group Games

Arrange class in groups of ten. Play crosscourt basketball or other modified basketball games (sideline basketball or Russian basketball).

Summary   This chapter has attempted to give further insights into the sequential introduction of the Movement Education approach. With each successive chapter, an informal atmosphere, the teaching progression, and the problem-solving method should become more firmly established in the Movement Education approach.

Figure 6.52   Crosscourt basketball.

Chapter Seven

Gymnastics: Building a Movement Vocabulary

Phase One: **Existing Program**

Phase Two: **Introducing the Movement Education Vocabulary**

Phase Three: **Building Themes**

Movement Education is an approach to teaching that permits greater freedom on the part of the learner. Such freedom, however, is based upon several important prerequisites on the part of the teacher as well as the learner. The teacher must be able to instruct children in an informal atmosphere, use the voice for control, and employ the problem-solving method with confidence and ease. The learner must be responsible for personal safety as well as the safety of other members of the class. Finally, each child must also learn to progress according to his or her own rate and level of ability.

Chapter six has laid the foundation for these prerequisites. The medium of games was used to introduce the Movement Education style of teaching and format of learning. Chapter seven contributes to this transition in several important ways. Within the medium of gymnastics, children have usually been taught formal or Olympic-style gymnastics. This has required the teacher to plan and present stunts, tumbling, and apparatus skills in a progressive manner, beginning with simple stunts and progressing to more complex skills and routines. Variations in the performance of any gymnastic skill, such as a headstand, squat vault, or kip-up, are ex-

tremely limited. Since each child is expected to perform a variety of standardized skills, a spotter has also been necessary to prevent accidents.

Teachers who are familiar with the problem-solving method may wish to apply this method to the teaching of gymnastic skills. However, the nature of a gymnastics program requires a few changes to be made. In order to encourage children to be creative and to move at their own rates and levels of ability, it is necessary to change the classification and structure of formal gymnastic skills to another system of movement classification.

The analysis of all skills in the Movement Education approach includes general categories of movement defined as "body awareness," "qualities," "space awareness," and "relationships." Within each of these three broad categories there are no standardized skills. Instead, there are movement terms that describe WHAT, HOW, WHERE, and RELATIONSHIP of skills. The teacher, using the problem-solving method, presents a verbal challenge to the learner, who in turn, creates a personal movement answer. Because there are no arbitrary standards, each child progresses at his or her own rate and level

Figure 7.1   The Movement Education approach allows children to develop gymnastic skills at their own rate.

of ability. In this new system of learning the child also becomes responsible for his or her own safety and the safety of others.

Chapter seven begins with a formal gymnastic lesson. Then, through the next eight lessons a Movement Education vocabulary will be introduced to the intermediate grade children. Previously-learned gymnastic skills are not eliminated from a child's repertoire of movement rather they are integrated with the new Movement Education vocabulary.

PHASE ONE: EXISTING PROGRAM

The structure of a formal gymnastic lesson is similar to a game lesson in that it has three closely related parts. In the formal gymnastic lesson illustrated in the accompanying chart, part one is used as a conditioning period with stress on running and specific calisthenic exercises to prepare children for gymnastic skills that will be performed later in the lesson. During part two students usually perform balance, tumbling, or agility stunts individually, with a partner, or with a small piece of equipment.

Part three is devoted to performing skills on large apparatus such as the vaulting box or climbing rope. Progression is based upon moving from simple to more complex skills or routines. The following chart illustrates the relationship between a formal and a Movement Education lesson.

Within the chart there are lists of small equipment and large apparatus. Note that it is not the equipment or apparatus that changes as the Movement Education approach is adopted, it is the lesson format, movement terminology, and the style of teaching that are involved in the transition.

A Movement Education lesson begins with the Introductory Activity which is similar in purpose, but not in style, to a traditional warm-up period of a formal gymnastic lesson. This period ranges from three to five minutes. Part two, Movement Training, allows children to learn new movement terms and concepts relating to WHAT, WHERE, and HOW the body can move. During parts one and two movements are limited to individual and partner activities with or without small equipment. Skills and movement patterns learned during part two are then performed on more challenging apparatus during part three, Apparatus Work.

Figure 7.2   Introductory Activity tasks.

◄────────── **FORMAL GYMNASTIC LESSON (30 minutes)** ──────────►

Part One: Warm-up	Part Two: Stunts	Part Three: Large Apparatus Activities
Conditioning exercises. three to five minutes.	Tumbling and small apparatus. ten to fifteen minutes.	 ten to fifteen minutes.

SMALL EQUIPMENT
Beanbags
Braids or rubber bands
Indian clubs or bowling pins
Wands
Chairs
Blocks of wood
Hoops
Traffic cones
Balls
Skipping ropes
Individual mats

LARGE EQUIPMENT
Tumbling mats
Balance beam
Springboard
Balance bench
Vaulting box
Horizontal bar
Stall bars
Climbing ropes
Jumping boxes
Planks and sawhorses
Agility apparatus

◄────────── **MOVEMENT EDUCATION LESSON (30 minutes)** ──────────►

Part One: Introductory Activities	Part Two: Movement Training	Part Three: Apparatus Work
three to five minutes.	ten to fifteen minutes.	ten to fifteen minutes.

Figure 7.3   Movement Training tasks.

Figure 7.4   Apparatus Work.

The following introductory gymnastic unit will illustrate how intermediate teachers can gradually introduce a new teaching format and a new movement vocabulary to intermediate level children. This unit is based on two important considerations. First, children in the intermediate grades have usually been taught gymnastic activities through a traditional approach. The second prerequisite requires that the children have previous exposure to the Movement Education approach through the soccer or basketball units described in chapter six.

Unit C: Gymnastics.
Grades: Four through six.
Skill Emphasis: Body awareness, qualities of movement, space awareness, and development of movement sequences.
Teaching Strategies: Direct, limitation, and indirect method.
Progression: From individual to small equipment to large apparatus activities with appropriate increases in the complexity of movement challenges.
Length of Unit: Nine lessons.
Length of Lesson: Thirty minutes
Small Equipment:

Minimum equipment
35 beanbags
35 braids or rubber bands
24 Indian clubs or bowling pins
35 wands or cones
24 chairs
35 blocks of wood
35 hoops
12 traffic cones
35 balls
35 skipping ropes

Recommended equipment
35 individual mats

Large Apparatus:

Minimum equipment
4 large tumbling mats
1 balance beam
4 balance benches

1 vaulting box
1 climbing rope
1 set planks and sawhorses

Recommended apparatus[1]
1 springboard
1 horizontal bar
1 set stall bars
4 jumping boxes
1 set of agility apparatus

In the previous soccer and basketball units the children have learned (a) to listen and react to the teacher's verbal commands, (b) to move about the instructional area with care and concern for other students, and (c) to work independently when given the opportunity. Shifting to gymnastic activities, however, presents some important considerations. Gymnastic activities, by their very nature, are potentially dangerous if taught incorrectly.

This unit is based upon the commonly accepted fact that children in the intermediate grades are used to performing standardized skills and to having a spotter present when practicing these skills. As a consequence, each successive lesson in this unit will illustrate how a teacher and class can gradually improve safety skills. The goal is to develop a conscious attitude about personal safety as well as the safety of every student in the class. This is gradually accomplished in sequence along with an introduction to the new movement vocabulary.

1. See Appendix C for list of equipment and apparatus supply companies.

Figure 7.5 "Run in different directions."

LESSON 1 BALANCE AND VAULTING

Lesson Outline

Introductory Activity Tasks
1. "Run in different directions."
2. "Run and touch floor."
3. Calisthenics with variations.

Movement Training Tasks
1. "Try individual balance stunts, such as *Turk stand, inch worm,* and *seal slap.*"

2. "Perform dual balance stunts, such as *Chinese get-up,* or make up your own stunt."
3. "Practice individual rope skipping, alternate step and make up variations of foot patterns."

Apparatus Work
1. "Work on vaulting activities: run, jump, hold balance, and jump off."

Introductory Activity

Explain to the class that you want them to run in different directions as they did in the previous soccer or basketball unit. As they run, call out "Move sideways . . . backwards. . . ." After a few minutes ask them to run and when they find an open space touch the floor with both hands, then run again and repeat touching the floor whenever they find an open space. Touching the floor will consciously and clearly demonstrate control of movement as children move through the general instructional area.

Arrange class in circle or squad formation for calisthenics in task three. Begin with a demonstration such as "Hands behind neck and bend trunk forward and backward on the count of two." Have class repeat the exercise several times, then ask them to perform the exercise at their own pace. Next say "Now keep your hands

Figure 7.6 "Touch the floor when you find an open space."

Figure 7.7 "How many ways can you stretch?"

behind your necks, and see how many ways you can bend and stretch."

Teaching Points   The modification in this presentation of calisthenics is a good way to introduce the problem-solving method to formal gymnastics. Children feel reasonably comfortable at the start and with practice will demonstrate unusual and complex exercises. It also allows the teacher to shift from beginning each task with "I want you to . . ." to presenting challenges in an informal and questioning manner.

Use such phrases as:

1. Can you . . . discover, add, make, find? . . . ?
2. Try to . . . add, vary, shift. . . .

Figure 7.8   "Can you discover a new way to bend and stretch?"

Figure 7.10   "Make up your own stunts."

3. How many different ways can you . . . ?
4. See if you can. . . .
5. Is it possible to . . . ?
6. Discover or invent a new. . . .

Movement Training

Ask children to find a space to perform individual balance stunts. When ready ask them to perform individual balance stunts such as a *Turk stand, inch worm,* or *seal slap.* After performing each stunt ask them, "Can you perform all three stunts, moving from one to the

Figure 7.9   "Change the position of your arms."

other without stopping? Now, see if you can vary or modify the position of your arms (or any part of your body) as you perform the turk stand." Watch and choose one or two unusual variations for a class demonstration.

In partners, present several dual balance stunts such as Chinese get-up, knee stand, or pig walk. Ask partners "Can you make up your own dual stunt?" Select a few for demonstration then move to skipping activities.

In task three, practice individual rope skipping. Each child should be given a rope and scattered throughout instructional area. Demonstrate and practice alternate steps. After a few minutes of practice, ask the class "Try the same skill and when you are ready, see if you can shift your free foot forward, to the side, or backwards. . . . Away you go!"

Teaching Points   These three activities may be too difficult for this part of the lesson. Select one you would like to try. Also, substitute other individual or dual activities if you feel they are more appropriate. The essential thing is to try to get the children to *think* about their movements and to invent variations.

Figure 7.11   Dual stunts.

Figure 7.13   "Shift your free foot."

Figure 7.12   "Alternate your steps while rope skipping."

Apparatus Work

To begin vaulting activities, arrange large apparatus according to the accompanying diagram. Substitute other apparatus that will provide a

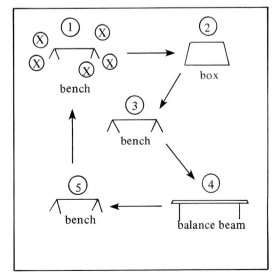

flat surface to jump on and off of. Chairs on a large mat are good substitutes for the small vaulting box. Divide class into five groups. Assign each group to one piece of apparatus and have them stand in scattered formation around the apparatus. (See diagram.) Ask each group to constantly keep on the move and when a free spot on the apparatus is available, jump on and hold balance, then jump off, and continue pattern. Add variations such as (a) one foot takeoff from floor, (b) jump off, make a stretched shape, land, and continue, (c) jump off with a half turn in the air, or (d) cross over apparatus without using your feet. Next, rotate each group to the right and repeat the above on new apparatus. Finally, allow children to use all the apparatus and to repeat their movements.

Summary   The apparatus activities should indicate that children can (a) safely share apparatus without "lineups," (b) jump off apparatus, bend knees, and generally land with ease and safety, and (c) move around the gymnasium, on and off apparatus without bumping into each other, and (d) move quietly enough to hear your voice whenever necessary. If you have not reached this stage, repeat this type of lesson until you feel ready to move to lesson 2. Also, if you feel your class is not ready to use the free time at the beginning of your next lesson, hold off for a couple more lessons. During the free period allow children to practice any skills learned in the previous lesson. However, do not allow practice on large apparatus during this practice period.

PHASE TWO: INTRODUCING THE MOVEMENT EDUCATION VOCABULARY

Skills and movement patterns in Movement Education are not classified according to standardized tasks such as those in games or gymnastics. In this new approach all movement is classified under the following categories:

CLASSIFICATION OF MOVEMENT			
Body Awareness (WHAT):	**Qualities (HOW):**	**Space Awareness (WHERE):**	**Relationship:**
the ways in which the body or parts of the body can be controlled, moved, and balanced	the ability of the body to move quickly or slowly, to perform strong or light movements, and to link one movement to another with control and efficiency	the amount of space a movement utilizes and the direction and level of movement	the relationships between the child and a partner, a group, and the apparatus
Stretching and curling Twisting, turning, and associated body shapes Jumping Traveling Hanging Climbing Pushing Pulling Swinging	Speed of movement Strength of movement Bound or flowing movements	Personal and general space Directions and pathways Levels	Matching and contrasting Following and leading Simultaneous and successive

Figure 7.14   "Cross over apparatus without using feet."

This chapter progressively illustrates how the concepts within the movement analysis can be applied to gymnastics. In addition, the safety skills of running, jumping, landing, and rolling, although part of each of these elements will be specifically emphasized in the first part of lessons 2 through 5. Thereafter they will be integrated within the general theme of the lesson. (See film *Introducing the Elements of Movement Education* in Appendix A.)

LESSON 2   BALANCE

Lesson Outline

Free play.

Introductory Activity Tasks

1. "Scatter beanbags, run around and jump over them."
2. "Demonstrate and practice log and side rolls."
3. "Five students per large mat: keep moving and perform log or side roll over mat. Join two or more groups and repeat."

Movement Training Tasks

1. Repeat balance stunts of lesson 1, then introduce balancing on different parts.
2. Invent ways of balancing on three, then two, then three different body parts."

3. "Hold hoop behind back and balance on head, knee, and foot."

Apparatus Work

1. Repeat apparatus work of lesson 1.
2. "Balance with one part on apparatus and two parts off. Balance with one part on floor and one part on apparatus. Balance with all parts on apparatus."
3. "Run, jump on to apparatus, balance on three parts, jump off and balance on three parts."
4. Rotate groups and repeat.

Introductory Activity

During the free-play period have the children practice with small equipment.

Scatter beanbags (or other small equipment) around the floor. Ask class to run in different directions around the beanbags. Add "Now run and jump over the beanbags. Jump over, touch floor, and continue."

"Find a space and sit on the floor." Explain that you realize that most of the class can perform a log and side roll. However, demonstrate both rolls on the floor—without mats. Ask class

Figure 7.15   "Run and jump over beanbags."

Figure 7.16   "Move from a log roll . . .

Figure 7.17   . . . to a side roll . . .

Figure 7.18   . . . back to a log roll."

to practice both rolls. Next, ask them to move from a log roll to a side roll to a log roll. Repeat rolling to one side, then back.

Teaching Points   Use mats only if you feel it is necessary because of poor skill levels or because mats are required by school policy. The purpose of performing the log and side rolls is to see if the children can work safely on a hard surface. If these rolls are performed correctly, no injuries will result.

Arrange class into five or six groups for task three. (One group per large mat.) Scatter each group around their mat. Now ask each group to keep moving around and over their mat, and when a free space is open on the mat, perform a log or side roll across it. Allow time for practice, then join two or more groups together. Repeat, using two mats. Allow practice, then let all children move anywhere and roll across any available space on a mat. Put mats away and get ready for part two.

Figure 7.19   "Move around and over your mat."

Movement Training

Ask the children to find a space. In scattered formation, have the children repeat individual balance stunts learned in lesson 1. After several stunts suggest "Show me if you can balance on two elbows and two knees." Choose one example, then try "Balance on your seat and hands." Continue the series of suggestions to help the class become familiar with developing their own balance positions.

Now explain that you are going to present challenges that will require a bit more thought. Ask them to balance (begin to use the phrase "take the weight on. . . .") on three parts of their bodies. Select examples for demonstration. Next "Balance or take the weight on two parts," and finally "See if you can find a new balance ("take the weight on. . . .") on three parts of your body."

Figure 7.20 "Can you balance on two elbows and two knees?"

Figure 7.21 "Balance on your seat and hands."

Figure 7.22 "Take the weight on three parts . . .

Figure 7.23 . . . on two parts . . .

Figure 7.24 . . . on three new parts."

Teaching Points   Taking weight on different parts of the body is the first part of Body Awareness. Presenting challenges, at first, may be a difficult and slow process for many teachers. With practice, however, the movement questions and suggestions will become a natural part of the teaching routine. The teacher will also be able to make the transitions between challenges quickly and effortlessly.

If time permits, ask the class to get out the hoops. Present a challenge such as "Hold the hoop with both hands behind back and see if you can balance on your head, knee, and foot." (See film *Using Small Equipment in Movement Education* in Appendix A.) Add other challenges such as:

a. "With the hoop looped between an arm and a leg, take weight on four parts."
b. "Find a balance position with the hoop as the highest part."
c. Ask each child to place a skipping rope on the floor in any pattern she wishes. Present a suggestion, "Find three different balance positions, change from one to the other while traveling on or over the rope."
d. Try some of your own challenges.

Figure 7.25   "Find a balance position with the hoop the highest part."

Figure 7.26   "Find three different balance positions."

Figure 7.27   "Change from one position . . .

Figure 7.28   . . . to the other."

Apparatus Work

Arrange apparatus in the same format as lesson 1 and repeat apparatus work for this lesson.

Have class return to their original groups and scatter around the apparatus. Ask them to find a position near the apparatus (side or ends). Pose the question "Can you place one part of your body on the apparatus and two parts off?" Allow for experimentation, then ask "See if you can start with a balance position on the floor, shift to a balance position with part of the body on the floor and part on the apparatus. Next balance only on the apparatus, then leap off."

In the same groups, pose the task, "Try to run and jump onto apparatus, balance on three parts, leap off, land, and end by balancing on three new parts." If time permits, shift groups and repeat the preceding two challenges. (See film *Using Large Apparatus in Movement Education* in Appendix A.)

Figure 7.29   "Balance on the apparatus."

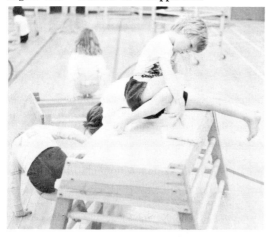

Figure 7.30   "Jump onto the apparatus and balance on three parts."

Figure 7.31   "Leap off . . .

Figure 7.32   . . . land and balance on three parts."

Summary   This lesson has further utilized the new lesson format and the new movement vocabulary. In the initial stages, teachers often find it difficult to think up enough movement tasks and to present them quickly enough to keep a steady pace throughout the lesson. Gradually, however, the ability to create interesting challenges will increase as the teacher becomes familiar with the new movement vocabulary.

LESSON 3   SHAPES

Lesson Outline
Free play.
Introductory Activity Tasks
   1. "Run, jump, and touch floor."
   2. "Run, jump, make shape, and touch floor."
   3. "Using mats, run, jump, land, touch, and roll."
   4. Introduce forward roll.

Movement Training Tasks
   1. Review balance on different parts.
   2. "Roll, balance, roll."
   3. Introduce stretched, curled, and twisted shapes.

Apparatus Work
   1. "Arrange small and large apparatus, perform stretched and curled shapes on apparatus."
   2. "Make up a sequence of stretched and curled shapes."

Introductory Activity
Have the children begin running in different directions, then add "Run, jump, land, touch floor, and continue."

Repeat task one, and add "Run, jump, make a shape in the air, land, touch, and repeat wherever there is an open space."

Scatter large or small mats around the gymnasium. Using the general space and available mats, ask class to "run, jump, land, and touch the floor near a mat, then roll across and continue running."

Teaching Points   If there is chaos, bumping, and lack of control, start with only half the class, then the other, and finally the whole class.

Review forward roll using large mats or floor. Allow children to practice this roll on a mat or on the bare floor.

Movement Training
Ask the children to find a space. Review balancing, or "taking the weight on," different parts of the body. "See if you can balance on two parts . . . three parts, include seat and an elbow . . . and now four." "Make up a sequence moving from a balance position on four parts to two parts to three parts."

Figure 7.33   "Run, jump, land, and roll."

Introduce a sequence with roll and balance. "Can you repeat the last sequence, only this time perform a roll between each balance position?" Allow lots of time for practice. Select a few examples for brief demonstrations. The balances should provide a logical preparation for a roll, for example, two hands and one foot leads to a forward roll. Follow the demonstrations with more practice.

Introduce stretched, curled, and twisted shapes. During the Introductory Activity children were asked to run and make a shape in the air. Although you were not concerned with specific shapes, it was a brief introduction to this part of the lesson. Now, it is time to introduce various shapes into the child's movement vocabulary. Stretching will be introduced first. It involves extending part or all of the body as far as possible. This is followed by a contrasting curling or tucking movement, which shifts the body into its smallest form. For older children begin with a reference point then gradually increase the children's freedom to find their own forms of stretch and curl. The following sequence will illustrate some possible movement suggestions.

1. "Begin with legs apart. Stretch upward as far as possible."
2. "Keep legs apart, now stretch to the side . . . back . . . low."
3. "Change the position of your legs and see how many ways you can stretch."

Figure 7.34 "Balance . . .

Figure 7.35 . . . roll . . .

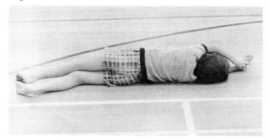

Figure 7.36 . . . and balance."

Figure 7.37 "Change the position of your legs and see how many ways you can stretch."

Figure 7.38   "Lie on your back . . .

Figure 7.39   . . . then stretch as high . . .

Figure 7.40   . . . as you can stretch."

Figure 7.41   "Can you move from a stretch . . .

Figure 7.42   . . . to a curl . . .

Figure 7.43   . . . to a new stretch?"

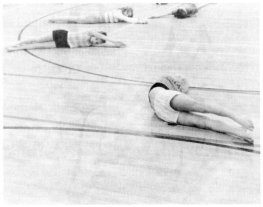

Figure 7.44   A twisted shape.

Figure 7.45   More twisted shapes.

4. "Now stretch on your side . . . back . . . stomach . . . on your back with legs reaching toward the ceiling."

5. "Can you make up a sequence of stretched shapes, moving from a position lying on your back to as high as you can stretch?"

6. "Roll, keeping in a curled position."

With stretching clearly in mind, introduce curling. Start with "Find a new stretched shape then curl or tuck up into a contrasting smaller shape." Find a good illustration and comment. From here pose questions such as, "See if you can stretch on your side then shift to a curl on your back?" or "Can you move from a stretch to a curl to a new stretched shape?"

If time permits, introduce twisting, holding one part of the body in a fixed position and turning other parts of the body across or away. Repeat the previous movement tasks with twisting.

Teaching Points   These three shapes can provide many movement possibilities. "Make up a sequence by moving from a stretch to a curl to a twist or, more complicated yet, balance on three parts and twist to. . . ."

Apparatus Work

Since it is recognized that many gymnasiums do not have enough large apparatus for groups of five or six students, large and small equipment will be combined in part three. Arrange apparatus as shown in the diagram on page 219 and assign five students to each set of equipment. You may substitute small equipment if the necessary apparatus is not available. Ask class to find a space on the equipment. Have them make a stretched shape and then a curled shape on the apparatus. Then ask "Can you make a sequence of shapes on your apparatus?"

Figure 7.46　"Can you make a sequence of shapes on your apparatus?"

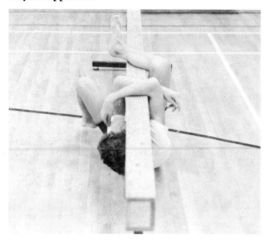

Figure 7.47　Stretched shapes on apparatus.

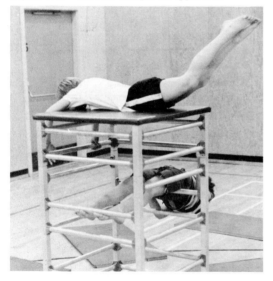

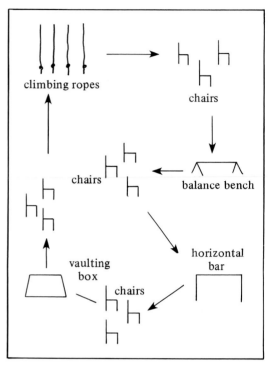

Summary　Many things have been accomplished in this lesson. The children have learned the forward roll, combined rolls and balances, shifted to shapes, and used a combination of small and large equipment. Though it may be repetitious, remember to allow the children to progress at their own rates. Also, additional lessons on shapes may be added if necessary before proceeding to lesson 4. The amount of progress made by each child will vary enormously at this stage. Use your own judgment and proceed according to the ability of your class.

LESSON 4　BALANCE AND SHAPES

Lesson Outline
Free play.
Introductory Activity Tasks
  1. "Move around floor on different parts of the body."
  2. "Run, jump, land, roll."
  3. Introduce diagonal roll.

Movement Training Tasks
  1. Review stretched, curled, and twisted shapes. Introduce wide and narrow.
  2. "Using small equipment, begin with individual shapes then add sequences."

3. "Partners, develop matching sequences."
4. "Partners, now make up contrasting sequences."

Apparatus Work

1. Arrange apparatus same as previous lesson. "Develop a sequence of matching shapes with one body part on the floor and one on apparatus."

Introductory Activity

Have the children begin running in different directions. After a few moments add (a) "Move around the gymnasium on two hands and one foot," (b) ". . . on one foot and one hand," or (c) ". . . on two hands and two feet." As children try to perform these movements, ask them to "see if they can perform a roll in between . . . for example, two hands, one foot . . . side roll . . . two hands and one foot."

Scatter large mats in task two. Review run, jump, land, and roll (log, side, and forward rolls).

The diagonal roll is introduced in task three. (See p. 60.)

Figure 7.49   "Lie on your back and make a thin shape."

Figure 7.48   "Move around the floor on different parts of the body."

Figure 7.50   "Show me a wide shape."

Movement Training

Review stretched, curled, and twisted shapes. Try several sequences with one sequence to include a roll. Introduce wide and narrow shapes. For example, "Lie on your back and make a thin shape. . . . Now, show me a wide shape. . . . Can you find another wide shape?"

Figure 7.51   "Find another wide shape."

Introduce small equipment. Ask each child to choose one piece of small equipment and find a space. Let us assume one third of the class has hoops, one third has traffic cones, and one third has individual ropes. Pose the following challenges:

Figure 7.52   "Practice stretched, curled, and twisted shapes, using small equipment."

Figure 7.53   "Develop a sequence of shapes using small equipment."

Figure 7.54   "Add balances to your sequence."

a. "Can you make up a sequence of stretched, curled, and twisted shapes while holding or touching your equipment?"
b. Repeat the sequence adding balances on two, three, and four parts of the body.
c. Repeat sequence with a roll added.
d. Add your own challenges.

Introduce partner activities. Arrange class in partners, then ask one partner to make a stretched shape and the other to match the shape. This is the beginning of matching and contrasting shapes. Next "Make a twisted shape while your partner matches it and finish with a curled shape." Let them practice their matching sequences. Now add "Work together and invent a matching balance sequence."

Repeat the sequence in task three with one partner making a stretched shape while the other partner forms a contrasting curled shape. Continue building upon these tasks to form a complete sequence.

Figure 7.55   "Make matching stretched shapes."

Figure 7.56   "Now make matching twisted shapes."

Figure 7.57 "Matching curled shapes."

Figure 7.58 Contrasting shapes.

Summary The most important new idea in this lesson is the use of partners. Virtually every movement, shape, balance, and form of traveling can now be added to partner work through the use of matching and contrasting sequences. Partner activities could even have been introduced in an earlier lesson. When children have not been exposed to Movement Education, using partner activities during the first or second lesson can often be helpful to those who lack confidence and creativity in developing movement ideas. Teachers must use their own discretion in deciding when to incorporate partner activities.

Figure 7.59 Confidence and creativity.

Apparatus Work

Arrange apparatus as in the previous lesson. In partners (one on the floor and one on the apparatus), develop a sequence of matching shapes. Allow time for practice, then ask partners to make sequences of contrasting shapes. Add your own challenges.

LESSON 5 RELATIONSHIPS

Lesson Outline
Free play.
Introductory Activity Tasks
1. "Move around on different parts. Run, jump, land and roll."
2. Introduce backward roll.

Movement Training Tasks
1. "Make one part the highest point."
2. "Invent a sequence of shapes with each shape having a different part the highest point."

3. "Use small equipment and make up a sequence of shapes."
4. "Partners, make bridge shapes."

Apparatus Work
1. One partner makes bridge shape on apparatus, other travels through. (Single bridge shape, single bridge with one part the highest point.)

Introductory Activity

Repeat Introductory Activities of lesson four.
Introduce backward roll.

Movement Training

Ask children to find their own spaces. Ask "Can
you think of a position on the floor keeping one
foot higher than any other part of your body?
Off you go." You will probably observe most
children on their backs, keeping one foot high
or on two hands and one foot with the other
foot held high. Cartwheels and handstands ap-
propriately meet this challenge. Choose a variety of ideas for demonstration.

Figure 7.60   "Make one foot higher than any other
part."

Figure 7.61   Cartwheels meet this challenge.

Individual sequences. Ask each child to
make up a sequence of three shapes, with each
shape having a different part of the body the
highest point.

Give students a choice of small equipment.
Pose the question, "Is it possible to make a
sequence of three shapes with the first shape
over the equipment, the second shape with the
equipment to the side of you, and the last shape
with the equipment on the highest part of your
body?"

Figure 7.62   First shape over equipment.

Figure 7.63   Second shape with equipment to side
of you.

Figure 7.64 For final shape make the equipment the highest part.

Ask one partner to make a "bridge" shape and the other to invent ways of traveling over, under, or through the bridge. Change positions and repeat the task. As they practice, encourage children to change directions as many times as possible and to go through the "bridges" on different parts of their bodies.

Figure 7.65 "Make a bridge shape."

Teaching Points The use of small equipment such as wands, canes, or hoops will further challenge children to make more complex bridges. Also, using three children with two of them forming a bridge adds more fun and complexity to the challenge.

Figure 7.66 "Form a bridge with three people."

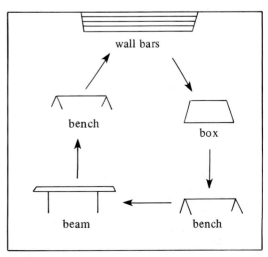

Apparatus Work

Arrange apparatus as shown in the diagram. You may substitute other available large apparatus. Assign two, three, or four sets of partners to each apparatus. One partner makes a bridge shape on the apparatus while the other partner travels through the bridge. Next "Make a series of bridge shapes with your partner on the

apparatus." Finally, "Make a bridge with your partner." This time, however, both partners must have one foot the highest point of the bridge. Rotate positions if time permits.

Summary   By now the movement vocabulary and inventiveness of your class should be reasonably well established. It is now time to encourage quality and form. Rather than shifting to new challenges as soon as one is finished, spend more time practicing the sequences to improve on quality and flow (on continuity) as the child shifts from one shape or balance position to another.

LESSON 6   QUICK AND SLOW

Lesson Outline
Free play.
Introductory Activity Tasks
   1. "Shadow game."
   2. "Run, leap, land, and do a slow controlled roll."

Movement Training Tasks
   1. "Individual shapes and balance."
   2. "Partners, make up a matching sequence; balance on three parts to quick roll, to a stretched shape with legs raised slowly."

   3. "Partners, repeat above with small equipment."

Apparatus Work
   1. Arrange apparatus as illustrated. Repeat same challenge as in (1) and (2) above.
   2. Individual sequences using all apparatus—stress shape and balance and quick and slow.

The term Qualities used in Movement Education is defined in the context of how the body moves. A child may move quickly or slowly and show strength in terms of the effort he exerts. He may also pause and hold the flow of movement, in contrast to movements which link or flow smoothly from one to another. Each of these elements represent one or more aspects of the qualities of movement.

   Lesson 6 and 7 will emphasize Qualities of movement or "how the body moves." Lesson 6 begins with quick and slow and adds this element of movement to the vocabulary learned in previous lessons. The next lesson will simply follow the same pattern adding strong and light movements to individual and sequential movements.

Introductory Activity
Begin with Shadow games in task one.
   Scatter large mats around instructional area.

Review run, change directions, leap, land, and roll. Now add, "Try running quickly, leap, land, and finish with a slow and controlled roll across the mat." Continue pattern.

Figure 7.67   Shadow game.

Movement Training

Practice individual shape and balance sequences. Continue task two in partners. "See if you can make up a matching sequence beginning with balancing on three parts . . . quickly roll forward to a stretched shape, then slowly raise legs as high as you can." Move from position to position until a full sequence is developed.

If you wish to add to this sequence include a change of direction as they move to each new position. Partners repeat the previous sequence with small equipment.

Teaching Points   If you wish to continue individual and small equipment activities, stressing quick and slow, try the following challenges:

Figure 7.68   "Begin by balancing on three parts . . .

Figure 7.69   . . . quickly roll forward . . .

Figure 7.70   . . . to a stretched shape . . .

Figure 7.71   . . . and slowly raise legs."

a.   Place small equipment on floor. Instruct the children to change pace as they run around the equipment.
b.   Practice individual sequences with small equipment, stressing shapes, rolls, and quick and slow.
c.   Partners, make up a sequence using small equipment, stressing quick and slow.

Apparatus Work

Arrange apparatus as shown in the diagram. You may substitute other available apparatus. Assign five to six students to each piece of apparatus. Repeat tasks one and two of the Movement Training. Explain to the class that they may modify or add to their sequences as they apply them to the large apparatus. If time

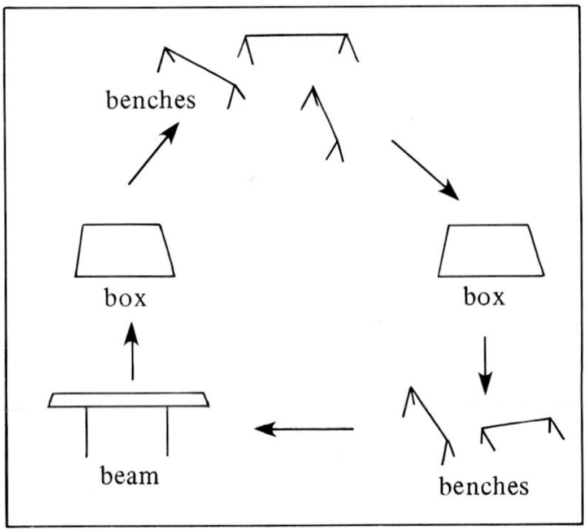
benches
box
box
beam
benches

permits, rotate groups to encourage more experimentation.

Explain to class they may now use all the apparatus. Ask them to develop their own sequences of shapes or balance positions and to use as many pieces of apparatus as they like. The only requirement is to include quick and slow in their sequences.

Summary Once students have the ability and a working knowledge of shape, balance, and sequence development, the addition of quick and slow is relatively easy. Students should now be able to make up complex sequences, individually, with a partner, and with small or large apparatus.

LESSON 7 STRONG AND LIGHT

Lesson Outline
Free play.

Introductory Activity Tasks
1. "Shadow game."
2. "Shadow boxing."

Movement Training Tasks
1. "Use small equipment. Invent ways to cross equipment; hands only, jumping over equipment, with partner holding equipment."

Apparatus Work
1. Arrange apparatus as in the previous lesson. "Run, jump on, jump off, land, and slow roll."
2. "One part on, one part off, and slow stretch, shift to light twist."
3. Repeat above and add quick and slow.
4. "Partners, make up matching and contrasting sequences."

In physical education, strength is defined as the ability to overcome resistance. It is a quality that is a virtual prerequisite to all physical activities. In Movement Education strength or force is defined in a similar way. It is the amount of effort required to perform a movement. At one end of the scale, we have very strong or forceful movements such as climbing and leaping, and, at the other end of the scale, there are soft and gentle movements such as landing and rolling (or any movement requiring a minimum of strength). Strength and lightness may also refer to the amount of tension shown in a particular movement, such as the holding of a difficult balance position or the forceful pull on all muscles when performing a twisted or stretched shape.

Figure 7.72 Strong movement of the arms.

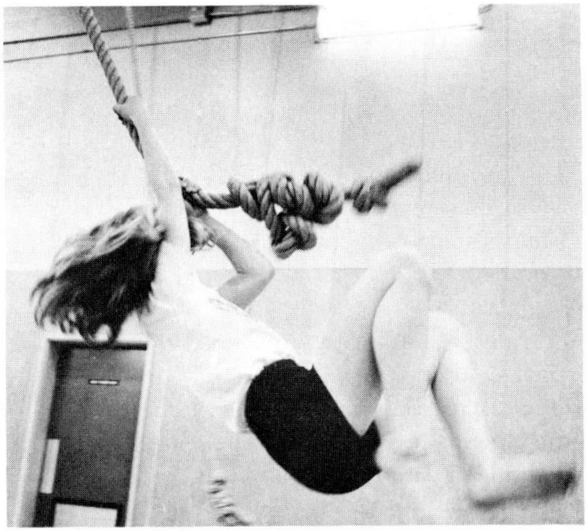

Introductory Activity

Repeat shadow game in task one.

Have the children choose partners, and explain shadow boxing to them. The children enjoy mimicking the actions of their favorite TV stars. Ask one partner to perform a forceful hitting or kicking movement, while the other partner takes the "fall." The latter should show a slow and collapsing downward movement. Allow time for practice and choose several examples to show the class.

Figure 7.73   Strong and forceful movements of the legs.

Figure 7.74   Strength also refers to the tension created by a twisted shape.

Figure 7.75   A forceful hitting movement.

Movement Training

Ask each student to get a beanbag, hoop, rope, or traffic cone and find a space. Pose the following tasks:

a. "See how many ways you can travel across your equipment."

Figure 7.76   Shadow boxing.

Figure 7.77   A partner takes the "fall."

Figure 7.78   "See how many ways you can travel over your equipment."

b. "Repeat above with hands only" (emphasizing strength of arms and shoulder girdle).
c. "Move around the floor and jump over hoop, land and make a slow roll. Continue pattern."
d. In partners, "One holds hoop off the ground, while the other partner tries to jump over or through the hoop."

Figure 7.79   "One partner holds the hoop . . .

Figure 7.80   . . . while the other jumps over . . .

Figure 7.81   . . . and through."

Figure 7.83   . . . and pulling . . .

Figure 7.84   . . . and light rolling movements."

e. In partners with one rope between them, ask "See if you can develop a sequence showing strong holding and pulling movements and light rolling movements."

Figure 7.82   "Develop a sequence of strong holding . . .

Apparatus Work

Arrange apparatus as shown in the previous lesson. Ask children to find a space, but not on the apparatus. Pose challenge "Run, jump onto apparatus, leap off, land, and roll." Allow time for practice, then ask the children to concentrate on a slow and gentle roll.

Task two involves individual work on apparatus. "Find a position with one part of your body on the apparatus. Stretch your body as far away from the apparatus as possible." (Some may stretch on the floor while others balance on top and stretch upward.) "Now shift to a new twisted position with part of your body contacting the apparatus." Ask the class to continue building their sequences, showing a forceful stretch, then shifting to a light and twisted shape, but always remaining in contact with the apparatus.

Repeat the sequence in task two and add quick and slow or a change of direction between each shape.

Join up with a partner and develop matching or contrasting shapes with one partner on floor and the other on apparatus.

Summary Strength as a quality of movement has been included in all previous lessons, particularly with the "run, jump, land, and roll" movements. This lesson has emphasized strength as an explosive force of the legs and arms. Balance positions and stretched and twisted shapes also demonstrate variations in tension and effort.

Figure 7.85 "Stretch as far away from the apparatus as possible."

Figure 7.86 "Shift to a new shape and develop a sequence."

Figure 7.87 Matching and contrasting shapes.

LESSON **8** FLOW

Lesson Outline
Free play.

Introductory Activity Tasks
1. Small equipment. "Run, jump over, shape, land, and roll."

Movement Training Tasks
1. Individual sequence development.

2. "Partners, develop matching or contrasting sequences using small equipment."

Apparatus Work
1. "Develop individual or partner sequences on available apparatus."

Flow may be defined as the ability of a performer to link one movement smoothly to another with control and efficiency. Reviewing the first few lessons, each shape and balance position was presented on an individual basis. We began, for example, by saying "Can you make a stretched shape . . . or, can you balance on one, two, or . . . parts?" These challenges represent bound or static movements. When asked to perform several shapes or balance positions, children at this stage often respond by statically shifting from one movement to another. A child who demonstrates a smooth, continuous transition between movements is utilizing the concept of flow or continuity of movement. Lesson 8 stresses this quality of movement.

Introductory Activity

Scatter traffic cones or other small equipment around instructional area. Ask class to "run, jump over cones, land, and roll." Add "Jump, make a clear shape, land, and roll."

Figure 7.88   "Run, jump over, land, and roll."

Movement Training

Set out a variety of small equipment (individual ropes, beanbags, chairs, hoops). Ask each child to select one piece of equipment, develop his or her own theme, and work on a sequence. After a few minutes of practice, point out good examples of flow.

Repeat task one in partners, but allow two or more pieces of small equipment.

Figure 7.89   Individual sequence of movements.

Figure 7.90   "Develop a sequence with your partner . . .

Figure 7.91   . . . showing flow . . .

Figure 7.92 ... and continuity."

Figure 7.94 ... roll ...

Figure 7.95 ... direction ...

Teaching Points A teacher may wish to stress another element of movement along with the element of flow such as weight or time. The following combinations of movements can provide the basis for future lessons.

Shape, roll, shape
Weight bearing, transference of weight, directions, and speed
Flight, roll, balance
Shape, balance, direction

Partners can use the above combinations of movements to make up matching or contrasting sequences.

Figure 7.93 Partners develop a sequence of balance ...

Figure 7.96 ... shape ...

Figure 7.97   . . . balance . . .

Figure 7.99   "Develop a sequence of matching shapes on the turrets or poles."

Figure 7.100   "How many ways can you travel on and off your apparatus?"

Figure 7.98   . . . and a wide shape.

Figure 7.101   "See how many ways you can cross your apparatus."

Apparatus Work

The movement challenges suggested in the Movement Training can be applied to large apparatus. The following photos are examples of children working individually or in partners. They illustrate how different types of large apparatus can be used to complement the movement task.

Figure 7.102 "Can you make up a sequence of shapes using the poles and ladders?"

Figure 7.104 "Perform a sequence of three shapes while on the trampet."

Figure 7.103 "Can you and your partner invent a matching sequence?"

Figure 7.105 "Can you make three different shapes on the rope?"

Summary   The movement tasks in this lesson illustrate what children can do with a repertoire of movement terms and challenging apparatus. As they gradually learn to use their bodies in a variety of ways, their ability to create imaginative movement sequences becomes almost un-limited. The teacher sets the tasks and creates the environment that encourages each child to work to capacity. The social climate should be one of cooperation not competition, and at the end of every lesson each child should feel physically extended and happy.

LESSON 9   LEVELS AND PATHWAYS

Lesson Outline
Free play.
Introductory Activity Tasks
1. "Run in different directions—backward, diagonal, zigzag."
2. "Run, jump, change directions in flight, land, and roll."

Movement Training Tasks
1. "With small equipment, make up sequence showing change of direction."
2. "Repeat above, stressing pathways of around, through, over, or under."
3. "Repeat above with a partner."

4. "Partners, join and make sequence including high stretch, low curl, and joint twisted shape."
5. "Repeat above with chair, one part on and one part off chair."

Apparatus Work
1. Assign students to a variety of apparatus. "Build individual sequences traveling from high to low."
2. "Repeat above with partner."
3. "Repeat above using small equipment and large apparatus."

Throughout the previous lessons there has been reference to Space Awareness. We have stressed working in your own space (personal or limited space). Challenges have been posed that require individuals or partners to move around and through the equipment or apparatus (using general space). Changes of direction such as moving forwards, backwards, and sideways have also been added to many movement challenges.

This lesson will add a few terms relating to directions, for example, moving across, diagonally, around, and through. And, finally, "levels" will be introduced. Levels involve performing movements with a conscious reference to where the body is in relationship to the floor, equipment, or apparatus. Teachers may require that students keep levels (high, medium, and low) in mind when creating sequences of individual shapes, balance positions, and ways of traveling.

Introductory Activity
To begin task one, have the children run in different directions. Change the directions to backwards, sideways, diagonal, zigzag.

In task two, add a change of direction in flight. The children may perform quarter- or half-circle turns while in the air.

Movement Training
Give each child three or four pieces of equipment. Ask class to make up a sequence that includes three changes of direction.

Ask the children to rearrange their equipment and make up a sequence that clearly shows a pathway of around and through or over and under.

In partners, repeat task two with four or five pieces of equipment. One partner should follow the other, matching each movement.

Figure 7.106   A sequence of pathways around . . .

Figure 7.107   . . . and over small equipment.

Perform task four in partners without any equipment. Explain that they must be joined in some way, with one partner making a high stretch while the other partner makes a low curl. Now make a "joint shape" with one partner performing a low twist while the other performs a high twist over the first partner. Ask partners to develop a series of joint shapes with one high and the other low.

Repeat task four using chairs. With one partner on the chair and one on the floor, have them join shapes in some way. Begin with individual stretched or twisted shapes, then develop them into a sequence.

Apparatus Work

Assign students to a variety of apparatus. Ask them to develop a sequence that includes traveling from low to high and a change of direction.

Repeat task one with partners. Next, combine small and large apparatus and repeat task one and two.

Figure 7.108   "Make up a sequence of traveling from high . . .

Figure 7.109   . . . to low . . .

Figure 7.110   . . . with a change of direction."

Summary   Lesson 9 represents the culmination of many things. Students have progressively built up a movement vocabulary and developed an ability to creatively perform extensive and complex movement sequences. Levels and pathways are not completely new terms. Rather, they are extensions and refinements of Space Awareness that include direction, pathways, and levels of movement.

To the teacher, lesson 9 also represents a gradual and systematic experience of presenting challenges and observing and assisting individuals, partners, and small groups as they develop movement sequences. During the last five lessons, the number of examples and suggestions have been reduced and more degrees of freedom have been allowed for teachers to experiment with their own ideas.

PHASE THREE: BUILDING THEMES

Phase Two can be described as a "smorgasbord" of movement ideas. Each lesson has briefly introduced one or more concepts of Body Awareness, Qualities, Space Awareness, Relationships. At no time, however, has there been a conscious or obvious repetition of one main element within two or more successive lessons. In the initial stages of Movement Education, each class's general lack of a movement vocabulary virtually dictates this procedure. However, by the end of the ninth lesson of this first gymnastic unit, the children should be ready for theme development.

If a class has been taught one games unit (soccer or basketball) and this smorgasbord gymnastic unit, their next gymnastic unit or "theme" should emphasize one or two short themes (three to four lessons) or, if ready, an extended theme of seven to nine lessons. The following chart will provide a basic format for developing short and extended themes. The illustrated stretch and curl theme will indicate areas where a series of challenges can be presented by the teacher. At this stage, however, each teacher must add, delete, or modify each theme to conform with his or her style of teaching as well as the level of interest and ability of the class.

The chart on page 240 can be used as a basic guideline for developing short or long themes. A theme is constructed by selecting one movement idea that will form the main emphasis throughout a series of lessons. Each lesson will also have one or more subthemes selected from any one of the four main categories. These subthemes will provide variety and interest within each lesson.

The more detailed chart on page 241 uses stretch and curl as a main theme with matching movements and changes of directions as subthemes.

Summary   By the end of chapter seven the teacher should possess a satisfactory understanding of the vocabulary of Movement Education. The teacher's knowledge and experience in presenting challenges using the problem-solving method should have developed to the point where it is easy to devise a series of challenges and to change emphasis or direction as the lesson unfolds. The teacher's observational techniques should allow each child to be seen as an individual and self-directed learner who may need special attention, correction, or additional challenges as his or her movement sequences indicate.

Also, the children should have developed an awareness of how their bodies can be used. They have learned to take on the responsibility of choosing among a variety of ways to answer each movement challenge. They should then be receptive to additional exploration through the medium of dance. The next chapter provides this opportunity.

Building Movement Education Themes			
Categories of Movement	Individual	Partners (small equipment)	Group (large apparatus)
1. BODY AWARENESS (what the body can do) a. Shapes the body can make: —stretched and curled —wide and narrow —twisted b. Positions the body can make: —on the floor —on apparatus and equipment	*Begin* by selecting one part ⟶ of an element as a main theme. ↓ Add part of another element as a subtheme.	*Continue* main and subthemes using partners, ⟶ hoops, beanbags, cones, wands, chairs, or other small equipment. Develop sequences which may be polished over a series of lessons.	*Continue* main and subthemes using vaulting box, benches, balance beams, climbing ropes, and agility apparatus, or combinations including small equipment. Develop sequences individually, with a partner, or in a group.
2. QUALITIES (how the body can move) —quick or slow —strong or light —static or flowing			
3. SPACE AWARENESS (where the body can move) a. Space: —limited or personal space —general space b. Direction and pathways: —forwards, backwards, sideways —around, over, across, and through c. Levels: —high, medium, and low			
4. RELATIONSHIPS —to equipment and apparatus —to other performers			

THEME: SHAPES			
	Introductory Activity	**Movement Training**	**Apparatus Work**
Lesson One *Main theme:* stretch and curl. *Subthemes:* matching and contrasting, change of direction.	Directional movements. Shapes in flight.	Review individual shapes. Individual sequences. *Subtheme:* change of direction. Partners matching shapes. Partners and hoops, and sequence of matching shapes.	Box, two benches, balance beam, three climbing ropes. Individual sequences. Partner sequences.
Lesson Two *Main theme:* stretch and curl. *Subtheme:* levels.	Repeat above.	Review partners and hoops theme, adding three levels to the sequence.	Develop new partner sequence, emphasizing stretch and curl, but require a change of levels within the sequence.
Lesson Three *Main theme:* stretch and curl. *Subtheme:* weight bearing.	⟶	Continue pattern as described in lessons one and two.	

Chapter Eight

Dance:
Using the Movement Approach

Phase One: Sequence Building

Phase Two: Phrasing and Rhythm

Phase Three: Accompaniment

Phase Four: The Lesson Plan
                    Folk Dance
                    Creative Dance
                    A Dance Drama

Movement which expresses a feeling or an idea or which mimes a situation or a character is part of the very essence of childhood. These expressive actions are the ingredients of dance and when carefully taught as part of the school curriculum can emerge as an enormously exciting art form.

There are two forms of dance which are suitable for the intermediate grades, and both forms should be included in the curriculum. The first is folk dance. This dance form includes square dancing, which is considered the folk dance of the United States. The other is creative dance.

Creative dance as it is defined within the concept of Movement Education is not the free interpretation of music; at least not until the children know a great deal about the structure of movement and how it can be applied to music.

Before they can write, children have a good working knowledge of spoken language and a reasonably large vocabulary. In dance, a move-ment vocabulary and some understanding of the "language" of movement are required before they can move with confidence and freedom. This is especially true with creative dance. To familiarize the children with the movement approach to dance, the teacher must draw upon the limitation or problem-solving method as well as the direct teaching method.

PHASE ONE: SEQUENCE BUILDING

As in gymnastics, actions are combined together in dance to form sequences or patterns of movement. Having decided upon WHAT actions will be used, the WHERE and HOW of those actions are considered. Attention is also give to possible RELATIONSHIPS. Take for example the movement sequence in lesson 2, pounce-creep-roll. The direction and level of the movement is already suggested by the words themselves but the concepts need reinforcing. The relative strength and speed of the three actions are also indicated by the words. However, these actions will need to be practiced many times before the movement sequence acquires definition and clarity as to the WHERE and HOW the body is moving. Creativity will not be inhibited by drawing out these qualities or by providing many opportunities for other teacher-directed sequences. In fact, such movement tasks are intended to provide the necessary framework for fostering creativity.

PHASE TWO: PHRASING AND RHYTHM

There is greater concern for phrasing and rhythm in a dance sequence than in a gymnastic sequence. An analogy with music may be helpful. A musical phrase has been described as the sound which comes from a single breath. It can be a simple, complete sound or series of sounds. One phrase can build upon another to make the piece of music or song last any length of time. Each individual phrase may be short or long. If the phrases balance each other, the music takes on a recognizable and satisfying structure.

Think of a movement sequence as a phrase and begin by establishing its duration. Repetition will bring about rhythm. Having performed one movement phrase, we can balance it by making another of equal length. The teacher may do this instinctively, as such phrasing is common in both music and metered verse. In folk dance the music helps to structure the phrasing. Every phrase does not have to be of the same duration, but they should balance each other if form and structure are to be recognized. From here on, each sequence can be repeated *exactly*. This is important, as it is only through repetition that real fluency can be

achieved, leaving the body and the mind free to experience the dancelike qualities of the movement.

PHASE THREE: ACCOMPANIMENT

The accompaniment for folk dance is of course the music of a particular dance or country. The accompaniment for creative dance can include a wide variety of music, sounds, percussion, or the spoken word. A short list of records is given in Appendix A to help the teacher get started. Ideally, the teacher should tape the music to be used, so that the tapes become part of a personal music library. If the school has a reliable tape recorder, this is much easier, and cheaper in the long run, than teaching with records.

Percussion

In the beginning, teachers will probably find percussion the easiest and the most evocative accompaniment for creative dance. Percussion has many advantages. For instance, because teachers are able to play the instrument, it gives them direct control over the accompaniment. Also a single action can be repeated over and over again with the support of accompaniment. Trying to locate a specific passage on a record or tape for repetition can be difficult and frustrating. Also to be considered are the related qualities of percussion and movement. Both speed and energy can be expressed through percussion. A slow beat on the drum can contrast with rapid beating. The fingernails can slowly scrape the surface of the drum or tambourine. Castanets can produce a sudden, almost electrifying sound. The reverberations after a cymbal has been hit produces a slow deceleration. Soft and loud can also be associated with light and strong actions. With these attributes, the percussion accompaniment can encourage greater quality in the HOW of movements, in addition to leading and defining the duration of a given action or phrase.

Prior to beginning creative dance, the teacher should acquire a good quality drum, a fluffy-headed stick, a cork-headed stick, a tambourine, and two cymbals. Also castanets on a stick, a triangle, a Chinese gong, and maracas are all useful instruments. In addition to the percussive sounds of these instruments, the teacher will find that many ingenious and imaginative sounds can be made by the children themselves, vocally or with clapping and tapping actions. If the teacher has a tape recorder available, a new world of strange and exciting movement ideas can be created by using the fast and slow speeds of the tape recorder.

PHASE FOUR: THE LESSON PLAN

The lesson plans for dance follow the same general plan as that of games and gymnastics. A rather simple, but invigorating warm-up or Introductory Activity which usually involves some form of space training, sets the atmosphere and tone of the lesson. This is followed by a more challenging development that corresponds to Movement Training, often with a partner. In Movement Training, the major concept of the lesson is approached, and exploration and selection of movements leads to the development of sequences. Finally, the most complex part of the lesson (often in a group) gives meaning to the work that has gone before. Just as a game completes the games lesson, and apparatus work completes the gymnastic lesson, a dance or at least a satisfying sequence of dancelike movements should be experienced at the end of the dance lesson.

Before any of following lessons are attempted, stress to the children that tasks such as running and jumping should be performed energetically and vigorously. It is the teacher's responsibility to see that each child works to maximum capacity and has plenty of time to repeat and practice each task. The children enjoy being challenged,

and, providing that self-control is maintained, the teacher should expect the tasks to be performed with concentration and effort.

The lesson plans that follow are intended only as guides. The material within each lesson may be adapted and reorganized to suit the needs and interests of each teacher and class. In general, however, the teacher is advised to move fairly quickly through the early lessons. Once children are familiar with this approach to dance, they will require more time (rather than less), to work out their ideas. This being the case, the material in the later lessons should be allotted a longer period of time than the material in the first lessons.

The section on folk dance is a brief introduction to folk patterns and dance with material for four to six lessons. The next section on creative dance has lesson material for about six to nine lessons.

FOLK DANCE

The following lessons can provide a great deal of enjoyment in moving to music. They can also encourage self-confidence and stimulate the children's participation and involvement in developing their own dances. The tasks and the standards of work expected from the class must be sufficiently challenging for the children to have a sense of accomplishment at the end of each lesson and at the end of this series of lessons.

Children are capable of developing their own dances once they become familiar with some simple floor patterns and foot patterns or steps. This unit incorporates two folk dances. Once the children have mastered these dances, they may be ready to attempt more complex folk dances or begin creative dance.

Each lesson utilizes and gradually refines the following skills:

1. Careful listening and sensitive response to music, recognition of the main beat, rhythm and phrasing.

2. Development of foot patterns, hops, skips, jumps, gallops, and combinations of these as they fit with the music.

3. Development of partner and group dances using a variety of floor patterns. Circles, lines, squares, and concepts such as opposite, to-gether, and on the spot contrasted with traveling.

4. The conscious use of directions such as forwards, backwards, diagonally, and around as they apply to dance patterns and pathways.

5. Memorization of set dances.

LESSON 1 FLOOR PATTERNS

Lesson Outline

Introductory Activity Tasks

1. "Try *walking* your fingers to the music."
2. "Travel to the music. Try skips and gallops."
3. "Practice on-the-spot steps."

Movement Training Tasks

1. "With a partner invent a traveling step and an on-the-spot step."

2. "Put the two steps together in phrases of eight counts."

Development or Dance

1. "Make up a group dance involving these ideas adding *towards and away from each other*."

Accompaniment

For a musical accompaniment use any good reel or jig in a fast moving 6/8 or 4/4 time. Square dancing music without the calls is suitable, providing there is a clear beat and the tune is one that invites the feet to dance.

Introductory Activity

Have the children sit on the floor and listen to the music. As soon as it starts, have each child make two fingers walk on the floor in time to the music. They can move their fingers forwards, backwards, and sideways.

In task two, have the children jump up and find a space on the floor. Instruct them to move their feet in time to the music while they travel all over the room. Remind them to move at a good speed, but avoid bumping into each other. Emphasize firmly that there must be no verbal sounds, the children must listen to the music and keep their feet light.

Children should vary directions just as they did with their fingers on the floor: sometimes traveling forwards, sometimes backwards. Let them try going sideways as well.

In task three tell them to find a space and

Figure 8.1   "Listen to the music as you move."

practice jumping on the spot in time to the music. Ask them to invent steps that will fit with the music (hopping, feet apart and together, step swings, and jumping and turning).

Teaching Points   Keep the pace brisk, making this part of the lesson very energetic. Don't worry about footwork at this stage. Most children will run, skip, or gallop to the music. If they are heavy on their feet ask them to listen to their own feet and see how light they can make them.

Encourage good spacing at all times and make sure the children vary their directions when traveling. See that each child performs at least two different types of jumps on the spot.

If the children are slow to invent various movements, demonstrate several dance steps to help get them started.

Movement Training

Part two is concerned with the development of phrasing. Partners should work up a sequence of steps that travels for eight counts then stays on the spot for eight counts. The children may decide whether they choose to face each other, stand side by side, or have one follow the other.

Allow only a short time for the children to work out their ideas as the pace of lesson should be kept brisk. The partners should select two steps from their previous practice to make a

repeatable pattern by alternating traveling with their on-the-spot steps. The children must decide which step to use, what their relationship to each other will be, and which pathway they will use to travel. If developing such a sequence is too difficult for most of them, select and develop one of the children's ideas and use the direct-teaching method to demonstrate a simple pattern. Then ask the children to vary the pattern in some way.

Development or Dance

Instruct two pairs to join up to make a group of four. "The music is going to change, so sit down and find the beat by making your fingers walk on the floor again." Each group should make up a dance that has:

a.   An on-the-spot step.
b.   A traveling step.
c.   Steps which take you toward each other.
d.   Steps which take you away from each other.

Allow time for discussion and practice, but encourage groups to get going quickly. The group dance has added one more ingredient,

Figure 8.3   A group dance.

Figure 8.2   "Invent an on-the-spot step with your partner."

"going towards and away from each other."
This can be performed in a square, a circle or a
line. The music should be similar but distinct
enough for the children to realize that their
group pattern is quite different from their partner dance.

If time allows, have half the class perform
their group dances while the other half watches
and offers constructive criticism. Sometimes you
may also suggest that the children learn each
other's dances. Footwork is now important. Are
the children light on their feet while they listen
to the music? Do they invent interesting steps?
Are their formations clear? Indicate specific
skills for the observing group to look for.

If some children are ready to perform their
dance while others need more time, the groups
that are ready can simply be asked to add
another step to their dances.

As this group dance is based on patterns
similar to the partner dance and the only challenge is the larger number of people to organize, this final development should occupy only
the last ten minutes of the class.

Summary
> WHAT: Gallops, skips, jumps, hops, and
>   combinations of these.
> WHERE: A variety of directions. On-the-spot
>   steps contrast with traveling.
> HOW: Rhythmically with an emphasis on
>   flow.
> RELATIONSHIP: Partners and groups work
>   together. Matching movements and
>   traveling away from and towards each
>   other.

LESSON 2   ON THE SPOT AND TRAVELING

Lesson Outline
Introductory Activity Tasks
  1. "Practice your dances from last lesson."

Movement Training Tasks
  1. Clapping patterns. "Use different levels and
     different parts of the body."

Development or Dance
  1. "Make up a repeatable dance alternating clap-
     ping patterns and traveling."

Accompaniment
You may use the music from the previous lesson
or switch to a popular contemporary song with
a good beat, such as "Alley Cat." (See Appendix A.)

Introductory Activity
The children may move freely to the music, in-
venting at least two ways of using their feet.
Vary directions and watch for spacing.
  Practice the group dance from previous les-

son. If the children have lost interest in the
dances, have them follow the leader in their
group. The leader invents a step and the others
must follow. Every sixteen counts a new leader
takes over. The leader is also responsible for
taking the group around the general space and
avoiding other groups.

Movement Training
Instruct the children to find a partner and an
open space. Have them sit on the floor and

make up a clapping pattern to the music. They should use other parts of the body besides their hands. Can they bring in their elbows? Tell them to jump up and make their patterns much bigger. Vary the levels. Remember to stress their knees and heads, for these parts will cause them to change levels.

Development or Dance

Instruct the children, in groups of four, to make up a dance involving a clapping pattern. Have the children develop a clapping sequence for sixteen counts then travel for sixteen counts. Let them decide upon the shape of the group, the floor pattern, and the steps to be used when traveling.

They should be ready to clap and begin the dance again immediately after traveling, so that the pattern becomes ABAB.

LESSON 3 FOLK DANCE

Lesson Outline
Introductory Activity Tasks
1. "Practice your dance from last lesson."
2. "Show your dances to the class."

Movement Training Tasks
1. "Listen to the music of 'Seven Jumps.'"

2. "Learn steps of 'Seven Jumps.'"

Development or Dance
1. "Seven Jumps."

Accompaniment
Use "Alley Cat" as the accompaniment for the Introductory Activity.

"Seven Jumps" is from *All-Purpose Folk Dances* by Michael Herman. (See Appendix A.)

Introductory Activity

Children may practice their clapping dance from the previous lesson to improve or add to it. If the children wish to perform their dances for the rest of the class, several groups may perform at the same time to speed up the pace of the lesson.

If the groups understand that their dances are "on display" for each other, there is an immediate interest in refining and clarifying what they have done. A valuable opportunity presents itself for the class to observe each

other. If the teacher is skillful in evaluating and encouraging each group, the children will learn much from the experience. Emphasis can be placed on (a) the movements they are performing, (b) the footwork and the feeling of dance, (c) symmetry and clarity of the floor pattern, (d) response to the beat and rhythm of the music, and (e) starting and finishing positions.

Movement Training

The children should learn the steps of "Seven Jumps." The instructions are given in the folk dance album.

Development or Dance

Perform "Seven Jumps" in a circle.

LESSON 4   FOLK DANCE

Lesson Outline

Introductory Activity Tasks
1. "Clap hands to 'Tinikling' music."
2. "Jump, feet together twice, apart once."

Movement Training Tasks
1. "Practice first two steps of 'Tinikling' using ropes or poles." No music.

Development or Dance
1. "Put the steps to music. Arrange poles in a different design. Change music and make up own dance using the poles as a focus." Different music or selections from previous lessons.

Accompaniment
"Tinikling" is from *Special Folk Dances* by Michael Herman's Folk Dance Orchestra. (See Appendix A.)

Introductory Activity
Have the children sit on the floor and listen to the music of "Tinikling." Without the music, have them tap the floor with flat hands twice, then clap hands together once. Now do the clapping pattern with the music.

Let the children jump up and make their feet do the same pattern—two jumps with feet together, one jump with feet apart.

Figure 8.4   "Clap the pattern in time with the music."

Movement Training
Teachers should note that skipping ropes can be used instead of the bamboo canes. The instructions for this dance are supplied in the folk dance album.

Development or Dance
After one or two of the steps have been learned, they can be put to the music.

As a further development for this lesson or for the next lesson, the children can use their canes or ropes to make a floor design. The music should now be changed, perhaps to the square dance music that was used in the first lesson. The children can make up a dance in their groups of four utilizing the design of their canes. If they need help in getting started, they may be reminded to think of (a) traveling and on-the-spot steps, (b) meeting and parting, (c) turning and crossing, or (d) under, over, and through.

Further Development
For the teacher and class who have become interested in folk dance, there is a great range of dances, complete with instructions, in "The World of Folk Dances" series (see Michael Herman's Folk Dance Orchestra, Appendix A).

In order to keep this type of dancing lively and dynamic, the teacher should vary the methods of presentation. Sometimes the steps of a given dance can be taught first and the children then invited to arrange a dance pattern using the steps. On other occasions great care may be taken to teach the dance as accurately as possible and with attention to its cultural origins. Children can also be asked to invent their own dances, given some guidance through the careful selection of music or through a "problem" which involves formations and floor patterns.

Important as folk patterns and folk dances are, the teacher is strongly urged to read and consider the next part of the chapter on dance. Creative dance is a more personal and unique experience, which is less difficult than many imagine. Indeed, when the movement terminology has been understood, it can and should become a natural part of the curriculum.

Some teachers may prefer to begin with creative dance and move toward folk dance. Others will reverse the process. It is hoped, however, that all teachers will eventually feel at home in both areas and derive much pleasure from the children's responses.

CREATIVE DANCE

The first lesson in creative dance in intended to show that dance is as exciting and energetic as games or gymnastics, if not more so. All the actions used in the following lessons are fundamental body actions that are shared with gymnastics. There will be greater stress on HOW these actions are performed, as speed, effort, and flow are the expressive qualities of all movement. As you follow these lesson plans you will appreciate the interrelationship of the movement vocabulary with games and gymnastics. At the same time, you will become increasingly aware of the unique contribution that dance can make to the overall Movement Education of the children.

LESSON 1   THE WASHING MACHINE
Analysis: Teacher directed.

Lesson Outlines
Introductory Activity Tasks
1. "Run and stop. Be sure to keep spacing in mind."
2. "Run and leap. This time be aware of spacing and control."
3. "Think up descriptive action words for a washing machine."
4. "Explore toss and twist. Toss your arms in the air. Now toss and twist your body, in the air, while running and leaping."

Movement Training Tasks
1. "With a partner, explore the actions of rising and sinking, spinning and collapsing."
2. "Combine your actions to form a filling cycle, a wash cycle, a spin-dry cycle, and a collapse."

Development or Dance
1. "Pretend you are a garment in a huge washing machine. During the wash cycle run and leap,

Figure 8.5   "Make your arms toss and twist."

and twist and toss in the general space. Your actions should be energetic. Join with a partner for the spin and collapse."

Stimulus

Children readily think up movement actions based on the stimulus idea of a washing machine.

Action Words

The action words used in this lesson are toss and twist, rise and sink, spin and collapse.

Accompaniment

The movement actions in this lesson may be performed to the accompaniment of a drum, cymbals, or tambourine.

Introductory Activity

Children may run anywhere in the room twisting and turning to avoid bumping. Tell them to freeze on the drum beat, then look to see if everyone is in a good space. Do not tolerate noise and discourage children from running around the edge of the room.

In task two, have them run and jump, then freeze on the drum beat. Encourage a slow, short run in order to promote high and controlled jumps. Keep checking the spacing. Work on this until the children are physically tired. A demonstration may be valuable to illustrate your teaching points.

Figure 8.6   "Run anywhere and freeze on the drum beat."

Have the children collect action words in response to a brief discussion of clothes being washed. The action words may be written on paper, or on a blackboard in the gym, or in the classroom prior to coming into the gym.

Figure 8.7   "Hang your arm as if it were an empty sleeve."

To introduce the children to toss and twist, ask them to sit and make one arm hang as if it was an empty sleeve. Next, ask them to move it a little. Finally, toss it very lightly up in the air.

Have the children jump up. Every time you hit the tambourine, the children should make their arms toss and twist. Think of all the action words that have been suggested. Discuss the quality of movement and encourage the children to use all the space around them—high, low, front, sides. Use the tambourine again and ask the children to watch their hands to see if their movements are light.

To further develop the task, have the children jump on the spot with a very light, tossing feeling. They may use their arms to add to the lightness of the action. Also, their heads should be lifted.

This is a very important stage as you are concerned with a jump that has a particular quality of feeling. As soon as a child has captured this feeling of lightness have him or her

Figure 8.8 "When I hit the tambourine, make your arms toss and twist."

Figure 8.9 "Watch your hands and make sure their movements are light."

Figure 8.10 "Prepare for it . . .

Figure 8.11 . . . then fling yourself into the air."

demonstrate. Encourage the arms to be flung up in a light, floppy way. Give the children plenty of practice and time to rest.

Finally, ask the children to run and jump all over the room. Their jumps should make them look like "old shirts" being tossed and stretched and twisted and flung about by the water.

Figure 8.12 Running and jumping.

The children have a lot to think about now: spacing, controlling their runs and jumps, and concentrating on a specific type of jump. Allow for sufficient practice, then let one half of the class demonstrate while the other half watches.

Movement Training

The tasks of the Movement Training section may be performed in partners. They can make up a movement sequence based on the actions of the washing machine. Their movements will interpret the actions of the machine as it fills, empties, and spin-dries.

In task one, instruct each child to put one hand flat on the floor and when he hears the rolling drum beat (or shake of the tambourine) to raise his hand slowly and smoothly.

Encourage a very slow but continuous arm action. Stop every now and again to see if they are listening. Vary the duration of the drum beat and sometimes go back down (sink) slowly and sometimes quickly.

Ask the children to join up with a partner. They can use their hands or other parts of their bodies to lead the rising and sinking. Partners should keep *exactly* in time with each other. Left to themselves, children may rise with their heads leading or alter their starting positions so that one or both feet lead the action.

Figure 8.13   "Keep your hands level and lift them very slowly."

Figure 8.14   "Use a different part of the body."

Figure 8.15   Rising and sinking with a partner.

We have now entered the spin-dry cycle. Partners join hands and spin for a moment. If they can control the spin, let them practice it a little longer.

There are a variety of ways of spinning, individually or with a partner, but for our purpose

Figure 8.16   Spin-dry cycle.

Figure 8.17   "Collapse in a 'spin-dry' shape."

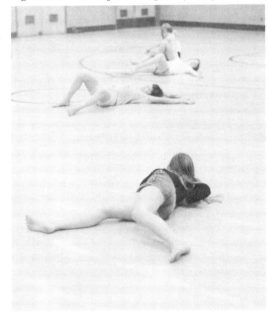

a double-handed spin with a partner is most satisfactory.

Instruct the children to make a flat, twisted, or curled shape to indicate that the spinning has stopped and they have been flung to the floor of the machine.

With their partners, have the children do a

slow spin, then separate and collapse into their final spin-dry positions.

Now have them perform the entire spin-dry cycle. The children will gather speed (instruct them to change direction if they get dizzy), then slow down and collapse.

Shake a tambourine, then bang it firmly for the collapse, or scrape two cymbals together for the spin and clang them together for the collapse. A running drum beat, followed by a loud bang is also possible. Practice this only once or twice as it is rather a demanding sequence and the children may get dizzy.

Development or Dance

In part three the various cycles are put together to form the final sequence. Have the children form small groups to decide how to combine all their actions. Let the children practice their dance sequences in their small groups without percussive accompaniment. Once they have mastered their sequences, allow the entire class to perform their dances while you provide the accompaniment. Remind them that their dances may occupy the space of the entire gymnasium.

The following example shows the typical development of a creative dance sequence. Have the children choose a starting position low to the ground. Do not begin until everyone is absolutely still.

Figure 8.18   "Practice dance sequence in small groups."

Figure 8.19   "Join washing machine actions together in a sequence."

Figure 8.20   "Make actions large and clear."

Eight counts for a rising action (a rolling drum beat or shake of the tambourine). Eight counts for a "delicate wash." Suggestions are twisting, tossing, reaching out, and curling up, but with minimal traveling on the feet. (A light 3/4 rhythm on the drum.) Sixteen counts for a "normal or dirty wash." Run and jump very energetically all over the gym. A great variety of body shapes and actions of the limbs should be seen. (A strong beating of the drum in a short-short-long rhythm.) Four counts for a rapid sinking action (draining), which can include a loose, swirling movement to link up with a partner. (Four clear beats on the drum or tambourine.) Three counts for the double-handed spin (cymbals, drum, or tambourine). One count for the final collapse (one very loud sound).

Summary   Naturally each teacher will enjoy departing from this outline and developing ideas that come from the class or from personal observation. The teacher will also be able to sense the children's interest and decide whether this lesson plan should involve two class periods or not. If the lesson plan is deviated from or even if it is strictly adhered to, the teacher should constantly be observing and commenting on the WHERE and HOW of the children's actions. The following summary may be helpful in this regard.

WHAT body actions: Jumping, tossing, twisting, running, rising, falling, spinning, collapsing.

WHERE the action took place: All directions. Changing levels from low to high to low again. On the spot and traveling actions.

HOW the actions were performed: Contrast light and strong actions in the wash. Contrasts in slow, sustained, rising, falling, quick, spinning, and collapsing actions.

RELATIONSHIP: Matching movements with a partner. Class works as one group or in small groups.

Classroom Work   To further develop this movement idea, ask the children to make up their own washing machine poems using action words and alliteration.

Figure 8.21   Follow-up activity in a language arts class.

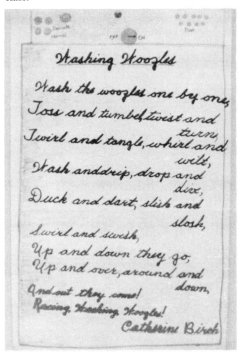

Figure 8.22   Washing machine poem using alliteration

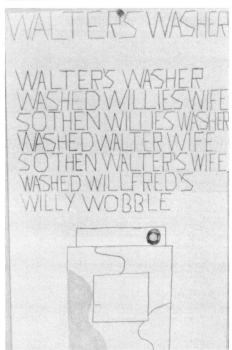

LESSON 2   SEQUENCE BUILDING

Analysis: Teacher-directed, followed by original partner work.

Lesson Outline

Introductory Activity Tasks

1. "Change speeds while running. Freeze when I beat the drum."
2. "Can you jump and turn in the air?"
3. "Start close to the floor and roll in any direction."

Movement Training Tasks

1. "Do you know how to pounce and creep?"
2. "Make up a sequence of pounce, creep, and roll."

Development or Dance

1. "Think of some action words to go along with pounce and creep."
2. "Make up your own sequence in partners."

Figure 8.23   "Begin your movements low to the ground."

Stimulus

The children can develop movement ideas based on connotations of the words themselves.

Accompaniment

The pouncing and creeping actions can be performed to the accompaniment of cymbals or a drum.

Introductory Activity

Instruct the children to run at various speeds without bumping and freeze on the drum beat to check spacing.

Begin task two with running and jumping. Emphasis should be light, springy jumps that turn in the air.

From a starting position close to the floor, roll in any way or direction you can and stop on the drum beat.

The Introductory Activities continue the work of the previous lessons. Cultivate control and sensitivity towards the ever shifting spaces created by the rest of the class. Constant reminders are needed to insure this. Require a quick response to the drum beat. The running can be made more interesting by varying the direction as well as the speed. When the children are performing rolls, keep the duration of each roll short and encourage a variety of directions as well as different types of rolls. The most easily-performed roll is a log roll, but some children will undoubtedly roll over one shoulder or do sideways tuck rolls or forward rolls. They should perform the rolls softly and slowly to avoid injuries.

Movement Training

Discuss the word *pounce*. Attention should be drawn to the *strength*, *power*, and *suddenness* of the action. The children will most likely associate the word with a predator. Thus a *focus* for the pounce and a specific direction will be important. Suggestions can be considered as to how the class might perform this pouncing action.

Figure 8.24 "Pounce."

Every child should be in his own space on the floor practicing a pouncing jump. Have them practice jumping from their feet onto their hands. Next ask them to jump from feet to feet but with a deep landing that allows the hands to come in contact with the floor.

Tell the children to listen to the cymbals. The big clash represents the pounce and as the sound dies away, the children should creep forward very softly and prepare for the next pounce. This should be practiced until the children are proficient enough at pouncing that they show a real contrast between the sudden, strong action and the soft, slow, creeping movement.

"Listen to this running drum beat. When you hear that sound begin to roll. Ready? *Pounce* with the cymbal.
Creep forward slowly as the sound dies away.
Roll with the drum beat.
Pause to prepare for your pounce again as the whole sequence is repeated."

If there is time, each child should join up with a partner and repeat the sequence. They can decide whether to move together or separately and in what direction. They might also alter the order of the three words.

Summary

WHAT: Pounce, creep, roll.
WHERE: Mainly medium and low levels. A

Figure 8.25   "Creep."

Figure 8.26   "Roll."

specific direction for the forward pounce; the rolls may be sideways, backward, or forward.

HOW: Very strong and sudden movements contrasted with very light and slow movements. Bound flow contrasts with fluency in the rolling.

RELATIONSHIP: Individual. Possibly with a partner.

Development or Dance

Action words can be listed, with help from the children, under the following headings:

> *Strong* fighting actions: Punch, thrust, kick, leap, wring, explode
> *Light* actions: (think of birds and fishes) Float, flick, dart, hover, glide, slither
> Actions which take place *on the spot:* Tremble, balance, melt, sink, expand

Partners should select three words, one from each heading and put them together in a sequence. They can use each word several times and in different ways before moving on to the next word.

As the children set to work, you have time to help any pair that might be slow in starting. Those children who are quicker at putting their ideas together can extend their sequences by adding more action words.

In part, the fighting words are to encourage children who may have lingering doubts about this type of work. Most boys and girls enjoy a mock fight. They see so many fights in mime on the television screen that they can very quickly improvise such a scene. Encourage larger-than-life actions and some slow-motion scenes. Mime builds upon the actual movement of the fight in action, not upon feelings of

Figure 8.27   "Practice action-word movements with your partner."

Figure 8.28   "Combine three action words to form a sequence."

anger. Furthermore, each child is working with a friend and the "fights" involve genuine cooperation.

As the teacher watches the children's sequences, their attention may be drawn to some of the following points:

1.   Are the strong actions really *strong?* Is the whole body participating in the action, particularly the back, shoulders, and legs? Are the light movements *light?*

Figure 8.29   "Explode."

2.   Have they made interesting use of changes of speed?
3.   Do their movements contain changes of direction?
4.   Do they match movements with their partners?
5.   Do they move one at a time in a "question and answer" relationship?

Figure 8.30   "Slither."

Figure 8.31   "Balance."

LESSON 3 INTERPRETING POETRY
Analysis: Teacher directed.

Lesson Outline
Introductory Activity Tasks
1. "Roll, alternating stretching and relaxing."
2. "Run and make a stretched jump."

Movement Training Tasks
1. "Melt and slump from a kneeling position, then from standing."
2. "Make a sudden stretch with one hand leading."

Development or Dance
1. "Make a strong, sudden, upward thrust followed by a slow melting."
2. "Match movements with a partner."

Figure 8.32 "With figure slumped, she slowly dwindled . . ."

Stimulus
Ask the children to discuss the movement imagery of "Candles" by Susan Heiffer (age 11, U.S.A.) from *Miracles*.

The candle screamed with fury,
Hot tears trickled down her face,
With figure slumped
She slowly dwindled in shadows
Darkness!

Action Words
Some action words the children can derive from the poem are thrust, slump, and dwindle.

Accompaniment
The actions of the candle may be accompanied by a verbal sound such as sharp hissing or by the percussive sounds of a tambourine, a drum, or cymbals.

When a poem is used as a stimulus for movement, we are concerned with symbolic action.

Line-by-line interpretation leads to a series of complicated and meaningless actions, destroying the power of symbolism. We must either use our own action words, which relate to the mood of the poem, or single out the most evocative and suitable words used by the poet.

Introductory Activity
Tell children to lie in an open space on the floor and stretch out tall and thin and tense. As soon as they are fully stretched, ask them to relax and go limp.

"Roll along the floor in a long, thin shape as the tambourine shakes, then relax on the tap of the tambourine." They should relax in a misshapen, twisted position, like melted wax. Encourage a wide variety of shapes. Have the children concentrate on making their bodies stretch to capacity before relaxing.

In task two, have the children run, jump high into the air from two feet, land, and run again.

The purpose of these activities is to allow the children to warm up, to review the spacing concepts, and to introduce two ways in which the body can stretch long and thin. Do not keep the children in an extended stretch for long. It is better to reach a maximum stretch, then relax immediately.

Movement Training

From an upright kneeling position ask the children to begin to slump. They should make their heads and shoulders heavy and relaxed. Now tell them to slump a little further.

Try this a few times, giving a tap on the tambourine for each slumping action. Then have the children "dwindle" smoothly to the tambourine accompaniment. Encourage the use of lopsided actions, twisted actions, and actions that involve different parts of the body.

Now let them try slumping and dwindling from a standing position. Their actions can be led by the shake of the tambourine. The children should stop moving when the sound stops.

Figure 8.33   Slumping and dwindling.

Figure 8.34   Preparing for a strong thrust.

Figure 8.35   Reaching high without losing contact with the floor.

They should remain in whatever position they are in, so the teacher can observe some of the different shapes.

Next, instruct the children to prepare for a very strong thrust, with one arm reaching up to the ceiling. When they hear the drum they should make this action sudden and strong, symbolizing the candle's scream.

The preparatory position should have slightly bent knees. The children must concentrate hard to focus on their hands as they make the strong, upward thrust. There is a greater feeling of stretch if the children finish on the toes of one or both feet. Practice several times as this is a difficult action involving balance as well as extension. If they jump into the air, they can-not sustain the stretch as easily, nor can they link the jumping action with the dwindling action smoothly and slowly.

Development or Dance

Now both action patterns are put together. When they hear the bang, the children begin to make their sudden thrust. After they have fully extended their stretch, they begin to melt to the scrape of the drum.

Make sure the children make maximum use of "melting" into twisted and curled shapes. The actions should be very slow and sustained, with conscious use of different body parts melting at different times. Each time they

"melt" have the children repeat the action even more slowly. They should freeze in their final positions when the tambourine accompaniment stops. Finally, you may ask the children to match and synchronize their actions with a partner.

Summary
WHAT: Rolling, thrusting, sinking, twisting, curling, kneeling.
WHERE: Up and down. Use of all levels.
HOW: Sudden and strong actions contrast with light and very slow actions.

Figure 8.36 "Melt and freeze, holding the final shape."

LESSON 4 INTERPRETING POETRY
Analysis: Children work on their own ideas.

Lesson Outline
Introductory Activity Tasks
   1. "Run and jump with turns and twists."

Movement Training Tasks
   1. "Work together in groups to interpret your poem." Each half of the class will work on a different poem.

Development or Dance
   1. "Show your ideas to each other."

Figure 8.37   Note witchlike shapes of head, back, shoulders, and hands.

Stimulus

Each half of the class will work on a different poem. The first poem is "Witches" by Linden (age 10, New Zealand) and the second is "Breeze" by Marie (age 11, Australia). Both are from a book of children's poetry entitled *Miracles*. See Appendix A.

"Witches"

A Star-white sky
Trees rustling as the wind lulls them,
Shadowy creatures slinking through the grass
Clouds sailing
Tattered and torn
Ragged and ripped
Suddenly
In the sky
Soaring
Zooming
Diving about
Flittering
Swooping into the air
Come witches
Cloaks ragged and torn
Streaming behind
Cackling, laughing
Fading into the darkness.

"Breeze"

Gentle as a feather
Cat quiet
Snow soft
Gentle, gentle as a feather
Softer than snow
Quiet as a cat
Comes
The evening breeze.

Action Words

The action words in "Witches" can be discussed in the classroom prior to coming into the gym. The most useful action words for movement will be

slinking, soaring,
zooming, flittering,
swooping, fading.

The action words for the second poem will be decided upon by the children in response to the mood and descriptive quality of the poem. Ask them what actions might be done very gently and softly. In order to avoid vague movements with flapping arms or burlesque tiptoeing, the children should initially be guided into actions that take place low to the ground such as:

creeping, crawling,
rolling, turning.

It may be interesting to withhold the name of the poem and the last line until many actions have been explored. This might help the children to think of a wider range of gentle actions.

Accompaniment

The actions of the poems may be accompanied by verbal sounds or by music, or the percussive sounds of a tambourine or cymbals.

Introductory Activity

Let the children run anywhere in the room and when they find a clear space, jump and turn in the air. On the spot, have the children spring high into the air and show a twisted shape with their bodies. Now, ask them to repeat their jumps, this time making a hideous face.

Figure 8.38   "Jump in a witchlike manner."

Figure 8.39   "Now make a hideous face."

Finally, instruct them to run again and show a variety of twisting and turning jumps.

There should be equal stress here on the strong thrust from the feet and legs to gain height, the shape of the body in the air, and a controlled landing. The running between jumps is for the purpose of finding an open space to jump into. However, be sure to stress jumping rather than running. Many children spend so much time running that they do not get enough practice at jumping. When the children begin to tire, have half the class rest while they observe the other half. The children who are observing should watch for three aspects of the jump already mentioned: the takeoff, the shape in flight, and the landing.

2.   Find another way of traveling, keeping close to the floor.

3.   From any starting position, transfer body weight smoothly to a second and then a third part of the body. Repeat this sequence in a slow, sustained, fluent way.

4.   Practice some of the variations that are provided by the class.

Movement Training

Some work with the class as a whole on light, gentle, flowing actions may be helpful for the movement interpretation of "Breeze." The following suggestions will give some movement ideas and indicate the standard of work expected. The teacher should demand complete concentration from the class with respect to the quality of movement.

1.   Roll in any direction showing some change of shape, but keep the roll fluent and light.

Figure 8.40   "Change your shape as you roll."

Development or Dance

Divide the children into groups of six. Each group is given one of the two poems. They must work on the specific action words of their poem. Some groups may be able to develop their own ideas without assistance, while others may require considerable help from the teacher. In any case, the teacher should draw the group's attention to the HOW, WHERE, and possible RELATIONSHIPS of their actions.

If it is possible to introduce some lighting effects into the gymnasium, these movement interpretations can be greatly enhanced. The room lit by a few flashlights or a red floodlight provides an exciting atmosphere and intriguing shadows.

The children should now decide upon the accompaniment that would best suit the movement composition. The sounds for "Witches" will probably include wailing wind sounds, cackling, and percussion. The lines of the poem may be read as part of the accompaniment.

The second poem, "Breeze," may be read as an accompaniment alternating with a gentle shake of the tambourine, a soft, rolling drumbeat, some verbal sounds, or music.

When the groups have completed their compositions, they should show them to the rest of the class.

Figure 8.41   Groups of five or six work out their own compositions.

Figure 8.42   Verbal or percussive sounds may be used as accompaniment.

Summary   The following is a summary of movement concepts illustrated by the poem "Witches."
  WHAT: Running, leaping, swooping, slinking, fading.
  WHERE: All directions and levels. Careful use of space to avoid midair collisions.
  HOW: Very strong, powerful actions. Slow, light, slinking, and fading actions.
  RELATIONSHIP: Working with a group of five or six.

Summary   The following is a summary of movement concepts illustrated by the second poem, "Breeze."
  WHAT: Creeping, rolling, turning.
  WHERE: Emphasis on moving close to the ground.
  HOW: Very light, gentle movements. Slow, but perhaps with some changes of speed.
  RELATIONSHIP: Working with a group of five or six.

A DANCE DRAMA: CHILDREN AND TEACHER WORK TOGETHER

The material for this dance drama has not been divided into specific lesson plans. Instead, a movement composition is outlined, drawing attention to some of the movement concepts which can be developed from the story. Ideas for exploration have been listed to help the teacher initiate and guide the children's work. As both teacher and children become involved with the drama, their own ideas will influence the structure and content of the lesson plans.

Classroom work that can develop from the dance drama is outlined on page 273.

The following story, taken from *The Book of Imaginary Beings* collected and edited by Jorge Luis Borges, is short and adapts well to movement.

Fauna of Mirrors

In one of the volumes of the Lettres edifiantes et curieuses that appeared in Paris during the first half of the eighteenth century, Father Fontecchio of the Society of Jesus planned a study of the superstition and misinformation of the common people of Canton; in the preliminary outline he noted that the Fish was a shifting and shining creature that nobody had ever caught but that many said they had glimpsed in the depths of mirrors. Father Fontecchio died in 1736, and the work begun by his pen remained unfinished; some 150 years later Herbert Allen Giles took up the interrupted task. According to Giles, belief in the Fish is part of a larger myth that goes back to the legendary times of the Yellow Emperor. In those days the world of mirrors and the world of men were not, as they are now, cut off from each other. They were, besides, quite different; neither beings nor colours nor shapes were the same. Both kingdoms, the specular and the human, lived in harmony; you could see through mirrors. One night the mirror people invaded the earth. Their power was great, but at the end of bloody warfare the magic arts of the Yellow Emperor prevailed. He repulsed the invaders, imprisoned them in their mirrors, and forced on them the task of repeating, as though in a kind of dream, all the actions of men. He stripped them of their power and of their forms and reduced them to mere slavish reflections. Nonetheless, a day will come when the magic spell will be shaken off.

The first to awaken will be the Fish. Deep in the Mirror we will perceive a very faint line and the colour of this will be like no other colour. Later on, other shapes will begin to stir. Little by little they will differ from us; little by little they will not imitate us. They will break through the barriers of glass or metal and this time will not be defeated. Side by side with these mirror creatures, the creatures of water will join the battle.

In Yanin they do not speak of the Fish but of the Tiger of the Mirror. Others believe that in advance of the invasion we will hear from the depths of mirrors the clatter of weapons.

Synopsis

The following movement interpretation of the story begins with the development of the unique creatures who live on the other side of the mirror. The class must first decide upon a *body shape* and a method of *traveling* for their creatures. Also ask them to think about a particular *character* for their creatures. The exploration of body shapes will include such concepts as *asymmetry*, lopsidedness, and making unusual *parts of the body high*. To differentiate the mirror creatures from the humans, the children must learn to move at unusual speeds. They can vary their speeds from *very slow* to very sudden. The contrasting speeds may be combined with movements that involve parts or all of the body or that take place at various levels.

Also, the children will have to develop movement sequences to represent "us," the people who live on this side of the mirror. Contrast "us" with the other creatures, emphasizing symmetrical movements and *uniform speed* of travel.

Next comes the fight between the rival forces. *Strong, violent actions* such as thrust, punch, and wring with a *direct focus* are practiced in an exciting battle scene, later referred to as the "turmoil." The children should practice their fighting movements in partners, emphasizing *action* and *reaction*.

The final movement sequence is based on the enslavement of the creatures who are condemned to mirror our actions. This sequence requires partners to relate to each other with exact, mirrorlike movements.

Accompaniment

See Appendix A. For the "creatures," any mysterious otherworldly music will be suitable. One suggestion is "The Dutchman" from *John Barry Conducts His Greatest Movie Hits.*

Possible accompaniments for the "people" might be "Little Man from Mars" from Perry and Kingsley's *In Sounds from Way Out* or "The Wrong Box" from *John Barry Conducts His Greatest Movie Hits.*

During the battle sequence, try the James Bond theme from the John Barry album mentioned earlier. For a more bizarre sound, try slowing down the speed of the tape.

The final sequence, the enslavement, may be accompanied by the same music that was used for the people.

Percussive sounds may be used as an alternative to music. Rhythmic patterns can be developed to accompany each phase of the dance drama.

Ideas for Exploration

Give the children some specific suggestions for movements of the creatures:

1. "Balance on three parts of the body, collapse slowly, and find a different three-point balance."

2. "'Find a balance position that allows you travel on three points."

3. "Make up a roll that involves twisting and untwisting."

4. "Run, jump, and twist in the air."

5. "Show me a strange, asymmetrical shape."

Emphasis on Body Shape   Make your body into the following shapes as soon as you hear the words:

round

a different round shape

wide

another wide shape

thin

twisted

feet higher than head

any point higher than the head.

Listen to the electronic music. Choose any starting position with a clear body shape. Transfer your weight onto a different part and invent a short sequence with a change of body shape that includes an upside down position."

If some children are uneasy about using their own initiative to develop movement sequences, ask them to begin by making a sequence of a three-point balance, roll, and another three-point balance. Allow the children time to develop their ideas, and point out various movement concepts as they work on their sequences:

WHERE: Levels, directions, pathways.

HOW: Changes of speed, effort, and flow.

Figure 8.43   "Balance on three points."

Figure 8.44   Moving and stopping with asymmetrical shapes.

See that the children keep their sequences short. Short sequences are easier to repeat and help the children gain confidence and skill. Emphasize clear body shapes with attention to toes, fingers, and head positions, as children so often forget about their extremities.

Ideas for Exploration

To develop "people" movements, concentrate on upright positions and symmetrical body shapes. Define symmetry to the children by using a simple example. If the body were to be split longitudinally, both halves would be identical. Thus, we are concerned with bilateral symmetry. Suggest some movement tasks that illustrate symmetry.

1. "Jump, on the spot, from two feet to two feet."
2. "Travel by jumping on two feet."
3. "Contrast four stride jumps (feet apart, then together) with eight steps or skips in any direction. Decide which action has symmetry.
4. "Run and jump, performing a symmetrical body shape in the air. Now try a different shape. Is it symmetrical?"
5. "Pounce from your feet to your hands. Then let your feet spring back to a push-up position. Lower your arms and roll sideways. Can you think of other actions that show symmetry?"

Emphasis on Body Shape   Make your body into the following shapes, keeping your body symmetrical:

round
thin
wide
another round shape.

"Listen to the music. Now design a short sequence where the main emphasis is on symmetrical body shapes.

Ideas for Exploration

To illustrate the relationship involved in *action-reaction* stand in front of the class with the drum. When you bang the drum you are "hitting" the children. They must react with the whole body, in such a way that indicates the

point of impact. Repeat several times, encouraging impact on a variety of body parts.

Work on strength and concentration here. The children should respond to the drum beat with a definite reaction, not simply a hand placed upon the "wounded" spot. Watch the children's natural reactions, and time the drum beat so that their actions maintain a steady pace. Stress to the children that their actions must show where they are being hit.

Now have the children become the strikers. "Punch in different directions when you hear the drum beat, using fists, elbows, and feet . . . vary your levels. Run and jump in the air, and

Figure 8.45   "Design a sequence of symmetrical body shapes."

Figure 8.46   "Move from one symmetrical shape to another."

give a kick or a punch with your fists before you land."

Ask each child to choose a partner. One becomes part of "the people," while the other becomes the "creature." Later they will exchange roles. Before engaging in dual combat, there should be a scene involving a great deal of action; a scene, in other words, of general turmoil.

Ideas for Exploration
Each person works out a way in which he or she can move with a fair amount of speed and energy while keeping in character during the turmoil. This is not to say that asymmetrical movements cannot be made by the people or that symmetrical shapes cannot be made by the creatures. The main emphasis is on vigorous activity with the different characteristics clearly recognizable. It may be decided that "the people" work at a high level and "the creatures" at a low level. Ideally, the scene should evolve from the ideas of the class.

The turmoil is followed by dual combat which ends in a clear victory for "the people."

Figure 8.47   The combat between the opposing forces.

Figure 8.48   Each maintains his basic body shapes.

Figure 8.49   Finally, the creature is defeated.

Ideas for Exploration
To begin the movement ideas of the enslavement, the teacher stands in front of the class and "draws" a very clear air pattern with one hand. This could be a letter of the alphabet or any other design. The students must mirror this action exactly.

Children enjoy doing this, but it is surprising how little attention they pay to the small details of "mirroring." For example, watch their fingers, which should reflect the position of your fingers; also their feet, head, and general stance. They will have to concentrate even more if you change the speed and the size of your gestures. Try curves, straight lines, and zigzag shapes in the patterns you trace in the air.

The two combatants are partners once again. The "people" (the first partner) must lead in any gesture, while the defeated "creature" (the second partner) must mirror it.

Having mirrored accurately with some interesting gestures, the children may enjoy working out a matching movement sequence involving gestures, traveling, or a short mime scene.

Development or Dance

The story is now put together. Starting positions and general spacing are decided upon. There should be a quick run-through twice, so that each partner has a turn at being the "creature." Finishing positions should be decided upon so that there is a definite end to the composition. It should not be allowed to fade away without a distinct moment of ending. A movement composition, like an essay, must have a begin-

Figure 8.50   "After the enslavement . . .

Figure 8.51   . . . the people develop a sequence . . .

Figure 8.52   . . . which the creatures must mirror."

ning, a middle, and an end. The clearer they are about each movement sequence, and the more they have worked to capture the movement qualities of each stage of the story, the more satisfying the dance drama will be. Making the drama more exciting, through the use of carefully chosen music and interesting lighting effects will add to the children's absorption in the story.

Summary
The Creatures
One to three minutes.
Mysterious music or sounds.

WHAT?
Transferring body weight onto different parts
of the body, using balancing, rolling, and
traveling on several parts of the body. Stretching, curling, twisting, upside-down and
asymmetrical shapes.
WHERE?
Low levels and a variety of directions.
Careful use of space.
HOW?
Extremes of speed. Emphasis on light actions
and flowing movements sometimes held in
stillness.

The People
One to three minutes.
Bright, cheerful music or rhythmic percussion.

WHAT?
Jumping, rolling, moving into positions which
show symmetrical body shapes.
WHERE?
Levels could vary, but emphasis on occupy-
ing the normal, upright amount of space.
Vary directions.
HOW?
Maintaining a rhythm which does *not* have
any dramatic changes of speed or effort.

The Fight
One and one-half to two minutes.
Mysterious music or the people's music played
at a different speed.

WHAT?
Thrust, punch, wring, pounce, lunge, collapse,
and roll.
WHERE?
Traveling or on the spot.
Change levels and direction.
HOW?
Very strong actions and sudden changes
of speed.
RELATIONSHIP?
Action-reaction in pairs, following, chasing.

The Enslavement
One to one and one-half minutes.
Lyrical music or a repeat of the cheery people's
music.

WHAT?
Gestures, some traveling.
WHERE?
Concentration on varied pathways of the
gestures. Varied use of levels and directions.
HOW?
Sudden changes of speed and flowing and
rhythmical movements.
RELATIONSHIP?
Action-reaction, mirroring.

Classroom Work These movement concepts can be related to mathematics through the study of asymmetrical and symmetrical shapes and their lines of axis. Reference can also be made to symmetry in nature. Another example of applying movement concepts to other areas of the curriculum can be found in art. The children can develop a variety of ways to create designs showing symmetry and asymmetry. Making or painting the creatures is an excellent class project. (See film *Free to Move* in Appendix A.)

These movement concepts can also be related to the language arts. Ask the children to describe the creatures through poetry or descriptive paragraphs. Emphasize adjectives (how they looked) and verbs (how they moved). Have the children describe their own creatures by reading aloud and taping the story. Find synonyms and antonyms for the creatures' and the people's movements. Act out the emotions of happiness and anger using bodily and facial expressions. Show differences in the way people convey attitudes to each other.

The following poems are written by children in a fifth and sixth grade class immediately after work on the dance drama.

The Creature
Murky, unearthly
A pulpy, pulsating beast
Roving, raving, harsh.

Patty (haiku)

People
People
Symmetrical, straight
Walking, jumping, running
Happy, gay, glad, carefree
Humans

Bob (cinquain)

Mirroring
Looking Alike
Moving Together, Same
Symmetrical, New Enslaved,
Exact Image

Keith (cinquain)

Further Development The list of ideas, action words, poems, and stories will grow imperceptibly for each teacher. The following lists may be used to extend the children's movement vocabulary and provide a storehouse for sequence building and dance compositions.

Nouns	*Action Words*
wind	hovering
volcano	darting
graveyard	spreading
Halloween	shrinking
machines	exploding
sea	drifting
designs	creeping
fireworks	melting

Space Words	*Sensations*
meeting	sharp
parting	prickly
around	smooth
over	happy
across	sad
through	aggressive
above	anxious
below	fearful

Teachers should listen to a wide variety of music and encourage the children to bring favorite records to school. Short passages of highly descriptive music are very useful. Also, the theme songs from popular films and television shows are often a helpful link to a relatively unfamiliar subject. A few suggestions for descriptive music are made in Appendix A. If the teacher has a tape recorder available, the class will enjoy the process of making their own tape recordings with words, sound effects, and musical extracts. These can be used for simple movement sequences or for complete dance dramas.

Each classroom teacher will find that there are many ideas and topics which have movement potential. The first step is to relate any part of the movement analysis to the topic. Next, examine the idea, be it story, natural phenomena, sculpture, or a piece of music, for relationships with the HOW of movement analysis. Once the amount of time, effort, and flow has been decided upon, the most suitable actions must be selected. Keeping in mind these actions and the way in which they are to be performed. the teacher must finally consider WHERE in the general space they will be performed and what RELATIONSHIP would be most appropriate.

All this is not to suggest that the teacher must have a complete picture in mind of the final outcome. Ideas will evolve in the course of teaching and the most satisfying ones are those which come from the children themselves. However the teacher must have a firm base and a set of guiding principles in creative dance, just as in any other subject. Dance is not a mystical experience which only a few people can teach. It is an important art form, which any teacher can learn about. The most successful teachers of dance are those that enjoy their teaching and understand the importance of expressive movement in children's lives.

Section 4

Appendixes

Appendix A: **Bibliography and Films**

Appendix B: **Definition of Movement Education Terms**

Appendix C: **Apparatus, Equipment, and Supply Companies**

Section 4 is a resource file of appropriate
written materials, films, and addresses of manu-
facturers and suppliers of equipment and
apparatus used in Movement Education
programs.

Appendix A:
Bibliography and Films

WRITTEN MATERIALS

Written materials on Movement Education are listed under a variety of topics. Several authors use terms such as "educational gymnastics" or "basic movement" to describe this approach to teaching physical education. Generally speaking, they are similar to Movement Education in meaning, content, and methods of instruction advocated.

Bilborough, A., and Jones, P. *Physical Education in the Primary School.* New York: International Publications Service, 1968.

Boorman, J. *Creative Dance in the First Three Grades.* Don Mills, Ontario: Longman Canada Ltd., 1971.

Borges, J. L., and Guerrero, M., eds. *Book of Imaginary Beings.* Baltimore: Penguin Books, 1974.

Buckland, D. *Gymnastics.* London: Heinemann Educational Books Ltd., 1970.

Cameron, W. M., and Pleasance, P. *Education in Movement.* Oxford: Basil Blackwell, 1971.

Carroll, J., and Lofthouse, P. *Creative Dance for Boys.* New York: International Publications Service, 1969.

Cope, J. *Discovery Methods in Physical Education.* London: Thomas Nelson and Sons Ltd., 1967.

Eastman, M., and Mettler, B. *Creative Dance for Children.* Tucson, Arizona: Mettler Studios, 1965.

Elliot, M. E., Anderson, M. H., and LaBerge. *Play with a Purpose.* 3rd ed. New York: Harper & Row, 1978.

Hackett, L. C., and Jensen, R. G. *A Guide to Movement Exploration.* Mountain View, California: Peek Publications, 1966.

Howard, S. "The Movement Education Approach to Teaching in English Elementary Schools." *Journal of Health, Physical Education, and Recreation,* January, 1967.

Inner London Educational Authority. *Educational Gymnastics.* London: 1966.

Kirchner, G. *Physical Education for Elementary School Children.* 4th ed. Dubuque, Iowa: Wm. C. Brown Company Publishers, forthcoming in 1978.

Laban, R. *Modern Educational Dance.* Boston: Plays Inc., 1974.

Laban, R., and Lawrence, F. C. *Effort.* Boston: Plays Inc., 1974.

Laban, R., and Ullman, L. *The Mastery of Movement.* Boston: Plays Inc., 1971.

Lee, D. *Bouncing Song from Alligator Pie.* Toronto: Macmillan, 1974.

Lenel, R. M. *Games in the Primary School.* London: University of London Press, 1970.

Lewis, R., ed. *Miracles: Poems by Children of the English Speaking World.* New York: Simon and Schuster, 1966.

Locks, L. F. "The Movement Movement." *Journal of Health, Physical Education, and Recreation,* January, 1966.

Ludwig, E. A. "Towards an Understanding of Basic Movement Education in the Elementary Schools." *Journal of Health, Physical Education, and Recreation,* March, 1968.

Mauldon, E., and Layson, J. *Teaching Gymnastics.* London: MacDonald and Evans, Ltd., 1965.

Monsour, S., Cohen, M. C., and Lindell, P. E.

Rhythm in Music and Dance for Children. Belmont, California: Wadsworth Publishing Company, 1966.

Murray, R. L. *Dance in Elementary Education*. New York: Harper & Row, 1963.

Mussorgsky, M. P. *Night on Bare Mountain*. San Francisco: Japan Publications Trading Center Inc., 1971.

Nichols, E. *Orff Instrument Source Book*. vol. 1. Morristown, New Jersey: Silver Burdett Company, 1970.

Redfern, B. *Introducing Laban Art of Movement*. London: MacDonald and Evans, Ltd., 1965.

Russell, J. *Creative Dance in the Primary School*. London: MacDonald and Evans, Ltd., 1965.

Sendak, M. *Where the Wild Things Are*. New York: Harper and Row, 1963.

Slater, W. *Teaching Modern Educational Dance*. London: MacDonald and Evans, Ltd., 1974.

Stanley, S. *Physical Education: A Movement Orientation*. Second Edition. New York: McGraw-Hill Book Company, 1977.

Stokes, E. M. *Word Pictures as a Stimulus for Creative Dance*. London: MacDonald and Evans, Ltd., 1963.

Thackery, R. M. *Music and Physical Education*. New York: Harper and Row Publishers, 1963.

Zemach, H. *The Judge*. New York: Farrar, Straus, and Giroux, Inc., 1971.

MUSIC

Barry, John. *Tenth Anniversary James Bond Superpack*. Recorded on United Artists UXS-91.

———. *John Barry Conducts His Greatest Hits*. Recorded on Columbia CS 9508.

Briscoe, Desmond, and Gray, Vera. *Listen, Move, and Dance*. Record 4. ("Electronic Sound Pictures," "Machine," "Witches, Wizards, Alchemists, and Sorcerers") Recorded on HMV EMI CLP 3531.

Bizet, Georges. *Jeux d' Enfants*. Recorded on London STS 15093.

Dalbey, John. *Pageant of Dances*. ("Machinery") Recorded by McDonald and Evans Educational Recordings, Ltd., ME-EP 30.

Dukas, Paul. *Leonard Bernstein Plays for Young People*. ("The Sorcerer's Apprentice") Recorded on Columbia MS6943.

Grieg, E. *Peer Gynt Suite*. ("The Hall of the Mountain King") Recorded on 6580-056.

Herman, Michael. *The World of Folk Dance Series*. (All Purpose Dances, "Seven Jumps," "Pop Goes the Weasel") Recorded on RCA Lpm 1623.

———. *Special Folk Dances*. ("Tinikling") Recorded on RCA Lpm 1619.

Heynssen, Adda. *Modern Dance Series*. Record 3. ("Machine Rhythms") Recorded by McDonald and Evans Educational Recordings, Ltd. ME-EP 21.

Holst, Gustav. *The Planets*. Recorded on Angel 36420.

Ibert, Jacques. *Divertissement*. Recorded on London STS 15093.

Mussorgsky, M. *Leonard Bernstein Plays for Young People*. ("Night on Bald Mountain") Recorded on Columbia M.S. 6943.

Oram, Daphne. *Listen, Move, and Dance*. Record 3, Side 2, bands 2 & 3. ("Ascending and descending sequences") Recorded by E.M.I. Recordings, Ltd. HMV 7EG 8762.

Perry and Kingsley. *In Sounds from Way Out*. Recorded on VSD 79222.

Rogers, Bernard. *Leaves From Pinocchio*. Recorded on Desto DST 6424.

Saint-Saëns. *Danse Macabre*. Recorded on London STS 15093.

Stephenson, Geraldine. *Listen and Move*. Record 4. ("Mechanical Doll") Recorded by McDonald and Evans Educational Recordings, Ltd.

FILMS

The accompanying list of films has been previewed by the writers and/or recommended by leading experts in the field. Wherever possible, we have listed the price and other facts relating to preview fees and geographical rental restrictions.

Series C: Movement Education

Series C has recently been produced by Dr. Glenn Kirchner and contains four films which sequentially introduce the Movement Education approach. This series is specifically designed to be used as in-service films for teachers of grades one through six or for use in teacher training programs.

Title: **Introducing the Elements of Movement Education** (Film No. 1)

Details: 16 mm., color, sound, sixteen minutes.

Distributor: Canfilm Media, 522-11 Ave. SW, Calgary, Alberta, Canada, T2ROC8.

Description: This film describes each of the basic safety skills of running, landing, and rolling and the four elements of "body awareness," "qualities," "space awareness," and "relationships." It also illustrates how each safety skill is sequentially introduced during the first part of each lesson, then followed by a similar introduction of the elements of Movement Education during the remaining portion of the lesson. Brief sample lessons, examples of teachers presenting verbal challenges, and numerous teaching ideas are provided in this film.

Title: **Using Small Equipment in Movement Education** (Film No. 2)

Details: 16 mm., color, sound, eighteen minutes.

Distributor: Canfilm Media, 522-11 Ave. SW, Calgary, Alberta, Canada, T2ROC8.

Description: The purpose of this film is to describe how a variety of small equipment such as hoops, beanbags, and individual ropes can be effectively used in a Movement Education program. The first part of the film describes where small equipment is used in a Movement Education lesson. The second part shows how this equipment should be used to extend a child's movement potential and creative response. Ideas

relating to task cards, station work, and instructional techniques are also provided throughout this film.

Title: **Using Large Apparatus in Movement Education** (Film No. 3)

Details: 16 mm., color, sound, fifteen minutes.

Distributor: Canfilm Media, 522-11 Ave. SW, Calgary, Alberta, Canada, T2ROC8.

Description: This film illustrates how a variety of different types of large apparatus are used in Movement Education programs. In the first part of the film vaulting boxes, climbing ropes, benches, and agility apparatus are used to show how children use their creative abilities as they develop movement patterns involving the elements of flight, traveling, and balance. The latter part of the film illustrates how large apparatus and small equipment may be used together, the application of task cards, and suggestions relating to the design and arrangement of large apparatus.

Title: **Theme Development in Movement Education** (Film No. 4)

Details: 16 mm., color, sound, sixteen minutes.

Distributor: Canfilm Media, 522-11 Ave. SW, Calgary, Alberta, Canada, T2ROC8.

Description: A theme in Movement Education is defined as a central idea or focus that is stressed in a lesson or a series of lessons. This film illustrates how to develop short themes of three to four lessons and extended themes of six or more lessons. Each theme is developed lesson by lesson to show how the central idea is stressed within each part of the lesson and throughout a series of lessons. A different sub-theme is also introduced into each lesson of the theme to provide variety and additional movement challenges.

Individual Films

Title: **Free To Move**

Details: 16 mm., color, sound, thirty-four minutes.

Distributor: National Audio-Visual Aids Library, Paxton Place, Gipsy Road, London SE279S4, England

Description: This film illustrates the way children move and the relevance of this understanding to a child's total education. It shows excellent relationships of classroom dance and gymnastic activities.

Title: **Teaching Game Activities to Primary Children**

Details: 16 mm., color, sound, seventeen minutes.

Distributor: Canfilm Media, 522-11 Ave. SW, Calgary, Alberta, Canada, T2ROC8.

Description: This film describes how to plan and organize a primary games program that will develop skills through individual, partner, and group activities. Numerous teaching suggestions relating to class organization, lesson planning, and teaching methods are provided. The problem-solving method and creative games approach are given major emphasis throughout this film.

Title: **Teaching Games to Intermediate Children**

Details: 16 mm., color, sound, eighteen minutes.

Distributor: Canfilm Media, 522-11 Ave. SW, Calgary, Alberta, Canada, T2ROC8.

Description: This is a companion film to *Teaching Games to Primary Children.* It illustrates how individual, partner, and group activities may be used to teach such games as soccer, basketball, softball, and field hockey. Numerous examples are provided to show how to effectively use the problem-solving method and the inventive games approach with upper elementary-school children.

Title: **Children in Action**

Details: 16 mm., color, sound, twenty-four minutes.

Distributor: Divisional Education Offices, Education Offices, Market Street, Nelson, Lancaster, England.

Description: This film was directed by Percy Jones (co-author of *Physical Education in the Primary School*) and shows upper elementary school-age children participating in various aspects of a Movement Education lesson. There are excellent illustrations of individual and partner sequences. Apparatus arrangement is also worth special attention. The presentation of movement tasks as well as methods of increasing the challenges on the floor and apparatus has been exceptionally well illustrated.

Title: **Movement Education in the Primary School**

Details: 16 mm., color, sound, twenty-six minutes.

Distributor: Somerset County Film Library, Mount Street, Bridgewater, Somerset, England.

Description: The basic elements of *space, weight,* and *time* are illustrated in this film. Children ranging in age from seven to eleven are showing developing movement skills during the movement training and apparatus parts of the lesson. The concepts of space, weight, and time are closely described and illustrated. Teachers will find many ideas relating to technique and the creative use of apparatus throughout this film.

Title: **Junior School Physical Education Lesson**

Details: 16 mm., color, sound, twenty-five minutes.

Distributor: County Film Library, 2 Walton's Parade, Preston, Lancashire, England.

Title: **Movement Experiences for Children**

Details: 16 mm., black and white, sound, seven minutes.

Distributor: Department of Instructional Media Distribution, 114 Altgeld, Northern Illinois University, DeKalb, Illinois.

Description: This short documentary film on the need for children to move and to learn to move well includes delightful pictures of children in natural outdoor activities, followed by a view of an experimental indoor program using a problem-solving approach.

Title: **Movement Experiences for Primary Children**
Details: 16 mm., color, sound, seventeen minutes.
Distributor: Department of Instructional Media Distribution, 114 Altgeld, Northern Illinois University, DeKalb, Illinois.
Description: This film includes a comprehensive coverage of how ideas of Movement Education are taught to elementary school children. Children are shown developing movement ideas on the floor and later on a wide variety of apparatus and new agility equipment. Emphasis is given to appropriate teaching methods used in Movement Education.

Title: **Movement Education in Physical Education**
Details: 16 mm., black and white, sound, twenty minutes.
Distributor: Hayes Kruger, Louise Duffy School, 95 Westminster Drive, West Hartford, Connecticut.
Purchase Price: $145.00; *Rental:* $25.00.
Description: This film interprets Movement Education through narration in question and answer form. Two teachers from the program provide much information on a variety of activities from kindergarten through grade six. The film demonstrates the methodology of the problem-solving approach, emphasizes the importance of a well-structured environment, and discusses the relationship to good traditional programming.

Title: **Movement Education in Physical Education**
Details: 16 mm., black and white, sound, seventeen minutes.
Distributor: The Audio-Visual Center, Division and Extension and University Services, University of Iowa, Iowa City, Iowa. (Films not available for rental or preview outside U.S.A.)

Description: In this film emphasis is placed on present movement patterns based on skills for daily work and play activities of children in the first grade and the relationship of these patterns to their activities throughout the elementary grades.
Purchase Price: $50.00; *Rental:* $3.00

Title: **Time and Space Awareness**
Details: 16 mm., black and white, sound, eight minutes.
Distributor: The Audio-Visual Center, Division and Extension and University Services, University of Iowa, Iowa City, Iowa. (Films not available for rental or preview outside U.S.A.)
Description: This film illustrates a sample lesson emphasizing time and space, two components of movement which are then transferred to a game situation.

Title: **Movement Education—Guided Exploration**
Details: 16 mm., black and white, sound, eight minutes.
Distributor: The Audio-Visual Center, Division and Extension and University Services, University of Iowa, Iowa City, Iowa. (Film not available for rental or preview outside U.S.A.)
Description: The teaching techniques used as children explore with hoops, jump ropes, and balls are highlighted in this demonstration film.

Title: **Movement Education—The Problem-Solving Technique**
Details: 16 mm., black and white, sound, twelve minutes.
Distributor: The Audio-Visual Center, Division and Extension and University Services, University of Iowa, Iowa City, Iowa. (Films not available for rental or preview outside U.S.A.)
Description: This film demonstrates keen fifth graders developing a dance using simple folk steps and music. The emphasis is on the teaching techniques of problem solving rather than on the finished dance product.

Title: **Movement Education—From Primary to College Level Programs**

Details: 16 mm., color, sound, twenty-four minutes.

Purchase Price: $240.00; *Rental:* $30.00 first day, $10.00 each succeeding day.

Distributor: Canfilm Media, 522-11 Ave. SW, Calgary, Alberta, Canada, T2ROC8.

Description: This film is a visual documentation of Dr. Kirchner's observations of educational gymnastic programs in England. The film illustrates the role and emphasis of educational gymnastics in elementary, high school, and college programs. In the majority of scenes, typical programs are shown to illustrate the methods used, levels of performance, and differences in facilities and equipment. The film also shows a few advanced educational gymnastic programs to illustrate the quality of performance that can be reached through this type of program.

Title: **Rhythmics in Movement**

Details: 16 mm., color, sound, eighteen minutes.

Purchase Price: $270.00

Distributor: Canfilm Media, 522-11 Ave. SW, Calgary, Alberta, Canada, T2ROC8.

Description: This film describes how the basic movement skills relating to games, dance, and gymnastic activities are taught to the accompaniment of music. The film illustrates how moving to rhythm begins with simple hand clapping and foot movements and progresses to partner and group routines. Numerous ideas relating to teaching strategies, use of small equipment, and selection of music are also provided.

Title: **Creative Folk Dance**

Details: 16 mm., color, sound, seventeen minutes.

Purchase Price: $225.00.

Distributor: Canfilm Media, 522-11 Ave. SW, Calgary, Alberta, Canada, T2ROC8.

Description: The film illustrates how folk dance activities can be taught using creative teaching strategies. Children are gradually introduced to each basic step and pathway through progressing from individual to partner to group dance patterns. Numerous ideas relating to lesson plans, musical accompaniment, and teaching techniques are also provided.

Appendix B:
Definition of
Movement Education Terms

The following terms will appear in many publications concerned with Movement Education. More extensive definitions of each term may be found within this text. (See the index or the references listed in the bibliography of written materials.)

agility apparatus: refers to all types of indoor and outdoor climbing apparatus.

Apparatus Work: the third part of a gymnastic lesson is concerned with the application of movement ideas to large and small apparatus.

asymmetry: a position or movement which is characterized by unevenness of one part of the body to its opposite side. Using a line drawn through the vertebral column, all positions of twisting, curling, or held positions, where greater stress is given to the limbs on one side, would be asymmetrical positions.

balance: the ability to hold the body in a fixed position.

body awareness: the way in which the body or parts of it can move (stretch, bend, twist, turn, and balance).

continuity: a situation where movements follow each other in succession.

direct method: in this method of instruction, the teacher structures the classroom organization, chooses the type of activity, and prescribes what each child should perform.

flight: the ability to propel the body into the air.

flow: the ability to link one movement to another with control and harmony.

general space: the physical area in which a movement takes place.

indirect method: in this method of instruction, the children are given the opportunity to choose the activity or movement idea to be practiced. Class organization and teacher involvement are unstructured.

Introductory Activity: the first part of a Movement Education lesson is concerned with general warm-up, lasting approximately five minutes.

level: the relative position of the body or any of its parts to the floor or apparatus. Levels are divided into low, medium, and high.

limitation method: in this method of instruction, the choice of activity or movement is limited in some way by the teacher.

movement idea: a movement concept related to one or more of the basic elements of qualities, body awareness, space, or relationships.

Movement Training: the second part of a Movement Education lesson is concerned with the development of movement patterns, on or off apparatus.

pattern: the arrangement of a series of movements in relation to shape, level, and pathway.

personal space: the area around an individual which can be used while keeping one part of the body in a fixed position on the floor or apparatus.

qualities: refers to how the body can move. It is the ability to move quickly or slowly, to perform light or heavy movements, and the flow with which one movement is linked to another.

relationship: applies to the position of the body in reference to the floor, apparatus, or to the interaction between partners and groups.

safety training: refers to the ability of children to move and land in a safe and efficient manner. In a broader context, it refers to the individual's safety on or around apparatus and his or her concern for the safety of other participants.

sequence: a series of movements performed in succession.

shape: the image presented by the position of the body when traveling or stationary.

space: the area in which a movement takes place.

stretch: moving the body or parts of it from a flexed to an extended position.

symmetry: in Movement Education, symmetry is used to describe a movement or balance position where both sides of the body would look identical if an imaginary line were drawn through the middle of the body.

theme: a central movement idea.

time: the speed with which a movement takes place (quick, slow, sudden, or sustained).

traveling: moving in various directions by transferring the weight from one part of the body to another.

turn: rotation of the body which may involve loss of the initial fixed point of contact e.g., turning in a full arch).

twist: one part of the body is held in a fixed position on the floor or apparatus and the rest of the body is turned away from the fixed position (e.g., twisting trunk to the side and back).

weight: the degree of muscle tension involved in the production of a movement, or the maintenance of a static position involving tension.

Appendix C:
Apparatus, Equipment,
and Supply Companies

The following companies are listed on the basis
of manufacturing and/or selling agility apparatus (indoor and outdoor), equipment (large
tumbling mats, springboards, etc.), and supplies (hoops, beanbags, etc.).

A. G. Spalding & Bros. Inc.
Chicopee, Massachusetts 01014 — *Equipment*

American Gym Company, Inc.
Box 111
Jefferson, Iowa 50920 — *Equipment*

American Gym Company, Inc.
Box 131
Monroeville, Pennsylvania 15146 — *Equipment and agility apparatus*

Atlas Athletic Equipment Co.
2339 Hampton
St. Louis, Missouri 63139 — *Equipment*

Big Toys
3113 South Pine
Tacoma, Washington 98409 — *Outdoor adventure playground apparatus
or and indoor portable agility apparatus*
Big Toys of Canada, Ltd.
18697 96th Avenue
Surrey, British Columbia, Canada

Childcraft
155 East 23rd Street
New York, New York, 10010 — *Climbing ropes and gymnasium apparatus
and equipment*

Creative Playthings, Inc.
Princeton, New Jersey 08540 — *Playground apparatus*

Game-Time, Inc.
Litchfield, Michigan 49252 — *Agility apparatus*

Gym Master Co.
3200 South Zuni
Englewood, Colorado 80110 — *Equipment*

Gymnastic Supply Co.
247 West Sixth Street
San Pedro, California 90733   *Equipment and supplies*

Lind Climber Company
807 Reba Place
Evanston, Illinois 60202   *Agility apparatus*

Madsen Gymnastic Equipment, Ltd.
Unionville, Ontario   *Agility apparatus*

Mr. J. A. McLaughlin
Director of Industries for Commissioner
Ottawa 4, Canada   *Agility apparatus*

Olympic Gymnastic Equipment
(Murray Anderson)
128 Dunedin Street
Orillia, Ontario   *Agility apparatus*

National Sports Company
360 North Marquette Street
Fond du Lac, Wisconsin 54935   *Equipment*

Nissen Corp.
930 27th Avenue SW
Cedar Rapids, Iowa 52406   *Agility apparatus and equipment*

Porter Athletic Equipment
Porter Levitt Co., Mfgr.
9555 Irving Park Road
Schiller Park, Illinois 60176   *Equipment*

R. W. Whittle, Ltd.
P.V. Works
Monton Eccles
Manchester, England   *Agility apparatus*

The Delmar F. Harris Co.
P.O. Box 288, Dept. J
Concordia, Kansas 66901   *Agility apparatus*

The Mexico-Forge Climbers
R.D. 1
Reedsville, Pennsylvania 17084   *Outdoor apparatus*

W. J. Volt Rubber Corp.
Subsidiary of American Machine and Foundry
Company, New York
3801 South Harbour Boulevard
Santa Ana, California 92704   *Equipment and supplies*

Index

Accidents, prevention of, 51, 58.
    See also Collisions
Action words, 121
Activity room, 28. *See also*
    Facilities
Adaptations for classroom
    teaching
    games, 163, 164
    gymnastics, 28, 41, 42, 49, 51,
        56, 72, 88
Adding to range and understand-
    ing. *See also* Themes
    dance, 49, 53, 58-76
    games, 155-58
    gymnastics, 49, 53, 58-76
Agility, 44, 52, 55
Apparatus tasks. *See* Lesson
    outlines
Arm strength. *See* Strength
Attitudes
    of the children, 35
    of the teacher, 32

Backwards. *See* Directions
    diagonal roll, 54, 59, 65, 81
    somersault, 76, 83
Balance
    beam (or bar), 67, 83, 84, 91
    gymnastics, 10, 48, 58, 59, 64,
        67, 69, 72, 74, 77, 79, 81,
        83, 85, 88, 92, 95, 96,
        100, 101, 211
Balloon, 133
Balls
    games, 156, 158, 160, 165
    gymnastics, 42, 44, 53, 55, 59,
        63, 70, 85, 90, 95, 96
Bands, 49, 85, 86
Bare feet, 35, 49, 56. *See also*
    Footwork
Beanbags
    games, 156, 158, 165
    gymnastics, 42, 47, 49, 50, 53,

55, 59, 63, 64, 69, 72, 74,
    77, 79, 84, 90, 95, 98
Benches, 44, 52, 59, 62, 64, 67,
    74, 77, 79, 83, 85, 89-91,
    93, 95, 97, 232
    rules for carrying, 46
Bend-stretch-twist
    dance, 121
    gymnastics, 53, 62, 64, 79, 92,
        96-97, 101
"Bird's Nest," 78. *See also*
    Somersault
Body alignment, 63, 73, 76
Body awareness, 10, 41, 44, 49,
    85, 88. *See also* Themes
    parts of the body
        dance, 106, 114, 117, 118,
            126, 130, 141
        games, 156, 158, 160, 165
        gymnastics, 59-60, 62, 65,
            69, 72, 79, 83, 85, 92, 96,
            101
        "patches and points," 64,
            67, 70, 72, 89
        whole body, 59, 62, 102,
            142, 149, 156, 160
Bounce, 63. *See also* Games;
    skills
Boundary ball, 176
Bowling pins
    games, 165
    gymnastics, 59, 77, 79, 85
Box, 52, 57-59, 63, 67, 69, 77,
    79, 83, 85, 89, 93.
"Breeze," 264
Bridges. *See* Shape
Bunny jumps. *See* Jumps

Canes, 52, 54, 85, 87, 90
Care of apparatus, 57
Cartwheels, 68-73, 101
Catching, 42, 55, 57, 74
C.A.V.E. or Cave, 66, 86, 90

Chairs, 51, 54, 85, 87, 90
Changing clothes, 36, 51, 53, 66
Clapping, 115
Class control, 32, 74
Classification of movement, 210
Classroom, 32, 83, 134, 153. *See
    also* Adaptations
Climbing, 52, 85, 98
    ropes, 52, 54, 63, 67, 76, 78,
        80, 85, 87, 89, 93
    safety rules, 61
Collisions, avoidance of
    dance, 106
    games, 148
    gymnastics, 38-41, 44-48, 58,
        79, 81, 83, 85, 88, 90, 97
Competition, 6, 147, 157
Confidence, 28, 65
Consideration, 35, 37
Construction paper, 49, 51, 56,
    72
Cooperation, 35, 42, 55, 66, 147,
    164
Coordination
    hand-eye, 39, 44, 45, 147-66
    foot-eye, 59, 147-66
Crawl, 86
Creativity, 6, 70, 100
Creatures, the, 121, 223
Crouch jumps. *See* Jumps.
Curl, 88, 92. *See also* Bend-
    stretch-twist

Dance, 105-144
    creative, 251
    drama, 266
Decision making, 41
Demonstrations, 53, 70
Development or dance tasks.
    See Lesson outlines
Diagonally. *See* Directions
Directions
    dance, 124, 126, 128, 130, 141

games, 150, 158-66
gymnastics, 52, 55, 57-59, 63,
    68, 72, 76, 81, 83, 85, 88,
    91, 100
Discipline, 47
Discovery, 38, 83
Dodgeball, 159
Down. *See* Directions
Dribbling, 177. *See also* Games
    skills

Empty the Basket, 147, 156
Equipment, 37, 39, 42, 48, 52,
    70, 88, 92, 96, 99, 101,
    155, 222. *See also*
    Apparatus
Evaluation, 22
Experimentation, 58, 155
Exploration, 37, 100

Facilities, 28
"Fauna of Mirrors," 267
Flexibility, 79
Flight, 11
Float, 137, 140
Flow. *See* Qualities
Follow the Leader, 109
Foot trap, 175
Footwork
    dance, 106, 119, 138
    games, 153, 164
    gymnastics, 40, 48-50, 56, 63,
        77, 96
    shooting feet, 62, 97
Force. *See* Qualities
Form, 37
Formal gymnastics, 204
Forward. *See* Direction
Forward roll. *See* Rolls
Four corner dribble, 179
Free play, 149, 155, 156, 158,
    160, 165
French Cricket, 161

Gallop. *See* Locomotor skills
Games
    lessons, 147-66
    skills, 147, 155
        bouncing, 153, 165
        catching, 153
        dribbling, 59, 60, 165
        fielding, 158
        hitting, 160
        kicking, 153, 160
        rolling, 153, 158
        running, 156, 160
        throwing, 156
    Groups. *See also* Sections
        dance, 137, 140, 143
        games, 159

gymnastics, 28, 57, 66, 78, 90,
    99, 101
Group work, 19
Gymnasium, 28, 32, 33, 34

Handstands, 68-72, 101
Hanging, 58
Headstands, 69, 72, 101
Height, 36, 52, 68, 84, 97, 100
High. *See* Levels
*Homer Price and the Donut
    Machine*, 142
Hoops
    games, 42-44, 53, 55, 59, 62,
        64, 69, 72, 74, 77, 83, 87,
        90, 95, 98, 230
    gymnastics, 149, 156, 160, 165
Hop. *See* Locomotor skills
Hopscotch, 51
How. *See* Lesson outlines and
    Movement analysis
Hump and hollow, 74, 90

Imagery, 105
Imagination, 94, 100, 102
Independence, 57, 70
Individual help, 148
Individual mats. *See* Mats
Integration, 130, 138, 140, 143
Intermediate grades, 68
Introductory Activity, 18
    tasks. *See also* Lesson outlines
Invent, 66, 69, 76, 102, 160, 165
Inventive games, 184
    by students, 187, 189, 191

Jack-in-the-box, 88, 92
Judge, The, 121, 122, 129, 130,
    132
Jumps. *See* Locomotor skills

Keep Away, 188
Kindergarten, 32, 36, 42, 47, 60,
    64, 66, 78, 83, 88, 92,
    100, 101

Laban, Rudolph, 9, 140
Landings, 48-50, 52-55, 59, 62,
    72, 77, 81, 84, 90-92, 96,
    97, 140
Language, 106
Large space. *See* Space
Leap. *See* Locomotor skills
Learning process, 32
Leg strength. *See* Strength
Lesson outlines
    intermediate
        creative dance, 251, 257,
            261, 263
        dance, 246, 248, 249, 250

games, 173, 177, 180, 183,
    185, 188, 190, 192, 194
gymnastics, 207, 211, 216,
    220, 223, 226, 228, 232,
    237
primary
    dance, 106, 108, 111, 112,
        114, 117, 119, 121, 122,
        126, 130, 132, 133, 137,
        140
    games, 141, 142-43, 149,
        150, 153, 156, 158, 160,
        162, 165,
    gymnastics, 27, 33, 44, 52,
        55, 59, 62, 64, 67, 69, 72,
        74, 77, 79, 81, 83, 85,
        88, 90, 92, 95, 97, 101
Lesson planning, 17, 171, 204,
    205, 243
Letters, 92, 101, 102
Levels, changes of,
    dance, 124, 126, 137, 142
    gymnastics, 52, 55, 62, 64, 72,
        81, 83, 85, 88, 90, 92-96,
        99, 237
    high and low, 48, 64, 88, 89,
        92, 100, 124, 126
Light. *See* Qualities
Limited space. *See* Space
"Listen and Move," 142
"Listen, Move, and Dance," 126,
    142
Locomotor skills
    dance, 106, 110, 113, 141, 147
    galloping, 88, 111, 113
    games, 149, 150, 154
    gymnastics, 55, 56, 70, 73, 81,
        88
    hopping, 55, 58, 59, 113
    jumping, 36, 39, 48, 50-57, 62,
        69, 72, 76, 80, 84, 88-97,
        101, 113, 117, 123, 124,
        143, 162
        crouch (or bunny jump),
            68, 71, 90, 98, 164
        leap, 48, 54, 57, 72, 81, 85,
            90, 97, 137, 140
    running, 38, 41, 45, 49, 52,
        59, 62, 69, 74, 77, 79, 81,
        83, 85, 88, 90, 95, 97, 99
    skipping, 39, 41, 44, 55, 87,
        95, 108, 112, 147
    sliding, 113
    walking, 41, 55, 58, 64, 68,
        84, 88, 98, 112
Log roll. *See* Rolls
Long shape. *See* Shape

Machinery, 142
Manipulative skills, 59

Matching shapes, 223
Mats, 47, 53-57, 60-63, 72-80, 81-84, 90, 96
Methods of teaching, 20
 direct, 20, 42
 indirect, 20, 42
 limitation, 21, 42
Mobility, 76, 97
Monsters, 128
Motor skills, 48
Movement Analysis. *See also* Lesson outlines
 patterns, 58, 74, 102
 principles, 58
 tasks, 58, 60, 71
Movement Education, 3
 concepts and skills, 9, 203, 210
 role of, 3
 values, 4-6
Movement Training, 18, 203
 tasks. *See also* Lesson outlines
Musical Bumps, 38, 111

Narrow shapes. *See* Shape
Nerf balls, 156, 160
Night on Bald Mountain, 137
Nine Lives, 69, 74, 111, 147, 149
Noise, 32, 36, 57, 70
Number game, 188
Nursery rhymes, 108

Observation
 games, 154, 164
 gymnastics, 23, 39, 44, 62, 66, 70, 71, 72, 73, 75, 82, 97, 101, 102-3
On the spot. *See* Space
Orff, 105
Organization, 42, 148

Partner work
 dance, 110, 112, 128, 132, 143
 games, 153, 156, 160, 164
 gymnastics, 41, 46, 48, 49, 55, 62, 64, 67, 72, 81, 83, 85, 88, 92, 95, 98, 101
Pass and trap, 173
Pathways, 141, 237
Percussion, 244
Personal space. *See* Space
Phrasing and rhythm, 244
Physical skills, 58
Pick-a-back, 68
Pig-in-the-Middle, 153, 158
Planning programs, 24
"Points and patches," 64, 67, 70, 72, 89, 95. *See also* Body awareness and Weight bearing
Pop Goes the Weasel, 111

Practice, 148, 149, 159
Praise, 39
Primary lesson outlines. *See* Lesson outlines
Problem solving, 70

Qualities of movement, 14, 40, 94, 133, 140. *See also* Themes
 flow
  dance, 106, 118, 121, 122, 126, 130, 133, 140, 141-42
  games, 156
  gymnastics, 81, 94, 100
 space, 94, 96, 156
 direct and flexible, 106, 122, 130, 132, 133, 140, 141, 142
 time, 14, 94, 106, 122, 130, 133, 140, 141, 142, 156
 quick and slow, 79, 92, 95, 114, 121, 126, 133, 236
 sudden and sustained, 96, 99, 101, 121, 132, 133
 weight = force
  strong and light, 62, 94, 96-97, 106, 122, 130, 132-33, 140, 141-42, 156, 238
Quality, 81, 95, 100, 102, 117
Quoits, 69

Range of movement. *See* Themes
Relationships, 15, 223
Relays, 147, 156
Releave-Oh, 149
Repetition, 38, 102
Responsibility, 35, 42, 53
Rhythm, 106, 109, 113, 114, 119, 137, 152
Rising and falling, 124, 126, 128, 137
Rock, 59, 60, 92
Rolling, 58, 63, 67, 76, 79, 81, 84, 90, 92, 95, 101, 140
Rolls
 backward, 54, 59, 65, 78, 81
 butterfly, 64
 forward, 64, 78
 log, 40, 44-46, 53, 55-57, 65, 68
 sideways safety, 36, 44-50, 52, 54, 61-63, 71, 81, 90
 somersaults, 68, 76, 83
Ropes. *See* Climbing and Skipping
Running. *See also* Locomotor skills
 in the air, 124, 144

Safety, 33, 41, 49, 53, 56-59, 61, 65, 68, 75, 79-81, 90, 149, 156
Safety training. *See* Themes
"Seals," 68, 97
Sections, 37, 41-44, 47, 50, 66. *See also* Groups
Self confidence, 42
Self control, 40, 42
Self discipline, 35, 42
Sequences, 16-17
 dance, 109, 118, 138, 140, 143, 243, 257
 gymnastics, 37, 65, 72, 77, 79-83, 85, 88, 93, 95, 100, 101
Shadow boxing, 230
Shadow game, 181, 197
"Shaggy Dog." *See* Hump and hollow
Shape
 bend-stretch-twist, 53, 62, 64, 79, 92, 96, 97, 101, 138, 217
 bridges, 37, 51, 61, 73, 92, 121, 123, 130, 132, 235
 curl, 89, 92, 136, 217
 dance, 121, 123, 130, 132
 gymnastics, 37, 51, 61, 73, 92, 216
 long and thin, 40, 55, 92
 narrow and wide, 92, 93, 100, 132
Sharing, 35, 42
Shin trap, 175
"Shooting feet." *See* Footwork
Sideways. *See* Directions
Sideways roll. *See* Rolls
Sitting, 39, 41, 55, 69, 76, 85, 92, 95, 101, 155
Skipping. *See also* Locomotor skills
 ropes, 42, 48, 54, 57-59, 64, 69, 72, 77, 79, 85, 96, 119, 150, 161, 162, 164
 correct length of, 151
Slashing, 124, 137
Slow. *See* Qualities
Slow motion, 73
Small. *See* Space
Smooth. *See* Qualities
Solutions, 68, 72, 100
Somersaults. *See* Rolls
Space. *See also* Qualities and Themes
 general, 13, 52, 55, 72, 74, 76, 95, 99
 dance, 108, 112, 134, 137, 142

games, 150, 153, 156, 160, 162
large, 40, 85, 94, 128
on the spot, 59, 62, 64, 67, 69, 95
dance, 130, 142
games, 156, 160
outdoors, 57, 148
own/personal, 13, 40, 62, 64, 72, 76, 95, 134, 142, 153, 162
pathways, 14, 141
small/limited, 40, 56, 72, 85, 88, 91, 94, 128
use of, 42, 45, 52, 55, 61
words, 55, 62, 66, 70, 72, 77, 83, 85, 90, 94, 99
Speed, 65, 79, 95, 100
Spotting, 33, 206
Stage, 50, 59, 61, 63, 90, 93, 98
Stamping, 139
Standards, 37, 38, 53, 77
Starting
and ending positions, 109, 115, 122, 127
Statues, 88, 99, 108, 117, 123, 144
Stimulus. See Lesson outlines; dance
Stocking bats, 55, 57, 148, 160, 161
Stopping
dance, 106, 110, 112, 118
games, 149, 150, 160

gymnastics, 38, 45, 48, 55, 64, 69, 72, 77, 83, 88, 99
Storage boxes, 42
Strength
arm, 44, 52, 55, 59, 61, 68, 96-98
foot, 50
leg, 52, 55, 92, 95, 97
Stretch. See Shape
Strong. See Qualities
Swerving, 83
Swinging
dance, 123, 141
games, 150, 161
gymnastics, 52, 54, 61, 77, 87

Tackling, 180
Tails, 33, 34, 85
Takeoff, 70, 96, 117
Tambourine, 106, 112, 122, 124, 139, 140
Targets, 156, 159, 160
Themes
Theme One: Safety Training
dance, 106-14
games, 149-55
gymnastics, 31-57
Theme Two: Adding to Range and Understanding
dance, 114-24
games, 155-58
gymnastics, 58-76
Theme Three: Understanding Space and Directional Movements

dance, 124-32
games, 158-66
gymnastics, 76-93
Theme Four: Qualities
dance, 133-45
gymnastics, 94-102
"Tinikling," 119
Traveling, 149, 150, 163, 165, 248. See also Locomotor skills

Units, 173
basketball, 195
intermediate gymnastics, 206
soccer, 173
Up, 85, 86, 92, 93, 97. See also Directions

Vaulting box. See box

Walk. See Locomotor skills
Wall bars, 52, 54, 76, 93
Warm-up, 40
Wastepaper basket, 57
Weight bearing, 88, 95, 98, 213. See also Body awareness, Patches and points, and Themes
Wheelbarrow, 68
Wide. See Shape
Witches, 133, 137, 138, 140, 141, 264
Wooden blocks, 54, 119

Zigzag, 39, 40, 77, 79